Death and Dying
in New Mexico

El Juicio Final by Charlie Carrillo

Death and Dying in New Mexico

Martina Will

UNIVERSITY OF NEW MEXICO PRESS
ALBUQUERQUE

Published in cooperation with the William P. Clements Center
for Southwest Studies, Southern Methodist University

© 2007 by the University of New Mexico Press
All rights reserved. Published 2007
Printed in the United States of America

First Paperback Printing, 2022
Paperback ISBN: 978-0-8263-4164-8

Library of Congress Cataloging-in-Publication Data

Will de Chaparro, Martina, 1967–
  Death and dying in New Mexico / Martina Will de Chaparro.
    p. cm.
  Includes bibliographical references and index.
  ISBN-13: 978-0-8263-4163-1 (cloth : alk. paper)
  1. Funeral rites and ceremonies—New Mexico—History. 2. Funeral
rites and ceremonies—Mexico—History. 3. Cemeteries—Social
aspects—New Mexico—History. 4. Cemeteries—Social aspects—
Mexico—History. 5. Burial—Social aspects—New Mexico—History.
6. Burial—Social aspects—Mexico—History. 7. New Mexico—Social
life and customs. 8. Mexico—Social life and customs. 9. New
Mexico—History—To 1848. 10. Mexico—History—Spanish colony,
1540–1810. I. Title.

  GT3210.N488 2007
  393'.9—dc22

                    2007002257

Front jacket art: *El Juicio Final* by Charlie Carrillo

Book design and composition by Damien Shay
Body type is Utopia 9.5/13
Display is Centaur and Avant Garde

Dedicated to the dead
reposing beneath the churches,
cemeteries, and streets
of New Mexico.

Rest in peace.

CONTENTS

LIST OF ILLUSTRATIONS

ACKNOWLEDGMENTS

I began my journey into colonial New Mexicans' death and dying in part by reading all I could about sixteenth- and seventeenth-century Spanish deathways. The literature, though abundant and certainly instructive in terms of methodology, left me wondering about the individuals who formed the foundation for the impressive quantitative research that characterized most of these studies. In writing about New Mexican deathways, then, I have tried to keep the individuals' stories central to the larger tale I am telling. In recovering the words of the woman whose husband tried to kill her, the man irate over the priest's callous treatment of his dying daughter, and the woman declared dead long before her body's biological death, I hope to recall not only the meaning of death to people in eighteenth- and nineteenth-century New Mexico but also the meaning that their lives held. To this end, I have done my best to accurately translate their words within the quoted text and include transcriptions of the original—but modernized—Spanish in the endnotes. In providing the original Spanish, I frequently include more than the precise quote so as to allow the reader to understand the larger context of a phrase.

Along the research and writing path I incurred many debts. From New Mexico to Texas to Mexico and to Spain, scholars, archivists, and friends offered encouragement, new points of view, and support. In the early stages in particular, the guidance of Linda B. Hall, John L. Kessell, Fr. Thomas J. Steele, SJ, and Marta Weigle helped me to formulate and refine my questions and findings. I am particularly appreciative of Father Tom's help with ecclesiastical history and several Latin translations found within the text. I frequently called on Robert Martínez, Larry Miller, and Felipe Mirabal for questions on the minutiae of New Mexico history; I deeply appreciate their readiness to share their encyclopedic knowledge. My good friends Miruna Achim,

Suzanne Stamatov, and Michael Anne Sullivan shared their passion for history as well as insights into their respective fields of history. Each furnished me a home away from home so I could visit libraries and archives in Mexico City, Santa Fe, and Albuquerque on a historian's budget. Their hospitality and camaraderie sustained me on many occasions. Among my many good friends in New Mexico, I wish especially to thank Arturo Sandoval, who has been unwavering in his support and encouragement. Thanks to all of you for making it feel like I'm coming home whenever I return to New Mexico.

At different stages of the research and writing, David J. Weber, Pamela Voekel, Ross Frank, Andrés Reséndez, Gary Laderman, Erik Seeman, Charlie Carrillo, Stanley Hordes, James Brooks, and Verónica Zárate Toscano offered me input on particular documents, chapters, and their respective areas of expertise. Statistician Rene Paulson deserves credit for helping me make sense of the statistics I gathered; I deeply appreciate her patience for those of us less mathematically inclined. Archaeologists Edward Crocker and Wolky Toll gave generously of their time and knowledge of Santa Fe's colonial and nineteenth-century archaeology. Richard Chapman and William T. Brown offered their insights on the Alameda cemetery excavation and allowed me to see the work in progress that represents the findings of this dig. A. Katie Harris and José de la Cruz Pacheco assisted me in securing images for the book that otherwise might not be included. Without the support of such a dynamic and diverse scholarly community, the present work surely would not be what it is.

Skilled archivists and library staff are essential to the success of any historical project. The wonderful staff at the Center for Southwest Research at the University of New Mexico assisted me on numerous occasions with requests for information. Nancy Brown and Ann Massmann in particular deserve kudos for their professionalism and helpfulness, even long distance. Rick Hendricks, Tim Blevins, and Dennis Daily at the Rio Grande Historical Collections and Special Collections at New Mexico State University likewise gave of their time, answering questions by e-mail and sending documents upon request. The archivists at the New Mexico State Records Center and Archives brought me cartloads of document boxes—one of which most memorably contained the still-bloodied knife from a believed suicide—and showed genuine interest in my work, offering opinions on some of the more challenging colonial handwriting. I am especially grateful for the consistently upbeat Melissa Salazar and Daphne Arnaiz-DeLeon, who made the archives a truly pleasant place to work. Russell Martin III, director of Southern Methodist University's DeGolyer Library, graciously agreed to acquire a microfilm collection I needed during my fellowship year, allowing me to continue my research from my new base in Dallas. Thanks also to the editors of *Catholic Southwest*, the *New Mexico Historical Review*, and *Relaciones* for their permission to publish selections previously published in their pages.

Institutional support, of course, made this project possible. At the University of New Mexico, the Department of History, the Latin American and Iberian Institute, the Center for Regional Studies, and the Dean of Graduate Studies' Deans' Dissertation Fellowship all provided essential financial support in the early years of my research. The Pew Program in Religion and American History at Yale University awarded me a crucial summer fellowship that launched the writing process. In 2001–2, the Clements Center for Southwest Studies at Southern Methodist University furnished me the opportunity to devote a wonderful postdoctoral year to begin the dissertation's transformation into the book before you. Finally, the extremely collegial Department of History and Government along with the Office of Research and Sponsored Programs at Texas Woman's University have been instrumental in helping to ensure that the project did not lose its momentum despite the usual demands on junior faculty.

Though I have here left them for last, in reality, it is my family who always comes first and to whom I especially want to express my gratitude. While not always sure about what I was doing, my parents and siblings provided me with many wonderful opportunities to escape the Texas heat and in many ways reminded me of the meaning of what I was doing. Though seemingly bewildered by both my choice of topics and the project's duration, my parents, Leonard and Wilma Will, instilled in me the importance of education, which is in some sense where this work really began. María Edith Rodríguez, my dear mother-in-law, reviewed Spanish transcriptions for me and cared for my daughter so that I could work on revisions. Finally, I thank my daughter, Isabella, for the love and laughter she brings. These have helped me maintain perspective while making the journey a most rewarding one.

Dallas, Texas
August 2006

INTRODUCTION

I n the New Mexican hamlet of Bernalillo, a few weeks before Christmas 1877, María Dolores Longina Chávez de Perea made her last will and testament. She undoubtedly suffered from an illness at the time, for she died within days of its completion. Chávez did not itemize her property, asking only for its distribution among her twelve children and her husband of thirty-five years, José Leandro Perea. She focused on her spiritual welfare rather than the disposal of her goods, providing meticulous instructions for suffrages on behalf of her soul, including annual masses to St. Gregory to be said for five years after her death. She also instructed her estate's executor—her husband—to pay for two annual *novenarios*, or two series of nine masses, to benefit her soul for as long as he lived, dedicating one to the Virgin Mary and the other to St. Joseph. Finally, she requested interment beneath the floors of Bernalillo's parish church.[1]

María Chávez's will possesses elements both unusual to and representative of late nineteenth-century New Mexican wills. Most New Mexicans who wrote wills prudently left a detailed list of their goods, however meager. Though she did not carefully describe her possessions, Chávez made it clear that she sought their equitable distribution among her children. She deliberately chose her devotions, including pious bequests for both the Virgin Mary and St. Joseph, each of whom had a special significance at the hour of death. Among Roman Catholics, Mary represented the Queen of Mercy. As the principal intermediary between mankind and God, she was the most popular advocate identified in wills. Her husband, St. Joseph, served as the patron saint of the good death. Her devotion to St. Gregory, patron saint of music, though less obvious, may indicate a familial devotion, as suggested by another will from a Bernalillo Perea. The relative popularity of these figures notwithstanding, Chávez's will is noteworthy because of her requests for masses and her choice of burial location, both relatively rare for a late nineteenth-century will.

While not unusual in colonial Spanish-American wills, by the time María Chávez wrote in the Territorial period (1848–1912), requests like these had become an anomaly. The colonial emphasis on masses and other suffrages for the dead had largely eroded, and people only infrequently requested interment within the church. By 1877, New Mexico's urban landscapes had rendered the worlds of the living and the dead. No longer welcome within the church's floors or its adjacent graveyard, people relegated the dead to cemeteries on the outskirts of town. These new suburban cemeteries did not share the social significance of earlier burial sites, which had served as public gathering places. Their distance from the very heart of the community of the faithful—the church—underscored the segregation between the worlds of the living and the dead that now prevailed. A few people, however, adhered to the traditional ways. They might, as María Chávez, employ a civil document to request a faith-infused baroque model of burial and memorialization. What in 1877 made Chávez's will unusual were the very elements that only a half-century before had been commonplace in New Mexico.

In referring to the baroque, what is meant here is less a historical period than that period's religious sensibility. The Spanish baroque relied on the senses to communicate the divine. The parish priest acted as mediator between the individual and God, as did the Virgin Mary and a panoply of saints, who responded to petitioners' earnest requests. Communal and participatory in nature, baroque piety resulted in the proliferation of religious brotherhoods, public processions, and extravagant material, architectural, and artistic demonstrations of the divine made possible by the gold and silver mined in the New World. While in the late eighteenth century in central Mexico a new interiorized piety promoted a more direct relationship to God and distanced itself from excessive display, in New Mexico popular piety remained more baroque than modern in character, evident in the emergence of the Penitente Brotherhood and a resurgence in the popularity of the saints in this same period.

New Mexican deathways originated in the baroque world of Roman Catholic Spain and as a result incorporated the community into death in numerous ways. Settlers and Franciscan friars from Spain and New Spain brought the model of the good death with them to New Mexico, where it endured through much of the nineteenth century. This model required pious meditation and preparation for death, the physical presence and spiritual support of community members, and the priest's administration of the last rites of the Roman Catholic Church. While the nature of life on the periphery of the Spanish empire made it impossible to apply seamlessly the baroque model in its entirety, people adapted and transformed elements of the model in a necessary concession to local conditions. Thus, their religious lives and their death customs differed from those in central Mexico, resulting in harsh criticism from Mexican ecclesiastical officials visiting in the late eighteenth and early nineteenth centuries. The present work considers both cultural continuity and regional adaptation, examining Spanish-American traditions as practiced in New Mexico in the colonial period (approximately 1700–1821) and during its Mexican era (1821–48), with some consideration of the early Territorial period (1848–80).

Dramatic changes took place in New Mexico in the decades between 1820 and 1880. The complexity of deathways, however, means that change rarely follows a direct or linear trajectory. In fact, contradictory beliefs and practices often coexist. As much as we try to generalize about the transformations that took place in New Mexico, a document like María Dolores Longina Chávez de Perea's will underscores the challenges in categorizing popular beliefs. To be sure, in New Mexico asymmetry characterized the pace of change in the nineteenth century. Rural populations accommodated less readily to change than their urban countrymen or paisanos in places like Albuquerque. This study of death and dying sheds light on models of behavior, deviations from those models, changes in deathways, and the varieties of opposition to change. As a study of popular piety, it builds on previous studies of deathways in the United States, Europe, and Mexico.

Using death as a lens to view the past has allowed historians of the United States to produce a compelling array of studies addressing everything from piety to the medicalization of society. One recent work goes so far as to claim that the very development of citizenship in the nineteenth-century United States can only be understood through a study of death.[2] While some writers have considered African-American funerary rites under slavery, most scholarship continues to focus on Protestant groups in the antebellum North. We must take care, though, as David Weber cautions, not to "mistake regional history for national history."[3] These studies often mistakenly imply that there existed an "American way of death" and that Protestantism defined it. Too often relegated to the fringes of both United States and

Latin American history, researchers have overlooked the Spanish borderlands in their inquiries into "American" deathways. By examining
the most populous of borderlands communities, this study demonstrates that there was no single American way of death, and I hope
challenges scholars to look beyond the Northeast.

Grave markers are emblematic of the differences between Roman
Catholic New Mexicans and Protestants in the northeastern United
States. The Puritans brought the use of headstones with them to North
America and even reproduced images of grave markers on broadsides
commemorating the deceased's virtues. Requiring the employment of
skilled masons, the weighty stone markers grew more and more elaborate over time, even as artisans transformed the skull and crossbones
into winged cherubs. Those markers stand yet today in graveyards
throughout New England, testaments to the masons' artistic accom-
plishments and the survival of individual graves. Though European settlement in New Mexico predates the earliest permanent English
colonies in North America, New Mexico does not preserve such a
legacy. Unfortunately for historians, who do not have this rich resource
to draw on, most of New Mexico's colonial dead received anonymous,
unmarked burials within their adobe parish churches. The relatively
small proportion of the population interred in graveyards garnered
only insubstantial wooden markers, which deteriorated as quickly as
the cadavers they identified. Had seventeenth-century New Mexicans
dotted their landscape with macabre stonework commemorating the
dead, the collective memory would likely find it much harder to ignore
the historical Spanish presence in our nation's always transnational
history. Likewise, tourists would—as they have in New England—find
yet another compelling reason to visit the Land of Enchantment.
Instead, most wander through the remaining colonial structures obliv-
ious to what rests beneath their feet.

Suggestive of the singular texture of life in the Southwest, the difference in the two regions owes as much to divergent conceptions of
the dead as to the absence of masons. In the Northeast, during the
course of the seventeenth century alone, Puritan austerity gave way
to increasingly elaborate death rituals that included gifts of gloves
and memorial rings to attendees. These trends continued through the
eighteenth century, and by the early nineteenth century, middle-class
Protestants in New England and the mid-Atlantic states carefully prepared the corpse and celebrated grandiose public funerals in order, in
the words of Gary Laderman, "to preserve their [the dead's] integrity,
to treat them according to inherited conceptions of dignity, and to

manage their remains in a manner that ensured familial or communal continuity."[4] The mid-nineteenth century saw new ways of memorializing and preserving the dead, and by the late nineteenth century an entire industry had begun to grow around the expert, professional care of the dead. As Roman Catholics, New Mexicans believed in the physical resurrection of the body. They therefore emphasized the importance of the dead finding rest in consecrated ground, whether or not the living would know an individual's precise whereabouts a generation later. No markers pointed out burial plots, and the body required no elaborate care prior to burial. They focused attention on providing for the soul's journey rather than the individual's memorialization. Once buried, the dead joined the parish's anonymous subfloor population. In keeping with Spanish baroque values, resting within this community of the faithful superseded individual identity and memorialization.

In contrast to Protestant groups in the British North American colonies, the Roman Catholics who represent the focus of the present work found solace not in ornate funerary monuments, sentimental literature, and embalmed and painted corpses but in the firm belief that they could affect the postmortem fate of their loved ones through private meditation and prayer, masses for the souls of the dead, and ritual, communal participation in confraternities. In their wills, they expressed their good fortune to be members of the "Most Holy Roman Catholic and Apostolic Church," which assured them of the communion of saints, and after serving their expected sentence in purgatory, a place in heaven. Culturally Spanish but racially a mix of principally Spanish and Indian populations, the New Mexicans who are the subject of this study acknowledged that their cadavers would become food for worms. They did not cherish the illusion of "death as sleep," with its corresponding lithographs, poetry, music, and self-conscious journal keeping. One has only to read any of the early nineteenth-century accounts by the first Anglo traders who traversed the Santa Fe Trail—which express shock at locals' brutal treatment of the dead and take offense at the festive nature of children's funerals—to see the glaring contrasts between the northeastern Protestant and New Mexican Roman Catholic traditions. No single "American" way of death has ever existed.

New Mexico likewise challenges what we know about Mexico in this period, though relatively little scholarship on colonial Mexican deathways exists. Much of what has been written focuses primarily on Mexico City and its environs, calling into question the validity of these findings for areas outside the Valley of Mexico. Though sharing in the Spanish Roman Catholic tradition, conditions in New Mexico differed radically from those in central Mexico. Frequently devoid of sufficient religious leadership, far from the seats of power, without a resident nobility, and deprived of ready access to luxury goods, New Mexicans lacked some of the mechanisms that defined and reinforced their contemporaries' ideas of the proper death and disposal of the corpse. Though New Mexico clearly had its own elite by the late eighteenth century, no matter how much wealth one accumulated, one could not pay for dozens of clergy to parade in a flamboyant funeral procession, because fewer than two dozen Franciscans served the entire province. While their counterparts in central Mexico enjoyed a long tradition of affirming social standing through ostentatious funerals and extensive pious bequests, New Mexican funerary ceremonies only occasionally presented anything classifiable as elaborate and were, at best, incidental in marking social standing. In general, burial practices support Oakah Jones's contention that New Mexico included essentially only two population groups: Indians and [non-Indians.[5]]

During the early eighteenth century, at the same time that U.S. Protestants began elaborating their high drama of funerary ritual, some Roman Catholic elites and the new merchant class in central Mexico increasingly moved in the opposite direction, rejecting the elaborate display of status-affirming funerals and embracing instead an interiorized piety.[6] Whereas dozens and even hundreds of paid mourners and religious routinely had formed the funeral corteges of Mexico's nobility and wealthy, some of these individuals now opted to spend their money on spiritually beneficial masses rather than squander it on lavish and ephemeral processions. They discarded dramatic funeral shows in favor of secret and even nighttime burials. New Mexicans, of course, seldom had indulged in or witnessed anything resembling Mexico City's or Puebla's baroque ostentation, making the changes in religious sensibility more subtle and difficult to observe hundreds of years later. Yet it is clear, even from this distance, that New Mexicans diverged in many ways from their Mexican counterparts.

Burial geography stands out as most emblematic of the differences between central New Spain and New Mexico in this period. Though the crown in the sixteenth and seventeenth centuries sought through royal edicts to ensure the availability of church burials for all Roman Catholics in the Indies, with the passage of time, a very different economic and social reality imposed itself. Ethnic, family, and corporate privileges increasingly manifested themselves in the church's burial geography, making the sacred space more and more exclusive. Confraternity membership with its exclusive tombs for members offered a solution for some, but generally churches reserved church sepulchers only for the most saintly or most affluent in New Spain. In New Mexico, by contrast, interment in one of these coveted plots beneath the church was a prerogative, available throughout the colonial period to all but the most downtrodden. Removed from—but certainly not unaware of—European ideas implicating the dead in the diseases afflicting the living, New Mexicans resisted the burial reforms authorities mandated in the late eighteenth century. Indeed, some New Mexicans would fight—figuratively and literally—to preserve their burial spaces within the churches for decades.

The backbone of this study consists of 469 wills spanning the years from 1704 to 1899; of these, just over 200 originate in the years 1750–1850, the period of this work's focus. I examined every will that I could find from 1750 to 1850; for the years before 1750 and after 1850, I used a representative sample of available wills. Almost half the wills are from Santa Fe, while the remainder were written in the jurisdictions of Albuquerque, Santa Cruz, and Taos. Women dictated approximately one-third of the wills. These testaments represent people from different social and economic ends of the spectrum; though few would have been considered among the most impoverished in their community, not all were wealthy, either.

The historian's ability to get at popular religious beliefs is undeniably somewhat hampered by the legal requirements and formulaic language of wills, the reliance on scribes, and—in the case of New Mexico—the relative dearth of surviving testaments. Spanish law strictly codified the writing of wills. In using wills to inform what is essentially a *mentality* study, it is essential to keep in mind the legal dictates and the individual whims of a notary. In New Mexico, the absence of official notaries means that there was perhaps a greater diversity of authors than elsewhere in New Spain.[7] Despite these variables, wills from New Spain, Spain, and New Mexico demonstrate a common organization and comparable language, similarities that at times transcend the centuries. Ultimately, the formulaic language and other parallels demonstrate the continuity over time and space of Spanish Roman Catholic eschatology. These commonalties, however, do not make wills any less representative of views and beliefs, be they societal or individual. Usually written in the midst of some life-threatening crisis, wills remain the source allowing historians the greatest proximity to people's beliefs about death. Indeed, by their very nature in this most critical of hours, wills may be more truthful historical documents than other intensely personal records. Although written with an eye to public consumption, wills were the final—and in many cases, the first—opportunity New Mexicans had to make their mark and leave a personal document for posterity. Used in conjunction with other sources, even the relatively few surviving wills offer tremendous insight into popular religious practices and world views.

The burial registers housed among the sacramental records of the Archives of the Archdiocese of Santa Fe, though more formulaic than wills, represent another major source for understanding New Mexican deathways. Though Michael Carroll's provocative recent study claims that "the surviving documentary record simply does not say very much about the religious beliefs and practices of Hispano settlers in colonial New Mexico,"[8] the present work defies that assertion. Though New Mexico certainly lacks the wealth of archival material available to scholars in places like Mexico City, an abundant—if tedious—paper trail does survive. Each burial book includes mind-numbing rows of names, dates, and occasionally, burial locations. Since individual priests varied greatly in their record keeping, however, these records are often incomplete as well as a challenge to decipher; in some cases, entire years are absent. Rich as these sources are, then, the research is monotonous and time-consuming, offering no immediate rewards but only a glimpse at what took place in a single parish in a single year. Yet when compounded with information from other parishes and other years, the burial registers offer significant insights into New Mexican piety. Considered alongside the information gleaned from wills during this same period, for example, the burial books can substantiate—or undermine—what people wished for in their deathbed testaments.

I examined three-year samples of burial book entries from Albuquerque, Santa Fe, and Santa Cruz for the years 1730 through 1850, in twenty-year increments (e.g., 1730–32; 1760–62; 1790–92). In some cases, priests meticulously recorded the characteristics of individual interments, including precise burial locations within the parish church. Less diligent friars allowed weeks or months to pass without a single entry, suggesting a lapse in record keeping. More typically, vague language obscures what we might otherwise learn about mortuary practices. Despite their inconsistencies, the approximately two thousand entries analyzed offer a good approximation of practices and changes over time. In addition to these, I reviewed thousands more burial entries from other communities, including numerous northern New Mexico pueblos. These records seemed to vary even more greatly in quality than those of the Spanish *villas*. I have incorporated anecdotal evidence gleaned from these burial registers as appropriate.

Along with wills and sacramental records, correspondence, material culture, and archaeological sources permit us glimpses at New Mexican deathways, creating a picture at once complex and contradictory. Precisely because death rests at the crux of all human experience, it often requires more than a single system of conduct or single set of rules. A multitude of shifting responses, beliefs, and practices materialized and sometimes coexisted.[9] In New Mexico, as in sixteenth-century Spain, people faced death with the "dialectic between confidence and anxiety."[10] Hopeful of God's benevolence, they lived and died in terror of the judgment and relied on the efficacy of post-mortem suffrages to promote their salvation and ensure their rapid deliverance from purgatory. Faith meant that as much as one anticipated heavenly rewards, one also lived in fear of God's judgment. While elements of this history remain lost to us forever because of destroyed or poorly kept documents, what we do know considerably broadens our understanding of what it meant to live and die in this most densely populated region of northernmost New Spain.

The picture that emerges reveals a fundamentally pragmatic faith. Though theologians and friars instructed people that they lived in a sort of spiritual borderlands, their lives tenuously perched between the here and the hereafter, New Mexicans did not obediently heed the dictates of their church so much as they did the dictates of their immediate reality. Though epidemics, the bloody life-size Christ sepulchered in their parish churches, and the repeated disinterment of the dead from beneath their parish church's earthen floors served as frequent reminders of death, death still caught most people off guard. Because they were more occupied with the necessities of day-to-day living than with actively pursuing their salvation through meditation and other exercises, faith informed but did not define their lives. Like Elena Olguín, who found herself desperate for a cure for a suspected tumor, headaches, and chills, individuals might turn to methods the church considered heretical.[11] The here and now in such a case carried as much sway as concern for the hereafter. Hoping that they would outlive an illness, many New Mexicans likewise ignored theologians' prescriptions to make a will to smooth the road to salvation. Rather than part with hard-earned crops and livestock in payment for a priest's services, they might avoid calling one until the last possible moment. Thus New Mexicans routinely took what they could use from their faith and discarded or deferred those elements they deemed impractical or contrary to their immediate reality. More pressing considerations often outweighed spiritual concerns. This is not to say, however, that New Mexicans were impious. It simply means that their brand of piety looked different than what we might expect—or hope—to find among our ancestors in a state where today even the government tourism department showcases religious and "spiritual" attractions. Their faith guided but did not rule them.

CHAPTER ONE

The Good Death

After years of marriage to an abusive husband, *vecina* María Manuela Ramírez came forward in San Juan de los Caballeros to complain of her spouse's tyranny and especially his most recent actions, which had nearly killed her.[1] In spring 1823, Ramírez testified that her husband, José Antonio Martín, routinely violated the sanctity of marriage by beating her. On the occasion in question, she had incurred his wrath by refusing to eat the meat of a sheep he had stolen. Infuriated, Martín attacked his wife with such violence that she resigned herself to death, begging him to call the priest to come and confess her. Martín responded that he would not summon the priest "were the devil himself to come" for her.[2] When Ramírez implored him to allow her to leave, stating that she wished for nothing more than to be allowed to die anywhere but under his roof, Martín denied his wife, observing that his very purpose in marrying her had been to make her life miserable.

Though few accounts of deathbed scenes from New Mexico survive, criminal cases such as this one offer a richly suggestive window onto death. This particular case exemplifies the very antithesis of contemporaries' conceptions of the model death or good death: Ramírez's experience was violent, sudden, and unattended by a priest or sympathetic persons who might assist her through prayer and reminders of God's goodness. According to her own account, Ramírez implored her husband to call the priest—presumably not just to confess her, but to administer all the last rites. Though Ramírez thus exhibited the resigned attitude that theologians extolled as essential to the good death, her husband's refusal to call the priest in her hour of need endangered her soul. Without the priest's ministrations, Ramírez could not receive fortification for the spiritual journey that began at the hour of one's death. It is no wonder that Ramírez wanted so desperately not to die in her husband's home. Though his savage assault left her feeling ready for death, the relationship's animosity and violence hindered her ability to maintain the state of mind necessary to die well. Ramírez's testimony meant not only to evoke sympathy for her plight but also to signal to contemporaries her spouse's complete moral depravity, evidenced by his refusal to call the priest in what seemed would be the hour of her death.

THE CONTOURS OF NEW MEXICAN LIFE

Though residing on the periphery of what, until recently, had formed part of the vast Spanish empire, Ramírez—and New Mexicans in general—did not live in isolation from the ideas that circulated in the Spanish world. These arrived along with the incoming settlers, who came primarily from central Mexico—or New Spain, as it was known in the colonial period—to settle the fertile lands adjacent to the course of the Rio Grande. Arriving clergy, both from Spain and New Spain, likewise infused the province with news and ideas. New Mexico possessed an ethnically diverse population, including Pueblo Indians who occupied their ancestral homelands, nonsedentary Indians, Spaniards, and the mestizo offspring of these peoples. Not including the jurisdiction of El Paso, Fray Francisco Atanasio Domínguez estimated New Mexico's population in 1776 to be 18,344 souls, of whom less than a third possessed Spanish ancestry.[3] After 1779, the Hispanic population grew dramatically, eclipsing the Pueblo population, which had been devastated inordinately by the smallpox epidemic of 1780–82.[4]

The ethnic and racial identity of peoples in New Mexico continues to cause controversy in some circles and warrants a brief discussion here. As concerned as eighteenth-century intellectuals and government officials were with classification—as suggested by the well-known *castas*, caste paintings, and detailed census records— race perplexed them just as it does us today. Those designated as *españoles*, or Spaniards, in eighteenth-century New Mexico already included many different racial admixtures. Social mobility was fueled in part by the need for soldiers and settlers and by high rates of *mestizaje*, or racial mixing, which, according to Antonio José Ríos-Bustamante, meant for example, that "anywhere from 70 to 80 percent of the population of Albuquerque were mestizo in fact, if not in convention by 1790."[5] Marital exogamy ensured that this group of mixed-race or mestizo people would continue to grow. As the documents repeatedly affirm, "español" denoted a cultural rather than a racial identity, and it is in this sense that I will use the term, which I occasionally interchange with "Hispanic," in many ways an equally vague and contentious term. The "Spaniards" who are the focus of this study—as dictated by the sources—spoke Spanish but descended from a mixed ethnic heritage, including Spanish, Indian, and to a lesser extent, African elements. Our modern conceptions of race, which are based largely on phenotype and lineage, do not encompass what contemporaries would have considered in defining someone as "Spanish" or "Indian." Beyond physical characteristics and ancestry, an individual's *calidad*, or status, originated in what Magali Carrera refers to as one's "social body," which included behavior, temperament, character, and worldly circumstances.[6] Calidad was therefore subjective, and an individual's identity might shift over space and time. Keeping in mind the slippery nature of all ethnic descriptors, I use the term "Hispanic" in a much narrower fashion than it is employed in discourse today, using it as a synonym for these same "Spanish" New Mexicans. Though residents of colonial New Mexico thought in terms of local and regional identities, I apply the term "New Mexicans" when referring to the entire population of the province, without regard to caste differences.

Outnumbering Spaniards through at least the mid-eighteenth century, New Mexico's Pueblo Indians represented the province's other major population group. The documents sometimes but not always provide clues as to an individual's origins but frequently rely on the generic "Indian." In these cases, the place of residence may suggest someone's group or ethnic affiliation. This too, however, can be deceptive, as Indian migration to Spanish towns accounts for some of the Pueblo depopulation between 1750 and 1820, according to Ramón Gutiérrez.[7] Whenever the documents provide a qualifier that grants insight into an individual's tribal origins, I opt for the specific over the generic. Elsewhere, I employ the generic—and undeniably problematic—term "Indian." The term "genízaro" refers to detribalized Indians, often "redeemed" Plains captives who had served Spanish households in a labor arrangement that will be discussed in chapter 2. Occasionally, the documents identify someone as a *coyote*, meaning

3

an individual of Indian and mestizo parentage. Few of the other categories of race found in New Spain appear in the principal sources used in this work because people only infrequently designated themselves or others in this fashion. Fray Ambrosio Guerra, who at the time had been parish priest of Albuquerque for twenty-three years, in 1801 commented, "I have in my charge and administration 2,952 souls...their classes being mainly genízaros (which is a mix of various nations), mulattoes, coyotes, and very few Spaniards, though most consider themselves the latter although they are not."[8] In fact, by this time, many documents ignored ethnicity entirely, identifying people by their membership in a particular community. Though the term "vecino/a" suggested a non-Indian, settler status for much of the colonial period, by the late eighteenth century the word had become far more inclusive. Even non-Spaniards assumed this label as a means of distinguishing themselves from Pueblo Indians. Wealth and class increasingly eclipsed lineage in importance among vecinos.

Most Pueblo Indians remained in their ancestral communities along the Rio Grande. Spanish settlements likewise followed the river's flow to ensure each family's proximity to arable land. Subsistence agriculture occupied many, as did sheep ranching. A considerable local industry revolved around the production of woolen goods, and households engaged in carding, spinning, and weaving wool for the manufacture of blankets and other trade goods. Residents also practiced the crafts necessary to sustain local needs, including carpentry, masonry, and shoemaking. Most Spaniards resided in or near one of four villas, or Spanish towns—Albuquerque, Santa Fe, Santa Cruz de la Cañada, and El Paso del Río del Norte—spreading out to establish new communities in the last quarter of the eighteenth century as the vecino population dramatically increased. As the growing population exacerbated pressures on the land, the mounting proportion of landless residents found work as day laborers.

The scattered nature of early settlements combined with a rapidly growing population by the late eighteenth century complicated the administration of spiritual life. Robert Wright argues that historians have overemphasized the shortage of clergy and contends that the number of clergy only occasionally fell short of the number allotted for New Mexico.[9] While Wright effectively undermines this "black legend," the documents demonstrate that many New Mexicans in isolated ranchos and farms did indeed feel without spiritual succor at times. Both residents and ecclesiastical visitors from the cathedral chapter in Durango voiced their concerns. Visitor Fray Juan Agustín de Morfi, for example, complained in 1778 that people "are deprived of the benefit of the sacraments, a great many dying without this aid because one lone minister, who must take care of one, two, three or more towns at the same time, cannot attend to those who are so far away."[10] Echoing the friar's concerns, New Mexicans—Spaniards and Pueblo Indians alike—repeatedly complained to ecclesiastical officials, hoping to increase the number of priests serving the province. Political and military considerations took precedence, however, and the number of religious relative to the growing population actually dropped from 1750 to 1850.

Political life in these years illustrates the extensive changes that New Mexicans experienced. In the course of one hundred years, New Mexico's political status shifted from a distant province of the Viceroyalty of New Spain, to a territory and "department" of the fledgling Mexican nation, to a U.S. territory. When the bishop of Durango, Pedro Tamarón y Romeral, toured New Mexico in 1760, he witnessed a society that was still frontier in character, insulated in some ways from the transformations taking place in Spain and New Spain, yet itself on the threshold of dramatic changes. In the last quarter of the eighteenth century, New Mexico's vecino population experienced unprecedented demographic and economic growth, which in turn advanced the development of a commercial economy increasingly entwined with northern Mexico's.[11] By 1850, when Pope Pius IX designated the Vicariate Apostolic of New Mexico and made New Mexico part of the Archdiocese of St. Louis, traders from the eastern United States had been traversing the Santa Fe Trail for thirty years, bringing with them foreign goods, people, and ideas. When the future bishop, Jean Baptiste Lamy, arrived in Santa Fe in the summer of 1851, he saw a society very different from the one that his predecessor had visited in 1760. The last Franciscan had died in 1848, the same year that the Treaty of Guadalupe Hidalgo made New Mexico a part of the United States. Welcoming foreign goods as signs of progress and modernity, New Mexicans had embraced the consumer products brought along the Santa Fe Trail, happily imbibing imported brandy along with medicinal elixirs.[12] New Mexicans now would struggle to maintain their traditions and their lands in the wake of the U.S. invaders, whose conquest and transformation of the landscape was initially economic and only subsequently political.

As suggested, spiritual changes accompanied the economic, social, and political ones. Franciscan friars had shaped New Mexican Roman Catholicism during the colonial period, despite some concessions to ecclesiastical authorities in Durango. Though part of the Bishopric of Durango created in the early seventeenth century, the Franciscans who ministered to New Mexico had challenged the bishop's jurisdictional authority until about 1760.[13] In that year, needing an ally against the governor, the Franciscans welcomed Bishop Tamarón's visit, which ended with the recommendation that several missions be secularized. In 1767, the viceroy, Carlos Francisco de Croix (1766–71), echoed this decision and ordered the secularization of four missions. Yet three full decades passed before Albuquerque, El Paso del Norte, Santa Cruz de la Cañada, and Santa Fe were secularized in 1797. After only a few years of service, however, the diocesan priests—disgruntled for numerous reasons—all had left the province. Secularized in name only, from late 1803 until early 1816, no secular clergy served in New Mexico. Beginning in 1816, however, Durango sent new priests to the Spanish villas, and from this point forward, the secular clergy established a firm foothold. Though their incoming numbers could not keep pace with the Spanish population's growth, the 1820s to the 1840s nonetheless witnessed the erosion of Franciscan authority in New Mexican life and the friars' eventual replacement with secular or diocesan clergy.

While New Mexico's vecino population grew rapidly toward the end of the eighteenth century and the beginning of the nineteenth, the number of religious did not increase. In 1788, some thirty Franciscans tended to the population in its dispersed villas, pueblos, and ranches. In 1818, though the population had nearly doubled in size, no more than five secular priests and twenty-three Franciscans served this same area.[14] Undoubtedly, few secular priests felt inclined to risk the hazards and hardships of life in New Mexico, which could not compare to the more urbane life-styles and agreeable climates offered by cities like Puebla, where more than one thousand priests served at the turn of the nineteenth century.[15] When ecclesiastical visitor don Agustín Fernández de San Vicente secularized the parishes of Abiquiú, Belén, Taos, San Juan, and San Miguel del Vado in 1826, only nine Franciscans and five secular clergy ministered to the population.[16] The government expelled a few Spanish-born friars in 1828, but death accounted for much of the decrease among the Franciscans.[17] A clerical shortage in Mexico meant that replacements—regular or secular—only occasionally found their way northward and never in sufficient numbers. New Mexicans implored authorities in Durango to send more clergy to meet their spiritual needs, but the church had more pressing concerns as it struggled to face the challenges of the liberal Mexican government.

Some northern New Mexicans took matters into their own hands. Building on the Franciscan Roman Catholic tradition, they formed the Brotherhood of Our Father Jesus of Nazareth, commonly referred to as the Penitentes, sometime in the late eighteenth or early nineteenth century, with a stronghold in Santa Cruz de la Cañada. Assuming community and spiritual leadership roles in many rural areas of northern New Mexico, the Penitentes offered an avenue for pious expression at the very historical moment when formal leadership waned. Though mutual aid and religious service were central to their organization and to the communities they served, the brotherhood's Passion plays and other rituals would bring them notoriety and, eventually, condemnation from the bishop.

Political and intellectual shifts that originated far from Santa Fe prompted some of New Mexico's changes. The Bourbon monarchs in Spain stepped up their campaign to reform Spain and Spanish America after the mid-eighteenth century. Under Carlos III (1759–88) in particular, the crown sought to end corporate privileges, reduce church power, expand Spain's military presence, and increase revenues. These reforms had economic and political motives but were also the product of a state that increasingly sought to embody reason and modernity, albeit in a selective fashion. Regarding priests and the church as obstacles to progress, reason, and efficiency, in the late eighteenth century the Bourbons attacked corporate privileges and promoted policies that ultimately undermined the very sanctification of power on which the monarchy rested. In central Mexico, high clergy and parish priests alike expressed their displeasure with these reforms, which threatened the social order as well as their incomes.[18] New Mexicans felt these changes as well, primarily through Spain's growing military interest in the frontier, but also through secularization and modernization efforts.[19]

Like other rural areas of New Spain, New Mexicans resisted Bourbon reforms of local religious practices. As Spain removed burials from churches and ordered that towns construct meticulously planned cemeteries a safe distance from population centers, for example, some New Mexican communities aggressively defended their right to bury the dead within the church. While Spain banned flagellation and public penitential processions in 1777, these very practices received new life in northern New Mexico through the Penitentes. Their focus on salvation, use of skulls as memento mori, and self-flagellation during the reenactment of Christ's Passion challenged Spain's modernization program.[20] In short, elements of the baroque Spanish religiosity that had arrived with the earliest Spanish settlers endured in New Mexico.

Faith, however, comprised only part of the reality of New Mexican life. Colonial New Mexicans lived in a society plagued by smallpox and measles, intermittent Comanche raids, and high child mortality.[21] Violent deaths surface repeatedly in burial books and court cases, including murder and accidental deaths by gunshot in dangerous games like El Torderito.[22] Savage spouses and hostile Indians appear as a frequent cause of death in burial registers, while the archaeological record documents cranial and vertebral fractures and stab wounds from undetermined causes.[23] Less dramatic but far more insidious were general living conditions. Poor sanitation allowed diseases to spread rapidly.[24] Though New Mexicans did not reside in crowded urban areas like their European and Mexican peers, they often lived in close quarters where disease spread easily. Marc Simmons cites the case of a British traveler in the mid-nineteenth century, whose accommodations in Arroyo Hondo consisted of sharing a one-room house with fifteen people, of whom six suffered from measles.[25] Epidemics periodically wreaked havoc. Most notably, smallpox decimated the population in 1780–82, reducing some communities—especially Pueblo—by up to 50 percent. Even in the absence of epidemics, the burial registers suggest that at any given time at least 10 to 15 percent of the adult population was widowed. The figures tended to be higher for women, and in Santa Fe alone, wills indicate that 88 percent of women had at some point been widowed.[26] Intertwined through marriage and compadrazgo, or spiritual affinity, families shared the news of death, never anonymous or far removed from daily life.

Although by the first decade of the nineteenth century children received inoculations against the dreaded smallpox, individuals had few resources in their battle against other dangers. No hospitals or trained doctors fought contagion. Governments did little to promote hygiene or sanitation. New Mexicans appear to have been what can only be termed superstitious in approaching illness. The "Lazarus" image pictured speaks volumes: framed in wood is a curious assembly of a wax doll's head and a figure painted with spots meant to represent the pustules of smallpox or some other disease. Placed in the room of a patient, this object might divert the malady from the patient into the dolls.

Turning to the community's medical experts did not necessarily result in more scientific methods being employed. While *curanderas*

1. "Lazarus,"
Photo by Michael
O'Shaughnessy
from *A Land So
Remote*, Red
Crane Books,
Santa Fe, NM

(healers) and *parteras* (midwives) healed the sick and tended to women giving birth, at times people must have feared as well as welcomed their ministrations. Witchcraft and folk medicine might be closely linked, both in terms of their techniques and their practitioners, and people frequently attributed illnesses not to natural but supernatural causes.[27] At the same time that an ascendant class of professional doctors and enlightened intellectuals made the case for environmental causes of illness in Europe and Mexico, many New Mexicans continued to embrace popular beliefs dictating that witchcraft and supernatural forces explained their maladies. One Abiquiú incident suggests the fine line between witchcraft and popular medicine and the inherent dangers perceived in both. A woman identified only as Isabel confessed to the excitable parish priest that the devil had commanded her and Petrona la Come Gallinas "to injure everyone and everything in the village." They posed as curanderas and doctored the sick but instead of healing the ill actually caused people's illnesses to worsen.[28]

Such cases point to the fact that hope and fear inevitably met when one called a curandera, demonstrating the tension between popular beliefs and popular medicine. Because of the elusiveness and imprecision of medical knowledge, those who held the keys to life might very well also hold the keys to death. New Mexico's representative to the Cortes of Cadiz, Pedro Baptista Pino, tried to alert Spanish authorities to New Mexico's lack of preparedness in 1812:

> I repeat that in all the province one finds only a single trained physician, and he is supported by the treasury [to care for] the 121 [regular army] soldiers. If this doctor treats other citizens, he is paid by whomever consults him. But if the doctor himself falls ill, it is necessary to go 300 leagues distant to get help from another. And consider this: in what condition will a gravely wounded patient be when the doctor arrives? . . . Not even those citizens, who go on campaigns at their own expense [as militia], have the consolation of [medical services]—specifically a doctor to treat the wounds they may suffer while on duty.[29]

Pino noted that New Mexico had neither pharmacists nor drugs, forcing people to rely on "native cures" to remedy illnesses. While some of these remedies certainly surpassed anything contemporary medicine offered, people must have greeted any illness with considerably more trepidation than we do today. With Mexican independence, New Mexico experienced an influx of self-proclaimed "doctors" and medicines, both of which were unregulated and of dubious value.[30]

Folk healing, which although widely practiced was sometimes cited as evidence of witchcraft before the Inquisition, endured well into the nineteenth century in rural northern New Mexico. Writing about the six months he had lived in San Miguel around 1850, German-born Franz Huning recalled:

> A man came to town, a sort of wizzard [sic] who cured people by incantations and by "sucking." His cures were always made after dark. He invited the sick to his quarters and a crowd of other spectators would also attend. He filled a small flat earthen vessel with water then commenced his incantations in a low solemn voice, and at the same time poured some liquid into the water which formed all sorts of dark figures. Presently he would beckon one of the sick and commence his sucking operations on the arm, the neck or a cheek. As a result of his sucking he would pull out of his mouth a rag or a ball of strings, or a piece of raw meat, or even a button, etc. These objects he pretended to have

extracted, although the skin remained entire and that those objects were the cause of the sickness. The patient was now pronounced cured, and the patient believed it. Afterwards I tried to convince some of the people, that that man was a fraud. I attracted their attention to the fact, that the skin in spite of his sucking had remained unbroken, consequently those rags, etc. could not have come from the body, but that the so called Doctor had them in his mouth. But they refused to be convinced and I had to give it up.[31]

Whether sent by God or by malevolent forces, illness posed a dilemma. Thus, the overall picture of health care appears bleak, though perhaps not significantly worse than elsewhere at the time.

Like the paradoxical view of illness, determining how people perceived death is fraught with complications. Nowhere is this more evident than in the debate over mortality rates and emotional investment. Some scholars have argued, for example, that parents intentionally avoided forming an attachment to a child until it had survived the most vulnerable years of childhood. Connecting mortality patterns with emotional structure, however, presumes that people possess the capacity to control the depth of their feelings. Recent research, furthermore, calls into question the relationship between demographics and emotions, finding substantial evidence of bereavement even during periods of especially high mortality.[32] Though confident in children's depravity and comforted by the certainty of God's design, even New England Puritans grieved deeply when their children died. While a relationship between demographics and emotions may indeed exist in some communities in some time periods, to construe such a correlation as universal is inaccurate and obscures the myriad and complex variables involved.

Since New Mexicans generally failed to record their thoughts in diaries or journals and little if any unofficial correspondence survives, only by looking to more impersonal sources can we begin to explore their perceptions of death and estimate to what extent faith or other factors may have attenuated grief. Scholars frequently consider naming to gauge affection or attachment to children, a method at once richly suggestive and potentially misleading. Though little such scholarship exists for Mexico, a study of eighteenth-century Guadalajara notes that infants and small children "were often buried unnamed, with no identification as to parents, and without having received baptism or any other form of the sacraments."[33] Although offering no corresponding statistics, the author concludes that the failure to name children was based in the custom of not naming children until they had passed the greatest danger of childhood mortality. Just as likely an explanation might be the priests' negligence, for clergy did not take the time even to note parents' names in these same cases. New Mexico's burial registers, in contrast, demonstrate that virtually all children had been named, notwithstanding the likelihood that many would not live past infancy. Even foundlings received a name—though whether before death or upon burial is impossible to ascertain—rather than receive anonymous burial, underscoring the importance placed on social recognition of the life and the death of even the least members of the community.

Community and church rituals provided acceptable channels for people's grief as well as a formal structure for dealing with death. Living in a relatively closed society, New Mexico's complex familial, spiritual, and community connections may have heightened the impact of a single death. The intimacy of familial and social ties and the meanings ascribed to death in popular Roman Catholicism meant that people probably experienced death as a profound event, no matter how frequent its appearance. Whether paying for masses to reduce a dead relative's sentence in purgatory or attending a neighbor's burial in the parish church, death possessed a meaning beyond the immediate loss it represented. Popular Roman Catholicism emphasized the importance of the living maintaining a relationship with the dead to facilitate the dead's exit from purgatory. Even before death, the community was called upon to participate in the deaths of its members. When God saw fit to send an illness or deadly accident, it behooved family, friends, and neighbors to visit the sick and help them die well. The illness of one reminded all of their mortality. In visiting with and caring for the dying, one might reap great spiritual rewards while also becoming better prepared for his or her own death. Private space became a public space as the community called on the dying: priest, curandera, friends, neighbors, and scribe.

THE GOOD DEATH

New Mexicans knew what it meant to die well through the model of the good death, which was integral to Spanish Roman Catholicism. Often unable to cure an illness or ameliorate bodily aches, people could diminish some of an illness's pain and death's horror by focusing on the art of dying well. The model of the good death provided guidance to the family and the community prior to and in the wake of a member's death. Theologians instructed the devout that death represented a terrible struggle for the soul. If won, the battle would lead to salvation and if lost, to damnation. Roman Catholic thought ascribed supreme importance to how one died, contending that in dying well, one could compensate for the sins of this world, thereby reaching heaven. By the same token, even the godly, if not properly prepared for death, might falter in the crucial moment and be damned, for when the soul left the body—during the time of death known as the *agonía*—the devil pitted himself against the dying, employing an arsenal of tricks. Only the most resolute and fortified could withstand his fiendish machinations in the final contest that determined one's eternal destiny. Given the high stakes, theologians and intellectuals from the fourteenth century onward penned detailed instructions on how to die well.

The good death fortified Roman Catholics for this furious struggle for the soul. Following certain ritual steps—chiefly receiving the sacraments and making a will—both family members and the sick enjoyed the comfort of knowing that they had done everything possible to attain salvation. If successful, their efforts joined with Christ's redeeming blood would rob death of its victory. Though most people were believed to be destined at least temporarily for purgatory, the character of one's death could reduce that sentence. Likewise, since the fourteenth century, Roman Catholics had believed that actions taken by the living on behalf of one's soul—prayers, masses, and pious bequests—could minimize one's time in purgatory.[34] After proper preparation, one would meet death with quiet submission rather than violent anxiety. This attitude would in turn facilitate salvation, and death, idealized as emancipation from this miserable, worldly existence, would ultimately herald one's arrival in God's presence.

This idyllic view notwithstanding, the dying did not necessarily embrace death. Despite their hopes for something greater, one historian observes, "this does not mean that these men did not experience anguish before the threat of nothingness; it is that their enormous faith was transformed into a weapon—or a shield—of efficacious wounding before this threat."[35] Certainly, God's judgment might inspire as much terror as the idea of spending eternity in heaven evoked rapture. Inextricably tied to Spanish Roman Catholic eschatology, New Mexicans viewed death in terms that transformed baptized young children into little angels but conversely promised to reveal the most feared truths of one's existence. New Spain's plastic

arts demonstrate this dualistic view. Artists depicted death as everything from a scepter-holding skeleton on a throne, to a whimsical bal-
let figure, to a cherub grasping a key. Death engendered trepidation
and fear as well as hope and joy.

By following theologians' precepts, the faithful could conquer
their fears and meet death with serenity. Outward resignation to one's
death signified that the dying had prepared for the ensuing struggle
for the soul. The crowd assembled around the deathbed would watch
for signs of the dying person's mental state. Popular belief dictated a
direct relationship between the character of one's death and the quality of the afterlife. Death in a sense signified life's very pinnacle; tri-
umph or damnation occurred at this climactic hour. Manuela Ramírez
certainly knew these things as she pleaded with her cruel husband to
leave her and let her die in peace, with the holy sacraments. His physical abuse embodied only part of the story she recounted to the magistrates in San Juan de los Caballeros after surviving her close call with
death. Martín's vengeful resolve not to call the priest but to force his
wife to die under his hateful watch had jeopardized her very salvation,
representing the most vicious of all his blows.

LITERARY TREATMENTS OF THE GOOD DEATH

Manuela Ramírez, like other New Mexicans, absorbed ideas of the
good death that circulated in published literature and had found their
way into sermons and popular culture. In the wake of the Council of
Trent (1545–63), Spanish writers took great pains to explain how the
manner in which one died affected one's afterlife. The post-Tridentine
catechism instructed Roman Catholics to view death as a vehicle for
liberation and redemption. Rather than regard death with fear, one
should anticipate it with joy and hope, for it represented the opportunity to reside at last in God's presence. Theologians advised contemporaries how to approach death to reap its fullest rewards.
Seventeenth-century Jesuit priest Juan Eusebio Nieremberg contended that everyone is born owing death to God as payment for original sin, elaborating that "this life's path is not voluntary, like that of
pilgrims, but rather necessary, like that of those condemned to the gal-
lows when they leave prison for the plaza. You are condemned to
death, and it is to your death that you are walking."[36] Nieremberg
argued that the fear so many people experienced as they approached
death stemmed from the knowledge that they had lived in sin. He
advised that at the moment of death, however, one assume an attitude

of resignation: "If you fear that you have offended God, accept the pain of this and console yourself that once you are dead you will no longer offend Him . . . you will no longer sin."[37] One could further decrease the fear of dying by focusing on the desire to see God.

Franciscan theologian Antonio Arbiol cast additional light on the subject of the good death in the eighteenth century. Echoing other treatises on the subject, Arbiol viewed helping the ill to die well as the most important act of piety. In the absence of a priest, anyone could read his manual's prayers and follow its instructions to help the sick die well. Everything one said to the ailing should be edifying, a reminder of the misery of this mortal life and the glory awaiting the faithful in heaven. Arbiol admonished visitors from expressing anything negative at the deathbed, for such distractions only would aggrieve the dying, who had to focus on offering their lives up to God and His mercy. Like Nieremberg, he observed that in order to bring people to their soul's health, God often took their body's.[38] Not divine punishment, sickness acted instead as a catalyst for pious meditation.

Theologians and other writers of devotional tracts recognized that few contemplated death until faced with a serious illness, and they emphasized the importance of meditating on death throughout one's life. Sevillan author Miguel de Mañara, whose *Discurso de la verdad* was republished several times in the eighteenth century, commanded readers to contemplate mental images of worms feasting on one's own cadaver, the dark horror of the grave, the desiccation of one's hands, and the terrifying and horrific reduction of the body to mere bones:

What does it matter, brother, if you are important in the world, if death will make you equal to the insignificant? Go to an ossuary, full of the bones of the dead, and try to distinguish between the rich and the poor, the wise and the ignorant, the small and the large; all are bones, all are skulls, all have the same shape.[39]

The truth that Mañara relentlessly drove home is that all die, a theme recurrent in much contemporary literature. By employing the most brutal imagery possible, the *Discurso* tried to prepare readers for the good death by swaying them from lives of vanity and vice and reminding them of the folly of this world's empty riches and diversions.

The sheer quantity of writing on the good death indicates that theologians and laymen alike found people in dire need of reminding.

Though most publications originated in Spain, a singular literary work came from a Franciscan based in Zacatecas, Mexico. In 1792, Fray Joaquín Hermenegildo Bolaños penned a series of vignettes in the life of Death, tracing her birth, activities in the world, and repeated efforts to remind men and women of her significance. Like New Mexico's skeletal nineteenth-century death-cart driver, doña Sebastiana, Bolaños's Death was female. Perhaps her femininity was to have made her arrival more palatable to humanity or serve as recognition of women's life-giving qualities.

Although unique in both personifying and novelizing death, *La portentosa vida de la muerte, empeatriz de los sepulcros, vengadora de los agravios del Altísimo y muy señora de la humana naturaleza* possessed a message in keeping with the period's interest in reminding readers of death's importance and imminence. In Bolaños's work, Death acted as the central figure, grousing that mankind had condemned her to "a perpetual forgetting."[40] Despite repeated reminders from God's ministers, Death lamented, people continued to endanger their souls by ignoring priestly remonstrations. Echoing the prescriptive literature, Death insisted that people meditate on the unavoidable in order to "domesticate" it. By so doing, people would lose their fear, allowing them to greet death rather than live in terror and die unprepared. Death berated mankind for being ungrateful for the service she provided, each death of a friend or family member a reminder to benefit the living. Instead of learning from her presence, most people simply ignored her throughout their lives, only growing more fearful with her increasing familiarity and proximity as they aged. Though articulating some familiar themes, Bolaños's work represented a pointed response to Enlightenment ideas that had gained ground among a small group of New Spain's intellectuals. In their view, one should not think about or fear death, for this was the product of superstitious religiosity and "a savage and irrational irruption that endangers social harmony."[41]

Bolaños's Death thus sought to inspire not fear but mindfulness. In *La portentosa vida de la muerte*, Death acted as an incentive to live a righteous life, not as a punishment. Death appeared as breathtakingly beautiful and elsewhere materialized in wretched and hideous form, depending on the beholder. Death called on a rich man without warning, giving him no time to mobilize notary, doctor, and priest. She preached to the doomed man:

> If you had said to your soul: be happy my soul, because I already have enough that I can pay for many masses for

you and to comfort the needy poor and do many good
works and finally bring you to heaven, you would have
lived more than you thought and would not have the fear
that you now have and the pain at seeing your property in
another's power.[42]

While criticizing the rich man's miserliness, Death also pointed out
the folly and danger of attachment to earthly possessions and the
importance of preparation. Elsewhere, Death dressed elegantly to call
upon a just and pious man, who regarded her with the serenity of a
saint. Here, a resplendent Death delivered keys of gold and ambrosia
served in crystal. The devout man embraced the opportunity to
escape the prison of his mortal body. Resolute even in his painful
death throes, he withstood temptation. Nothing disturbed his soul's
remarkable placidity. Each vignette in the text articulated an obvious
moral, exhorting preparation for death's arrival.

Using a novelistic format, *La portentosa vida de la muerte* illus-
trated the same spiritual lessons that others had taught more point-
edly and didactically. Richly detailed images accompanied the text,
driving home the meaning. Conceptions of the good death remained
intrinsic to Roman Catholic piety, even though people clearly needed
reminding. Never tiring of the topic, Spanish and Mexican writers
ensured the endurance of this notion of death as an ideal. Many of the
most popular theological works from the seventeenth and eighteenth
centuries did not lose their currency, and publishing houses in Spain
and Mexico repeatedly republished their tracts.

Spanish and Mexican editions of books in part helped to dissemi-
nate these ideas in New Mexico. While New Mexico's missions often possessed only the essential missals and religious manuals, by 1776 the
library of the Custody of New Mexico held 256 volumes, including sermons, breviaries, the lives of the saints, regulations of the Franciscan
Order, and some canon law.[43] Wealthy individuals brought small
libraries with them from Mexico, including historical works on the Indies
and devotional materials. Joaquín del Pino, a native of Mexico City, listed
ten volumes by the Jesuit Pedro Murillo Velarde, author of a well-known
guide to making one's will, among his books in 1768.[44] He passed these on
to his heirs, and the next generation undoubtedly received them from
Pino's children. The overall scarcity of books meant that people
bequeathed existing tomes as well as lent out, traded, and sold volumes
during the owner's lifetime. While limited in number, books probably
reached a wider audience than numbers alone suggest.[45]

Certainly, however, the relative dearth of books combined with widespread illiteracy prevented most New Mexicans from actually reading devotional literature. For much of the colonial period, few opportunities for formal education existed in New Mexico. Albuquerque and Santa Fe census records show the presence of teachers in 1790, but it was 1803 before the first governmental primary schools were founded, and those were limited to boys under the age of twelve.[46] Bernardo Gallegos estimates that up to a third of Santa Fe's male population was literate, a figure that appears quite high for the colonial period, though the capital likely boasted more literate residents than more rural communities.[47] Wills from 1700 to 1800 demonstrate that in fact only about a quarter of all testators could sign their names—many in only the crudest manner—a figure a little bit lower than one seventeenth-century literacy estimate.[48]

Despite high levels of illiteracy, a rich oral tradition of sermons, stories, morality plays, and songs reinforced themes found in written texts and made these ideas accessible to the population. Key to this process of cultural instruction were the Franciscans who ministered to eighteenth-century New Mexicans and had received rigorous educations at one of the *conventos*, or monasteries, in central Mexico. Coming predominantly from urban areas, most also had served in one of the more cosmopolitan of New Spain's colonial cities—Mexico City or Puebla—and received instruction as missionaries at Santiago de Tlatelolco outside Mexico City.[49] By the time he arrived in New Mexico, the average friar was almost thirty-five years old, well versed in theology, and possessed of a world view shaped by a lifetime in central Mexico's dynamic urban centers. The friars educated New Mexicans on matters of faith, life, and death. Based on this faith, confraternities sponsored masses, processions, plays, and other communal events that fostered and reinforced the common body of knowledge. In addition, the *despedida*, a farewell song with details of an individual's life and death, probably offered examples of living and dying well.[50] Along with public readings and the tutoring afforded some New Mexican youth, a variety of written and oral traditions therefore transmitted cultural beliefs and values within families and across generations.

IMAGES OF DEATH

Communicating ideas, as any visitor to one of Mexico's dazzling baroque churches knows, relied on powerful images as well as sermons and songs. Images of death—good and otherwise—had long been integral to the literature. Detailed drawings of Death's pursuits accompanied Bolaños's writings in *La portentosa vida de la muerte*, and paintings and sculptures frequently adopted popular literary themes. Death-related imagery of course figured centrally in Roman Catholicism: depictions of Christ's death, the resurrection of the dead, the martyrdom of the saints, and the Virgin Mary's sorrows all offered opportunities to meditate on death. Christ's Crucifixion, with blood oozing from his wounds, served as churches' central fixture as well as the focus of the mass. Life-size statues of the mourning Mary, complete with glass beads simulating tears, offered vivid, heartrending focal points for parishioners. Canvases showed anguished souls burning in purgatory's fires while gory depictions of saintly martyrdom comprised an entire genre of painting. After the Council of Trent affirmed realism in religious art, artists developed painstaking techniques to make these pieces appear even more lifelike.

These popular devotional themes and the techniques to give the plastic arts a high degree of realism came to the Americas through books and artwork as well as through masters who worked in the colonies. Seventeenth- and eighteenth-century Mexican painters like Juan Correa and Miguel Cabrera emulated and built upon the rich Spanish tradition. They relied on the familiar religious and allegorical subjects, painting the death of the Virgin Mary with her face serene, the very embodiment of the good death. Mary also appeared as the Virgin of Sorrows, pierced by swords, and as the tear-stained Virgin of Solitude grieving her son's death. Like the life-sized, bloodied, and coffined *Santo Entierro*—Christ in the tomb—that occupied a prominent place in churches, these images offered believers a potent point of reference to their own lives.

Although the Council of Trent reminded people that religious images should not be mistaken for the saints depicted, in practice these paintings and carvings served as more than just representations of the sanctified. Artists' creations did not sit passively in the home or church. Like their Spanish and Mexican counterparts, New Mexican parish images participated in the many communal rituals that animated popular religious life. The changing seasons and the corresponding needs of an agrarian people determined some of these rites, while others corresponded to the liturgical calendar. Death and rebirth, the crux of Christian thought, united many of the rituals. The anointing of the forehead with ashes on Ash Wednesday reminded people of the temporary nature of the body while Holy Week processions enlisted the entire community in elaborate reenactments of

Jesus's death and burial. Using a life-size statue of Christ, the community created a mobile sacred space, and the multitude grieved Christ's death as though witnessing it first-hand. Individuals in their private devotions and the community in its parish festivities accessed the sacred through these devotional objects. These utilitarian pieces sat in home altars, where they became the locus of family members' appeals.[51] People ascribed power to the images, burying or facing toward the wall a santo who had failed to fulfill a petition. If the saint rewarded someone by granting a request, the faithful might reciprocate by paying for a mass in that saint's honor or making a pilgrimage to an area shrine.

Not merely polychromed wood or canvas, the images themselves held power, for they bridged the mundane and the sacred both symbolically and literally.[52] The faithful fashioned delicate clothes for the saints, who displayed their finery during Holy Week processions that snaked their way through the community. The living took solace in visiting with and praying before the objects of their devotions, and the dying gave personal items to their favorite images—jewelry to the Virgin, a trinket for St. Anthony—in hopes of intercession. When natural disaster threatened or struck, communities and individuals turned to their saints, enacting rituals designed to restore order. German immigrant Franz Huning described such a ritual as he observed it in San Miguel during an 1851 drought: "A lot of women got hold of their Saint San Miguel (the priest had loaned him to them), and went in procession to the fields, praying and chanting hymns."[53] The women's incantations resulted in the desired thunderstorm, affirming the saint's efficacy. The repository for generations of prayers, hopes, and secrets, the bultos, or statues, offered a tangible, physical site of spirituality.

Paintings, somewhat less portable than bultos, perhaps did more to instruct than to intercede. The model death appeared on canvases depicting tranquil male and female religious on their deathbeds. Saintly martyrdom, too, offered insights into how to die well, for painters frequently portrayed the saints blandly enduring the agonía in a moment of exquisite corporal pain. Though martyrs' deaths tended toward the savage, on canvas, even in the face of bodily violence, their faces conveyed spiritual peace. Juan Correa's *Martirio de Fray Vicente de San José*, for example, portrays the martyrdom of the Spanish Franciscan, burned alive in a fiery circle, his face composed and his eyes intent on the cross he holds. Prepared for death, Fray Vicente de San José registers no pain. In other works,

St. Lawrence roasts on the gridiron, St. Agatha offers her severed breasts on a platter, and a bound St. Sebastian stares impassively as arrows pierce his body. Even those who suffered upon death—most notably, those expiating their sins in the fires of purgatory—enjoyed the hope of relief and redemption in paintings that showed the Virgin Mary rescuing suffering souls from the flames. Migrants to New Mexico had seen these images and understood their message, even if comparatively few gilded statues and oil paintings graced the region's churches.

Themes of saintly martyrdom and the model death appeared in New Mexican art, likely inspired by engravings from books, which friars and artisans routinely copied as they recreated the world of their youth with locally available materials. Some pieces have been lost in all but the documents, fleetingly described in wills or other texts. We know, for example, from one U.S. soldier's foray into New Mexico, that before its destruction, Santa Fe's Chapel of Our Lady of Light included a stone carving of the Virgin rescuing a fortunate soul from Satan's jaws.[54] The images that survive in churches, museums, and private collections allow us to glimpse the world of ideas that informed New Mexican deathways. The Laguna Santero (1776–1815), whom Larry Frank asserts likely received his training elsewhere, painted an image (Illustration 2) of St. Philip of Jesus's martyrdom typical of the genre described. Though lances cut through his body and blood gushes from his torso, the Franciscan's face is placid as he dies on a cross in a foreign land. St. Apollonia of Alexandria (Illustration 3), by Pedro Antonio Fresquís (1749–1831), displays an equally calm visage. As the executioner rips the teeth from her mouth in a bloody torrent, the saint confronts the viewer's gaze with profound serenity.

Until the late eighteenth century, along with imports from Mexico and work local artisans created, the Franciscans themselves produced some of New Mexico's devotional art, re-creating favorite themes and images from their training in Puebla and Mexico City. Though most produced anonymously, among the earliest identifiable *santeros*—the artisans who painted or carved religious art—is Fray Andrés José García, the creole son of a blacksmith who arrived in New Mexico in 1760. He crafted sculptures, altarpieces, and furniture in Santa Cruz, Santa Fe, and Albuquerque that imitated the baroque styles he had grown up with in his native Puebla. Fray Domínguez's observations in his visit to the Santa Cruz church suggest the friar's enthusiasm and creative energy: "The altar screen, the image of Our Lady of the Rosary, the large Jesús Nazareno, the Holy Sepulcher, casket, and the

2. *St. Philip of Jesus* by Laguna Santero, courtesy The Museum of International Folk Art (a unit of the Museum of New Mexico, Santa Fe, New Mexico), photo by Michael O'Shaughnessy from *A Land So Remote*, Red Crane Books, Santa Fe, NM

3. *St. Apollonia of Alexandria* by Pedro Fresquís, Collection of the Museum of Spanish Colonial Art, Santa Fe, photo by Michael O'Shaughnessy from *A Land So Remote*, Red Crane Books, Santa Fe, NM

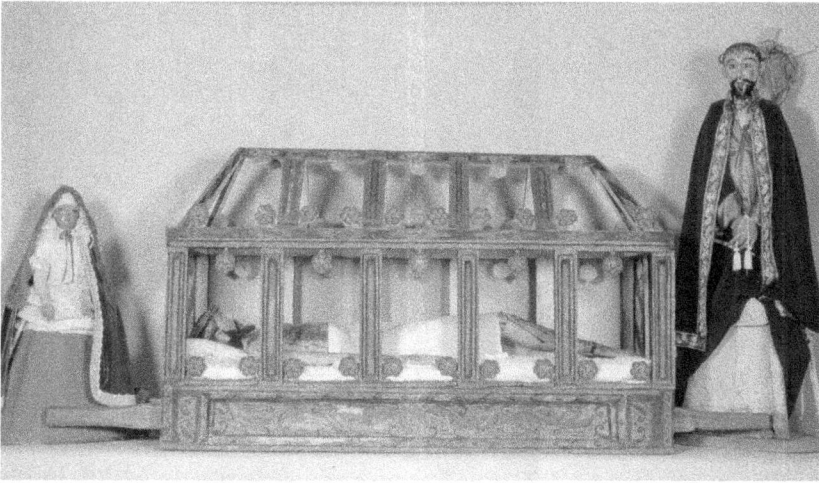

4. *Santo Entierro* by Fray Andrés García, parish church Santa Cruz de la Cañada, from the Collections of the Archdiocese of Santa Fe

balustrade in the sanctuary were made and designed by Father Fray Andrés García, who worked day and night with his own hands."[55] His *Santo Entierro* even today rests in the parish church at Santa Cruz de la Cañada. Other friars were probably also among the early santeros, but because they worked in anonymity we know them only by the names art historians have invented for them. Although santeros after 1790 would move away from the baroque and develop, according to Larry Frank, "original interpretations of religious iconography, made within the context of the social, cultural and spiritual influences of New Mexico," they would continue to rely on familiar baroque themes in their work.[56]

In the first quarter of the nineteenth century, the number of Franciscans in New Mexico declined, and a commercial santero tradition emerged to meet the growing population's devotional needs. Using pine, cottonwood, gesso, and tempera, the santeros relied on local materials and familiar subject matter from sermons, engravings, and existing artwork. Though uniquely New Mexican, the iconography and the themes reflect the santeros' roots in the Spanish tradition. By far the most popular images in New Mexico were those depicting the Virgin Mary in some form. She most frequently appeared as the Virgin of Sorrows, the mother grieving her son's death, depicted with one or seven arrows piercing her chest.[57] Mary, however, emerged as a subject in many guises and formats, including

5. *Our Lady of Mt. Carmel* by José Rafael Aragón, Harwood Museum of Art, University of New Mexico, gift of Mabel Dodge Luhan, photo by Pat Pollard

the buffalo hide paintings disparaged by early visitors to the province, described in Fray Domínguez's meticulous 1776 report. Suggestive of Mary's pivotal role in the afterlife, another favored Marian advocation, Our Lady of Mount Carmel, the patroness of the chapel in Santa Cruz's parish church, appears in a painting by José Rafael Aragón, rescuing a sinner from purgatorial fires.

Lacking the training and materials available to artisans in central Mexico, these images are two-dimensional and lacking in perspective. Yet while they appear less realistic or immediate than those found in Mexico City and Puebla in this same period, the santos often direct their gazes at the viewer, establishing a personal connection and even at times implicating the spectator in the images' experience. Traveling from village to village, the santeros created images that, though not as realistic as those in central Mexico, would have meaning in the community just as potent.

Like the santos' outward-directed gaze, communities' Holy Week rituals implicated the faithful in the events taking place. The parish would take the life-size Christ from the church to dramatize his death and burial. A removable crown of thorns, nails, a winding cloth, and other accouterments of Jesus's suffering made the unhappy image complete and offered a tangible connection to the divine, transforming spectators into eyewitnesses as the beleaguered Jesus wound his way through the multitude. Rev. Lewis Smith, an 1852 observer of such a procession, described it:

> The image [of Christ] looked like a corpse—the crown
> of thorns was upon its head—the nails were in its hands
> and feet—the head was fallen upon its breast—the face
> was the picture of intense agony, and blood seemed to be
> flowing from every wound. It was so constructed that its
> limbs worked after nature's pattern, and when it was taken
> from the cross, we could hardly divest our minds of the
> idea that it was really a human body upon which we were
> gazing. The women cried aloud, and the church resounded
> with sorrow. The body was laid in a glass case, covered
> with artificial flowers, and was to be paraded through
> the streets.[58]

Behind him trailed the grieving mother, the almost life-size statue of Our Lady of Sorrows, clad in her finest black gown for the occasion.

More than a simple reenactment, the sensational drama of Holy Week created a sacred space wherein New Mexicans actually witnessed Christ's suffering and gory death. Though culpable in his fate, participants also actively and vociferously mourned his death. As Smith observed, the stark reality of the image made it difficult to separate truth from fiction—even for a Protestant minister such as himself. A Good Friday sermon that Fray Manuel Antonio García del Valle delivered illustrates how the priest's vivid use of language reinforced the familiar images. Beginning with the biblical passage in which a soldier gashes open Jesus's side, the friar continued:

> What recollections, my fellow Christians, these words of
> my text introduce into our minds! Jesus suffering and hang-
> ing dead on the tree of the cross! Let us travel by meditation
> and contemplation to Golgotha, also called Mount Calvary.
> What do our eyes see in this sad, ill-fated, and mournful
> place? From every direction come the cries, laments, and
> voices of sorrow. Here the blood, tears, and cruel sorrows

of the best Son, the compassion of one of the Marys, the finest of them . . . [59]

Although speaking in 1821, García del Valle's approach might be characterized as baroque, for it sought to awaken the audience's visual senses and arouse its emotions by focusing on Mary's and her son's humanity. The friar did not merely ask the faithful to think of the horrors of the Crucifixion but besought the congregation to "meditate" and "travel" to Golgotha, visualizing the terrible darkness and the mutilated body, and thereby feeling the observers'—and in particular, the mother's—despair.

Parishioners experienced the darkness of Christ's death first-hand during the tenebrae services on Holy Thursday, Good Friday, and Holy Saturday. The parish extinguished fifteen candles over a period of time, finally leaving the faithful in a darkened church. The candles' gradual extinction signified the apostles' abandonment of Christ, the Stations of the Cross, and Christ's death and burial. The darkness reminded the community of the turmoil and void left in the world with Christ's death. As the community later relit the candles, they felt the hope offered by the resurrection and the promise of salvation.[60]

Mary figured prominently in the drama of Holy Week, both as the Virgin of Sorrows and the Virgin of Solitude. In García del Valle's sermon, she mourned her son, exclaiming:

Oh dead life! Oh obscured light! Oh defaced beauty! And what hands were they that have done so to your divine form? What crown is this that my eyes see on your head? What other wound do I see in your side? . . . My Son and my blood, whence rose this powerful storm? What kind of day has this been that you should be taken from me? Where shall I go? Who will care for me? Fathers and brothers came in their affliction to beg for their dead sons and brothers, and you with your infinite virtue and clemency consoled and assisted them. But I who see my Son and my Father, my Brother and my Lord lying in death—whom can I implore to help him? Who will console me? Where is the good Jesus the Nazarene, Son of the living God, that he might console the living and grant life to the dead?[61]

Again, the priest's language recreated familiar visual images while also reinforcing the drama to be played out before the community.

Mary's grief was palpable in the sermon, and her son's death must have resonated with New Mexican women and men, all too acquainted with high infant and child mortality.

New Mexico's elaborate Passion plays became emblematic of the Penitentes, who had emerged in rural northern New Mexico sometime around the turn of the nineteenth century to fill the increasing need for religious leadership, mutual aid, and communal ritual. Many of the brotherhood's religious practices had clear origins in the baroque world of Spain and Mexico, and death often figured prominently. Closely associated with the Penitentes was the death cart piloted by the ghastly doña Sebastiana—Death herself. Clinging to a bow and arrow, she was the heir to a long tradition of European memento mori. Her obsidian eyes reflected a New World element mixed in with the Old. Dramatic Holy Week processions in which brothers pulled her in her death cart comprised part of the Penitentes' more public forms of worship. Like the preponderance of skulls and Crucifixion images in the moradas, or meetinghouses, where the Penitentes worshipped, the death cart reminded the living to be mindful of death. Echoing Bolaños's and Mañara's rejoinders to humanity, doña Sebastiana spurred contemplation and preparation for death.[62] In the time-honored tradition of the good death, these practices would ensure that by the time one faced one's own death, years of pious meditation combined with judicious living would translate into a deathbed that was peaceful and resigned.

At the deathbed, secular and religious traditions united to dictate the actions of the sick and their family members. Though people certainly looked to what medical help was available to delay the inevitable or at least minimize discomfort, theologians discouraged the sick and friends and family from entertaining thoughts of recovery. Such distractions would only diffuse the suffering person's limited energy and thereby endanger the soul.[63] Family and friends were to remind the sick of God's glory, thus keeping them squarely on the path to salvation. Even for those like María Manuela Ramírez, who faced a sudden and violent death, the model of the good death offered order and guidance. In the midst of bodily aches, limited physical comforts, and what must have been an impending sense of loss among all concerned, the ideal of the good death provided hope for the dying and order for the living.

CHAPTER TWO

Releasing Worldly and Spiritual Concerns

Juliana Fernández probably had nursed enough other people in their final illnesses to recognize the signs that death would soon arrive for her. Or perhaps she merely had grown impatient with the ailment that confined her to bed. Whatever the case, in 1785 she realized that the time had come to put her spiritual and worldly affairs in order. She beseeched her husband to fetch someone who could record her last will and testament, along with witnesses to ensure that the document would be legally binding. After the arrival of José Maldonado and Pablo Sandoval—both officers from the garrison in Santa Fe—she began the process of distilling her life onto paper with a long, detailed profession of her faith. She acknowledged the virgin birth and the Last Judgment and consigned her soul to God, its "creator and redeemer." Charging her executors to shroud her body in the habit of St. Francis, she requested burial in the parish church of Santa Fe, wherever there might be room. Finally, Fernández instructed that her body be present at the funeral mass, reflecting her hope that her soul might benefit from her cadaver's presence at the service.

The dying woman's focus then shifted to her family. She had been married twice and widowed once. Though she had no living children of her own, she recognized her stepdaughter from her second marriage as her heir. She next listed her belongings—among them an unspecified amount of land, 50 sheep, 38 cattle, some silk, a coat, two comales or griddles, two copper sauce pans, a tablecloth, some boxes from Michoacán, and an armoire. Fernández left a delicate string of pearls to an image of the Virgin of Sorrows in the parish of Santa Cruz de la Cañada and divided the rest of her property among her husband, step-daughter, mother, and an Indian servant girl whom she referred to as "mi indita" or "my little Indian girl," likely a ransomed captive. She asked her executors to pay for four novenas, or series of masses for her soul. Her recent sale of 250 sheep would cover all funeral expenses, with the remainder designated to pay for masses to benefit the souls of her first husband, Miguel Ortiz, and their only child. Though already nine years into her second marriage, Fernández also left half the house and lands she had inherited from Ortiz for the benefit of his soul and that of their daughter, who had died several years earlier.[1] Neither death nor remarriage had severed these bonds.

Fernández's discussion of her business transactions—which she apparently conducted independently of her second husband—and her meticulous attention to the details of her funeral and suffrages reveal her firm convictions about both her commercial and her spiritual life. Her preparations for death necessarily included dispensing of material goods and contemplating how she might further her soul's welfare after death. Her carefully thought-out directions and the very act of drawing up her will indicate that Fernández aspired to die according to the model of the good death.

To die well went beyond ritual fortification for the final, deathbed battle for the soul. It also meant taking care of one's spiritual and material obligations. After a righteous life and contemplation of one's mortality, making a will constituted the next step in achieving deathbed serenity. Though ideally written while in good health, draft-ing a will was especially essential for the dying, for it formally released their hold on the temporal world. Once the sick had relinquished all earthly possessions and rectified areas in which they had been remiss during life, they could concentrate on spiritual matters. The commu-nity—family, friends, priest, confraternity members—might help in this by reminding the dying of spiritual truths and helping them to maintain their focus on God.

THE MECHANICS OF MAKING A WILL

Since New Mexico lacked public notaries, people usually asked that an individual of some local standing officiate and "interpose his author-ity" in the process of making a will. Typically the *alcalde mayor, teniente de justicia*, or *alcalde de paz*—all government officials—would lend his support and, if himself literate, pen the will.[2] In Juliana Fernández's case, Lt. José Maldonado from the garrison in Santa Fe noted that Gov. Juan Bautista de Anza had conferred upon him the authority to officiate. Maldonado acted not simply as a scribe, for in the absence of a notary, his presence placed the weight of the law behind the document. Scant evidence survives to indicate the price for this service, though in 1836 Gregorio Sánchez received four pesos for a will he penned on behalf of María de la Luz Pacheco. This figure included the cost of the official stamped paper, which New Mexicans routinely did without because of its scarcity.[3]

To be legally binding, a will had to be approved by the testator in the presence of several witnesses. Without an official *escribano* or notary, Spanish law required five witnesses rather than the usual three to validate a nuncupative or open will. New Mexican wills frequently do not include the requisite number of witnesses; often only two or three people signed or made a cross to indicate they had witnessed the will. Yet even with only a few witnesses, making a will remained a public process, the sickbed serving as a link between public and private as well as spiritual and legal worlds.

The will's text repeatedly established the public quality of the document. It often opened with a statement akin to "Know ye all who may see this testament" and ended with a sentence acknowledging the witnesses' presence. Since most people waited until they were at death's door before drafting a will, the sick room would be peopled with officials and witnesses, as well as the entourage of family and friends whom illness inevitably brought. Three witnesses accompanied presidial soldier Ramón García at his sickbed in 1768. The morning before her death, Rosa Bustamante's three daughters and her priest surrounded her bed. A servant who was in the room at the time later testified that "Said Señora was already on the path or agonía, as she was coming to terms with our Creator."[4] Merchant Juan Esteban Pino in 1838 observed that he made his will without the presence of a judge and before "only" five witnesses, for "finding myself having to make it at the point of Pecos Canyon, it was not possible to observe all the legal requirements."[5] Thus, as he lay dying, at least five individuals attended Pino, probably praying with him in addition to acting as witnesses.

Though theologians exhorted the faithful to draw up wills for their spiritual well-being, the desire to distribute one's accumulated goods certainly motivated many people. Roman Catholic doctrine dictated that all but those living in the most abject poverty craft their wills well in anticipation of death. Adherence promoted preservation of wealth, maintenance of social cohesion, and meditation on death. Whereas some Spanish synods in the early modern period actually had banned burial in sacred ground for Roman Catholics who died intestate, Spanish civil law simply fined the estates of the intestate. New Mexico's eighteenth-century *arancel*, or schedule of fees, affirmed this more immediate incentive: "Let it be noted with regard to the funerals of Spaniards who die intestate without designating a burial place that double fees must be paid even though the deceased be buried in the parish church."[6]

The prescriptive literature likewise impressed the importance of making a will. In their writings on the good death, Arbiol, Nieremberg, and others identified the will as central to fulfilling one's spiritual and material debts, and numerous texts guided the formal process of writing the will. The Jesuit Congregation of the Good Death in Mexico published a volume elaborating the basic rules of making a will in 1714. It emphasized the importance of drafting one while still in good health so as to devote the requisite attention and clarity of thought to this essential Christian endeavor.[7] The seventeenth-century bishop of Puebla, Juan de Palafox y Mendoza, emphasized the will's importance in a book describing Mother Francisca del Santísimo Sacramento's visions. The Carmelite Mother Francisca saw souls suffering in purgatory because they had died indebted, their worldly affairs unresolved.[8] Though we tend to think of the spiritual and secular worlds as distinct today, the two were in many ways one for contemporaries.

The most utilitarian of all the manuals was the *Práctica de testamentos en la que se resuelven los casos más frecuentes que se ofrecen en la disposición de las últimas voluntades*. Written by the Jesuit priest Pedro Murillo Velarde, it was first published in the mid-eighteenth century in Mexico City. Testament to its extensive reach and enduring value was its repeated republication, including a Santa Fe edition printed in 1850. More technical than spiritual in nature, the manual clarifies all manner of questions relative to inheritance, executors, and witnesses. While most of the volume centers on juridical matters, the eighteenth-century editions include a rhyme on the page facing the first page of text, which reads: "MEMENTO MORI/Dispose of your things of good fortune/That they may give you life in death."[9] Murillo composed this instructive book to give readers the know-how to make a will, so as to reduce the number of people whose souls were jeopardized by dying intestate. While lacking the elevated religious prose of other manuals, Murillo's slim volume addresses heirs' and executors' moral duties. If the deceased ever had expressed, even if only "by signs," that they wished to make a bequest for the good of their soul, for example, the heir or executor must step forward and let these wishes be known. Spiritual and material concerns were indivisible.

The actual exercise of writing a will served as a meditation on death. Certain of death's arrival but unsure of its hour, theologians encouraged people to cultivate an awareness of death's imminence. Mindfulness ensured a more peaceful transition to the afterlife and kept one in a constant state of preparation. Like ascetics who meditated with a skull in one hand, ordinary people could reap enormous spiritual rewards by making their wills. Theologians in sixteenth-century Spain actually instructed the faithful to revisit their wills after making them, for, as Carlos Eire observes,

> constant periodic reading of one's own testament was
> a highly meritorious form of devotion, not only as a prepa-
> ration for death but also as a means of enhancing the
> efficacy of the will's pious bequests, for if one renewed
> one's assent to the will over and over again, it could
> increase one's charitable disposition.[10]

In the process of making a testament one had to take spiritual inventory as well as dispense with one's goods and pay both monetary and moral debts. These steps prompted one to think about death and thereby facilitated a clear conscience and the proper temperament at the deathbed.

These ideas came to New Mexico like the structure of wills, which followed a template. Testators began by identifying themselves by name and place of residence. Occasionally they offered parents' names, attested to their legitimacy of birth, or indicated their calidad. For the will to be legally valid, the testator had to assert his or her mental competence. Frequently, the individual would offer the precipitating motive for making the will. People next made a profession of faith, which affirmed the individual's faith in Roman Catholicism and specific tenets, such as the belief in the holy Trinity, the Immaculate Conception, the Resurrection, and the Last Judgment. In Juliana Fernández's 1785 profession we find the following typical phrasing:

> First, I believe and confess in the ineffable mystery of the
> most holy Trinity, God the Father, God the Son, and God the
> Holy Spirit, three distinct persons and only one true God.

Second, I believe that Christ was made flesh in the blessed
womb of Our Lady the Virgin Mary, remaining virgin before
giving birth and after giving birth, ever-virgin and true
Mother of God. I believe that he suffered death and the
Passion in order to redeem and save us. I believe that he
rose on the third day. I believe that he will return to judge
the living and the dead, to reward and punish. Finally, I
believe and acknowledge all the mysteries of our holy
mother, the catholic, apostolic, Roman Church, in which
faith and belief I want to live and die.[11]

Circumstances sometimes dictated, however, that an individual—like
the unfortunate Juan Esteban Pino, for example—issue a hastier and
more abbreviated blanket statement of belief in "all the mysteries of
our holy faith."[12] Some further truncated the profession, confining their
statement as María Antonia Andrea Martínez did, to: "In the name of
almighty God and the ever-virgin Mary, conceived without the stain of
original sin. Amen."[13] Though examples of even these abbreviated professions of faith appear in the early colonial period, by the late eighteenth century there was a decided trend away from elaborate
professions of faith. By the late nineteenth century, even these
abridged professions of faith appear increasingly anomalous in a document that is otherwise wholly secular. Yet no matter how abbreviated,
even the distilled profession identified the dying as a member of the
church and thus set the stage for the will's remaining spiritual steps.

Many people next turned to Mary and the saints, imploring their
intercession both to evade the devil's tricks and temptations and garner
favor before God. To withstand better the epic moral dangers that would
face them in death, the dying called upon the aid of a variety of holy
intermediaries. Most New Mexicans invoked the assistance of the Virgin
Mary as intercessor, *abogada* or advocate, as well as some combination
of name saint, guardian angel, saints of special devotion, the apostles
Peter and Paul, St. Francis, and the rest of the heavenly court. Many
specifically asked that these figures intercede and help put their souls
on "the most certain path to salvation." Far from signaling finality, death
thus represented a spiritual journey as well as the commencement of
the soul's greatest challenge. In addition to referring to the judgment in
her profession of faith, Juliana Fernández observed that "if God shall be
served to call me to judgment, I order my testament in the following
manner."[14] Many people must have been acutely aware that God would
sentence their soul upon death, and awareness of God's impending

judgment gained a special resonance in the will, underscoring as it did the testator's looming appointment with the heavenly tribunal.

More imposing even than this judgment, perhaps, was the soul's singular vulnerability at death, when the devil would tempt and torment the dying in an effort to claim the soul for himself. The moment of death represented a battleground. This conception of death found expression in Capt. Joseph Baca's will, among others. At age fifty-four, Baca elected both St. Francis and St. Joseph to serve as his advocates "that they may defend us from our common enemy in death."[15] Gregorio Martín of Abiquiú likewise invoked the saints to help him combat the devil. Although already gravely ill, he renounced the folly and excesses of this life in exchange for the intercession of numerous saints, "so that in the hour of my death they may banish all bad spirits, for which end from now on and forever I renounce all the ostentatious vanities of this world."[16] Martín's unabashed attempt to bargain with the saints appears a natural extension of the "deals" people routinely brokered as they sought a better harvest or protection from a storm. His renunciation of earthly delights proved brief, however, for he died within a few months of pledging austerity.

The request for intercession served not only to identify a favorite devotion or signal one's piety but actually demonstrated that one was resigned to his or her death. The language used often conveyed humility, as people acknowledged their sinfulness and unworthiness before God. Others spoke of the debt they owed God, echoing the idea that mankind paid for original sin with death. Nieremberg, Bolaños, and other theologians had emphasized this belief by referring to human existence as a state of spiritual arrears. In this conceptualization, Death herself merely served God as a sort of debt collector. This view implied death's equity, not merely in the usual sense that death equalizes rich and poor but in that death is just payment for life. In San Antonio del Embudo, Juan Francisco Martín noted that "fearing and dreading death as a natural thing and a debt we have to pay, as ever, I take as my intercessor the ever Virgin Mary."[17] Martín did not resist, but resigned himself to paying his debt, in keeping with the ideal of the good death.

Though unquestionably formulaic in structure and language, when viewed over a long span of time, wills reveal the changing nature of New Mexican Roman Catholicism and the changing character of New Mexican society as a whole. For much of the eighteenth century, for example, wills retained their lengthy professions of faith and meticulous instructions for burial and postmortem masses. In time, however, detailed appeals for intercession from the saints fell off. Pleas to apostles Peter and Paul and even the venerable St. Francis, for example, slowly waned over the course of the eighteenth century. St. John the Baptist disappeared from view by the last quarter of the eighteenth century, and the Archangel Michael made his last appearance in 1830. In the late colonial and early Mexican periods, fewer and fewer people mentioned saints by name in their wills. Indeed, Mary's was the only name invoked with any consistency. Whereas about 90 percent of people had asked for divine intercession in the early eighteenth century, by the early Mexican period only close to 30 percent of New Mexicans requested the favors of a saint. In fact, from approximately the last quarter of the eighteenth century through the 1820s—the very historical moment when New Mexicans experienced unprecedented economic growth—requests for intercession dropped.

Though suggestive of an increase in secular over religious interests in an increasingly commercial New Mexico, the period from 1826 to 1875 shows a slight resurgence in these appeals for intercession that complicates what might otherwise appear to be a simple, linear tale of what scholarship terms "dechristianization." While wills clearly became increasingly secular documents throughout the nineteenth century, the noted resurgence coincides with the small but growing incursion of non–Roman Catholics and foreigners. Beyond the faith itself, then, Roman Catholicism increasingly formed part of a larger New Mexican cultural expression. Just as baroque forms of worship—e.g., the communal penitential practices of the Penitente Brotherhood—emerged during a period of dramatic social and economic change, social stress may have led some to return to a more traditional faith, not just for solace but also as a means of self-identification and community fortification against the encroaching outsiders. The Mexican government in this same period deliberately used religious rhetoric to promote nationalism and to distinguish between Roman Catholic Mexico and its Protestant neighbor.[18] Though the numbers are small, they suggest that faith offered a means of contesting the transmitters of Anglo culture, even as New Mexicans embraced much of the interlopers' material culture.

REASONS FOR MAKING A WILL

Like Francisco Martín, most New Mexicans accepted mortality as the requisite payment to God at the same time that they lived in fear of death. Resignation tempered their anxieties, however, with little variation in language. The 1767 will of Joaquín de Alderete, a vecino of El Paso del Norte, is typical. While confined to a bed in Santa Fe, Alderete declared himself "fearing death, which is natural, and not wanting it to catch me unprepared."[19] This formulaic language reveals great continuity with Spanish traditions despite New Mexicans' geographic distance. The most commonly used phrase "temiéndome de la muerte que es cosa natural" dates to at least the sixteenth century. Using this or similar wording, 37 percent of New Mexicans explicitly cited apprehension among their motives for composing a will in the years 1750 to 1850. Stemming in part from a centuries-old notarial formula, this statement of fear also represented the very real terror people experienced as they faced their mortality.

Despite theologians' exhortations, almost 90 percent of New Mexicans waited until gravely ill before drawing up a will. Both the model death and the formula of the will prescribed fear, but the immediate situation in which people found themselves—confined to bed by an illness or debilitated by an accident "that God had seen fit to send"— also warranted their fear. While the last-minute composition of wills suggests just how far from the model death most New Mexicans were, in this, too, they demonstrated their similarity to their counterparts elsewhere in the Spanish world. The scholarship demonstrates that from Seville to Mexico, less than a third of testators drew up their wills while in good health. Only among the nobility does this figure shift upward, to 39 percent, though people still tended to wait until declining health or a pregnancy threatened before making a will.[20]

Though likewise formulaic in expressing the belief that spiritual forces—in this case, God Himself—caused illness, regardless of etiologies, people's physical troubles motivated them to draw up their wills. They rarely, however, gave details regarding the nature of their afflictions. Only one Simón de Leyba related the cause of his pain, reporting that he had received a mortal blow from a horse. The force of the kick had so incapacitated him that he thought his body should not be moved from his small farm, where he believed he would die.[21] Perhaps in part because of medicine's inefficacy, the wills—like the burial books, which cite only the most violent causes of death—offered no details. In any event, the nature of one's illness was immaterial and focusing on it could only distract one from the real priority.

Wills suggest that the dying person's spiritual health ideally stood preeminent. Nicolasa Vigil, a resident of Santa Cruz de la Cañada, alluded to her illness and her receipt of the last rites as reasons for making a will.[22] Since only those certain to die were to receive extreme unction, hers is an unusual sequence of events. She had suffered an accident while in Chama, however, which may have caused people to call the priest more immediately than had she been suffering from a slow, progressive illness or had she had an accident at home. More common was the situation of Gerónimo López, who made his will while sick in bed "knowing that I am mortal and that I cannot know when God Our Father will see fit to call me to Him, and not wanting this hour to catch me off guard."[23] Reflecting calm and resignation, López's will indicates the frame of mind considered ideal at the deathbed.

Some people employed dramatic language to express their preparedness for death. Echoing the period's prescriptive literature, in 1746 Josefa Baca of Albuquerque asked for God's mercy even though "I know myself to be the greatest sinner, and without the anguish that I should have for offenses committed against my God and Lord."[24] Baca's manifest humility presumably served her well as she faced the heavenly tribunal. One hundred years later, Donaciano Vigil hoped his illness would take him from "this miserable world."[25] Although he lived another thirty-five years, in thus negating his attachment to the world, Vigil demonstrated that he was ready to die. The language of renunciation, however, belies the truth that for some, the property clauses of the will ranked as high in importance as any spiritual clauses.

Not all wills contained each of the spiritual elements identified, and some launched very quickly into a list of material possessions. Numerous testators made a lengthy profession of faith without requesting any intercession, for example. Others included only remnants of some spiritual clauses and discarded others completely. Those who were faithful to the formula, however, were remarkably so. Only occasionally did New Mexicans deviate from formulaic language as they commended their souls to God and their bodies to the earth "whence it came." Though never going so far as to invert societal expectations or roles, some New Mexicans here took the opportunity to express their unique understanding of Roman Catholic dogma.[26] Corp. Luis Jaramillo made his will from the sickbed in 1764, postulating that "the death of the soul was not part of the Lord Our Father's arrangement, but rather the evil ones sought it."[27] Gervacio Ortega of Chimayó observed in 1851 that "it is necessary to wait until the day of the Resurrection in order to be returned to form in order to never die again."[28] The infrequency of these curious personal asides reflects the fact that though they lived at the geographic periphery of the Spanish world, New Mexicans resided firmly within the Spanish-American religious realm. Even without notaries, they remained largely true to the sample will offered as a template in Murillo's book.

TEMPORAL AND MATERIAL CONCERNS

Though illness and fear of death impelled many to make their wills, people also cited a host of spiritual reasons for drafting a testament. Many expressed a desire to die with a clear conscience. Others hoped to receive God's mercy or put their souls on the path to salvation by preparing a will. Simply being prepared for death—essential to the construct of the good death—coupled with an illness or accident motivated others. Widow María Chaves dictated her will in 1765 following an accident, stating that she wished to be prepared for death.[29] Soldier Nicolás Mares, though sick in bed, sought God's mercy in making his will.[30] María Rosa Agustina Chacón had suffered an accident when she made her will in the fall of 1840. Though she thought she would die and feared death, she also wished her sins pardoned and her soul saved. Beyond these spiritual concerns, she sought through her will to excuse all debts owed her.[31]

After the first decade of the nineteenth century, New Mexicans less frequently cited their reasons for making a will, but those who did increasingly admitted their need to order and apportion their worldly possessions. Though wills had always been a principal means of disposing of property, in the period from 1750 to 1784, only two people expressed concern with the distribution of material wealth, and this stemmed in part from spiritual motives. Francisco Romero observed that he was making his will because he was "coming to the close or end of my days of life, in order to die as a Catholic Christian and with the disposition that is necessary for the greatest peace and tranquility of my soul and seeing as I have children to whom I must give my goods."[32] However modest their assets, from 1785 onward, people increasingly articulated the desire to distribute their goods, expressing as a goal the avoidance of family conflicts and litigation. Pablo Manuel Trujillo of Taos in 1810 wanted to ensure that his wife of forty years and their four surviving children received their rightful shares of his property, which included a house, a few livestock, and some land.[33] Though still representing only a small fraction of all wills, the rise in wills mentioning the disposition of property among their objectives is suggestive of a shift in values as both New Mexico's commercial economy and population grew, in turn placing greater pressure on land and other resources. Based on the burial books examined, the percentage of people leaving wills also rose in this period—from 10 percent in 1790–1809 to 26 percent in 1830–50—giving added weight to this interpretation of the subtle shift in reasons offered in the testaments.

While Spanish civil law fined the estates of those who had died intestate, it did not require that the poor leave wills. Those with little to bequeath perhaps made verbal arrangements for the disposal of their few goods. Presumably their poverty and suffering on earth ensured their spiritual well-being, thereby negating the will's spiritual functions. Burial records for Santa Fe, Albuquerque, and Santa Cruz indicate that from 1730 through 1850 an average of 15 percent of residents made a will, a figure considerably higher than might be expected for a province without so much as an official notary. It is likely that the actual number actually ran higher than 15 percent, but few priests provided all the information they were supposed to in the burial registers, making it impossible to gain a more accurate approximation. In those cases where priests specifically noted that someone had not left a will, they typically cited the sudden nature of the illness as the culprit, but in fully 96 percent of cases, clergy blamed poverty for preventing someone from making a will.

Those who were not thus excused from this moral and legal obligation sought both to pay material debts and atone for spiritual debts, which in some cases proved inseparable. Having given up on locating their creditors in Spain or in central Mexico, for example, a few people requested that masses be said on their creditors' behalf. Frequently, wills provided an opportunity to recognize "natural" children, pay for promised but unpaid masses to a devotion, or free slaves or household dependents known as *criados*, whom I will discuss below. Wills highlight people's ideas of fairness and justice, their moral infractions and personal foibles, and reflect the litigious nature of colonial society. Taken as a whole, it is the humanity of these individuals that emerges most clearly. Behind the lofty spiritual language and generous pious bequests lived a pragmatic people who loved life and had a difficult time releasing their hold on it, notwithstanding their ardent hopes of soon being in God's presence.

Seeking to avoid litigation and familial divisiveness, people took pains to be fair and precise in their distribution of goods. If a daughter already had received her share of the estate as a dowry upon her marriage, or if a son had received land or other goods upon reaching the age of majority, the will would note these items and leave instructions accordingly. The will might also recognize as heirs adopted children and others raised in the household but not legally entitled to a share of the estate. Juan Joseph Moreno, a childless settler from Seville with a long list of debts—including his servants' wages—named his niece, Antonia Roybal, as heir. He and his wife Juana Roybal had raised

Antonia during their twenty-three-year marriage, and he bequeathed her his clothes, a house, and sixty sheep.[34]

Faced with their mortality, numerous testators named a child born out of wedlock as among their legitimate heirs. Joseph Baca of Pueblo Quemado, for example, acknowledged an *hijo natural*, or natural son, in 1772 and ordered that the boy receive a share of the estate equal to that of Baca's other children.[35] Josefa Baca of Albuquerque freely admitted that while she had had no husband, "being a wretched, fragile sinner I had six children," whom she proceeded to name as heirs.[36] The process of recognizing one's indiscretions did not always come so readily, however, as the will of one of Santa Fe's leading citizens—Rosa Bustamante—reveals. The daughter of a former lieutenant governor, Bustamante made her will while sick, naming only the children of her fifty-one-year marriage as her heirs. Her conscience plagued her as she lay dying, though, and she sought her priest's counsel. She confessed that before her marriage, she had borne two natural children. Fray Francisco de Hozio encouraged her to make amends, which she did by adding a clause recognizing these children—and their progeny, for she was now a grandmother—as her legal heirs. Over a month lapsed, however, between her admission to the priest and this clause's composition. Just a few hours after its completion, at four in the morning the next day, she died.[37] Bustamante's protracted soul-searching suggests why so few wills identify natural children. Though baptismal records disclose the high incidence of births outside of marriage—almost 19 percent in Santa Cruz and close to 28 percent in Albuquerque in the eighteenth century—only a handful of wills mention natural children.[38] While it is impossible to know how many parents omitted known natural children from the pages of their testaments, certainly the process of identifying heirs could be both a spiritual exercise and a spiritual challenge. Doing so brought some, like Rosa Bustamante, closer to the model death, even as others' failure to do so made the good death more elusive.

Like the case of children born outside of wedlock, the family dynamics that surface in wills suggest people's notions of ideal behavior as well as the often harsher reality. To avoid disputes after death, people carefully identified both legitimate heirs and the property due them. Men and women who had remarried after a spouse's death and then raised a second or third family sought to ensure that their children from a previous marriage received their proper share of the parental estate. People divvied up individual houses according to rooms or areas measured in the number of vigas or roof beams, resulting in living arrangements that might include a criado having legal ownership to a room in a house that the former master's children otherwise owned. Children from a first marriage might find themselves living with a parent's second spouse. Manuel Pudillo in 1849 left half of his five-room house in Santa Fe to the six children who survived from his first marriage. The rest of the house remained in the possession of his second wife, doña Juliana García. The meticulous Pudillo even requested that his first wife's cow—though after over forty-three years, certainly not literally the same cow—be divided up among the children of this first marriage.[39]

Wills might reveal special affection for family members, living and dead, as well as reprimand those who had fallen short of expectations. Petra Paula Padilla, a poor vecina of Santa Clara's Plaza de San José, in 1816 left a small piece of land to her daughter María. Though her possessions were few and she had three other children to think of, Padilla believed that María warranted this special reward for having taken care of her as a mother would a child.[40] Whether Padilla meant thus to reproach her other children, who had not cared for her in the same selfless manner, the critique seems transparent. At his death, Juan Cristóbal Vigil recognized a stepchild's care for him during a twenty-year illness, "under my domain almost sacrificing its existence to benefit mine."[41] In exchange for its troubles, Vigil granted the nameless child a portion of his Santa Fe estate equal to that of his four surviving children. Thus, the spiritual debt Vigil owed the now-grown child would be paid upon his death.

People left many pious acts unfinished until death. Thus the most common spiritual debt was also in many cases a financial one: namely, money owed priests for masses, weddings, and other services. Mexico City native Joaquín Pino died owing Fray Agustín de Iniesta for a mass to St. Anne and the wax for candles for that mass as well as twenty-three low masses, a high mass, and the mass and candle wax for his son's funeral. In addition to these obligations, he owed Fray Manuel José Rojo for a sermon he had dedicated to St. Anne.[42] Clearly, patience was a necessary virtue for Franciscans serving in New Mexico, who might have to wait until a parishioner died before collecting on some accounts.

Like these debts that were both monetary and spiritual in nature, New Mexicans might also defer payments to confraternities until after death. Confraternity membership typically guaranteed a proper funeral, with full attendance by the association's membership. Reflecting the communal nature of baroque piety, confraternities also promoted the lasting bond between the living and the dead through anniversary masses for their dead members. While it is not surprising that people died owing the Third Order of St. Francis—undoubtedly the most popular religious association in New Mexico—their three pesos in membership dues, some adults in fact waited until after death to join the venerable organization, directing the estate to pay inscription costs.[43] Certainly, many paid into confraternities over an adult lifetime, but others did not join until after death. Their estates paid the membership fees, demonstrating how flexible popular conceptions of faith were and underscoring that the community of the faithful endured after death.

Not only priests and confraternities, but the saints themselves had to exercise patience as they waited for pledged masses and acts of charity. Many people died quite literally in debt to a saint or devotion. María Pascuala de los Dolores Romero of Santa Cruz ordered her executors to pay the twelve masses she owed for the souls in purgatory, along with masses dedicated to Our Lady of Carmel and Our Father of Esquípulas.[44] In addition to being popular devotions in the Santa Cruz area, each of these held special significance at death. Our Lady of Carmel offered scapulars to souls suffering in purgatory, facilitating salvation, while Our Father of Esquípulas was an image of Christ on the Tree of Life, representing spiritual regeneration. Thus, the debt's payment may have been all the more important at death. Juan Manuel Ortega, a vecino from Santa Fe, had promised the Virgin of Sorrows a mass in her honor, but finding himself suddenly ill, realized he had not fulfilled his obligation. He therefore instructed his estate's executors to take care of this oversight upon his death.[45] When she made her will in summer 1800, Teodora Gertrudis Ortiz owed Our Lady of Guadalupe a bull for her chapel, perhaps pledged as part of the chapel's building campaign.[46]

In taking stock of their spiritual estates, some people inevitably confronted their relationship to the local variety of human bondage. New Mexicans paid ransoms for war captives, who then served their redeemers for a term of ten to twenty years, or until adulthood, when they were to be emancipated. To be fair, only a fraction of wills refer either to criados or *esclavos* (slaves), corroborating Gutiérrez's findings that through the end of the Mexican period, fewer than 10 percent of Spanish households included either.[47] Though many people raised these ransomed war captives within the Roman Catholic faith and incorporated them into the household through compadrazgo or godparenthood, wills demonstrate people's ambivalence toward the criados living in their power and under their roofs.

The system of enslaving and ransoming war captives had deep roots in both Native American and Iberian traditions, and while the term "criado"—literally, "one who has been reared"—implies a paternalistic and even a familial bond, this connotation is misleading—perhaps intentionally so.[48] The criado-master relationship existed on a continuum that included extremes of both abuse and affection and that rested on a base of unequal power. Mónica Tomasa Martín, a vecina of Taos, left some black bracelets to Catarina, the daughter of María del Carmen, "mi india"—a criada whom she had raised and kept through adulthood. Although María was a mother in her own right, the possessive way in which Martín referred to her reveals the paternalism that informed her sentiments. Though the trinkets suggest affection for the young Catarina, Martín did not free either the girl or her mother and carefully noted that both her criada and her criada's sister owed her livestock.[49] At the same time that it reveals fondness for Catarina, then, Martín's will demonstrates the underlying dynamic of power defining the institution, however varied its manifestations.

Although in his classic study of New Mexico's population Oakah Jones defines criados as "servants," wills illustrate that criados might differ from slaves in name only.[50] In their testaments, people listed criados—often without names—as property brought into the marriage or as debts owed another vecino. Andrés Montoya, a vecino of Cieneguilla, for example, acknowledged that "I owe Ignacio Gonsales, vecino of San Buenaventura, an Indian boy, age seven . . . I owe a son of Tomás Madrid, vecino of San Buenaventura, an Indian girl, age six."[51] Elsewhere, criados appeared with a purchase price attached. Domingo de Benavides claimed that he had supplied the merchant don Clemente Gutiérrez two unnamed female Indians, each valued at fifty silver pesos in 1770.[52] Francisco Romero, whom accompanying documents identified alternately as an indio and a coyote, listed among his property a house and small farm with thirteen hundred varas of land in Trampas, a considerable amount of livestock, and "five indias criadas with eight little coyotes."[53] Romero clearly claimed his criadas' children among his assets. His use of the possessive pronoun—"mis coyotitos" or "my little coyotes"—may have signaled paternalism or simply indicated that these were literally his children, a common occurrence, according to Gutiérrez, who concludes that fully 82 percent of births recorded to Indian women enslaved in Spanish households took place outside of marriage.[54] Romero did not emancipate anyone in his testament, and one can only guess how his gifts of an old cow to each of these women and a yearling to each of their children were received upon his death. Though in theory vecinos emancipated their criados upon adulthood or after their term of service had expired, wills like Romero's indicate that this might not occur and confirm that the mother's status passed to the child.

Faced with their impending mortality, some New Mexicans tried to atone for what they realized at some level was spiritually problematic, though rarely is the atonement as black and white as we might hope to see through our twenty-first century lenses. The ambivalent nature of the criado-master relationship surfaced in the 1752 will of María de la Candelaria González, who first identified Asencio Antonio Trujillo only as a boy she had raised, and left him a parcel of land. Numerous New Mexicans raised the orphaned children of friends and family, and only González's words a few lines later reveal Asencio's status as a slave. In the same sentence that González emancipated an Indian named María Jusepa who had "served me well," she also gave Asencio Antonio his freedom.[55] Burial registers suggest similar tensions within the institution. In one 1786 entry, for example, Fray José Mariano Rosete identified a fifty-year-old Indian woman named María Antonia as a criada who had been purchased from the Comanches. He indicated that she was a vecina of Alameda, suggesting that she had established her own household; nonetheless, her identity remained tied to her origins as a captive.[56]

Burial practices likewise reflect the tremendous variety of master-criado relationships. Upon death, some criados received expensive funerals and first-rate burial plots within the church. Others, like Teresa, a seventy-year-old Indian who had served Felipe Sandoval for "only" a decade, were consigned to the cemetery because their masters refused to pay for a church burial.[57] Even the parish priest—who certainly knew the worst of his parishioners' traits—could not refrain from criticizing Sandoval in recording Teresa's burial. Within the same home, fates might differ radically. Capt. don José Ortiz had at least two Indian servants in his Santa Fe household. When Juan Miguel, an Indian boy he had raised as his own, died in May 1780, Ortiz saw to it that the servant received a charitable plot within the San Miguel Chapel. In the same month, when Ortiz's Ute servant Margarita died, she was assigned a charitable plot in the churchyard.[58] As James Brooks concludes: "Suspended somewhere between the status of patrimony and property, Indian slaves in New Mexico were simultaneously exploited and cherished, even within the same household."[59]

The widespread use of "criado" reflects not only that Spanish law prohibited enslaving Indians who had not been taken as war captives, but also suggests New Mexicans' discomfort with the term "esclavo" and their need to justify bondage with a more benign term that was

also suggestive of a Christian upbringing. In the early nineteenth century, a few New Mexicans used "esclavo" in listing their human property, indicating the presence of African slaves or perhaps reflecting the
shift in Indian slavery that had taken place around the turn of the century, when settlers raided Ute and Navajo communities for the express
purpose of acquiring slaves.[60] Though the crown in 1812 banned the
practice of placing Indians in servitude, the custom endured; both the
explicit references to slavery date from after the prohibition's arrival in
New Mexico. In 1814, Miguel Ortiz left his slave, Andrés Sandoval, two
small plots of cultivated land, the *solar de casa*, a yoke of oxen, and
other goods, without giving him his freedom. He did, however, emancipate Matilde Sandoval, but without any gift of property.[61] Diego
Montoya, originally from El Paso, freed his esclavo Baltasar and gave
him a bull and a calf in 1818.[62] Thus, facing their own mortality, the sick
rectified those areas in which they had been either morally or spiritually remiss. The church encouraged people to relieve any moral obligations in their wills so that they could die peacefully, consciences
unhindered by unfinished business.

Through the distribution of property, the will could further serve
as a mechanism for postmortem social control. Eduarda Rita Garduño
granted her husband the use of lands she owned in the Cañada del
Pino with the stipulation that at his death they be donated for the benefit of the Poor Souls in Purgatory.[63] Upon his death, Francisco Martín
freed three criadas. He qualified the payment of this spiritual debt,
however, by instructing the three to stay with his wife so she could
continue to care for them, thereby ensuring that they not become
"vagabonds."[64] In Santa Fe, Felipe Tafoya named his wife and two of
his sons executors, reminding his offspring that they should honorably
fulfill these duties, attending to their mother and other siblings. He
further directed his sons to "not do anything without their mother's
approval."[65] José Martínez of San Acacio named his wife universal heir,
instructing her to use his possessions for the benefit of their children,
"not allowing any son or daughter to enter into any vice, as all vice is
counter to God and the honor of one's father and mother." In turn,
their twelve children were to obey and support their widowed mother
and treat each other with "the greatest harmony."[66]

Some testators went so far as to withhold their postmortem blessing should their wishes go unheeded. The wealthy María Micaela
Baca divided her property equally among all her children, enjoining
them to maintain "above all peace and tranquility in order that they
may enjoy God's blessing and mine."[67] Testators beseeched their heirs

to faithfully adhere to their final wishes and avoid all strife and complaints among each other. One man named his nieces and nephews as heirs, since he had no children. He warned, however, that should any of them file a complaint regarding their inheritance, they would automatically lose their share of the estate, which would then go to pay for masses for his own soul.[68]

Inserting language to ensure adherence to one's wishes after death was one way in which people tried to maintain their grasp on life. The will thus represented both a looking forward to the afterlife and a compact with the material world. Ironically, while the will opened the path for salvation by clearing one's conscience and paying spiritual and material debts, the very steps that were to leave one unencumbered revealed people's profound attachments to "this miserable world" and their desire to exert control over it even in death.

Pious Bequests

Believed to abbreviate purgatory's torments, pious bequests allowed people to facilitate their salvation in a tangible way. Some individuals—like Gerónimo López, who trusted his wife and children to pay for masses for the repose of his soul "because she has been my companion for so many years and because they [the children] are my legitimate heirs"—put their faith in their survivors' arrangement of pious bequests.[69] Most, however, did not leave things to chance. Though in central Mexico people increasingly relied on their heirs to make these arrangements, New Mexicans specified the precise number of masses they wanted said and to which devotions. Typically, they requested masses dedicated to the souls in purgatory, the Virgin Mary, or a favorite saint. Men showed some preference for the souls in purgatory over Marian devotions while women were more likely to leave money to one of the many advocations of Mary. Others did not articulate how many masses they wanted but left a piece of land, clothing, or riding gear to be sold for masses. Fewer than 10 percent of men or women gave goods or money for one hundred masses or more, and on the whole, men granted larger amounts of money to the church at death. This appears logical given that men more likely enjoyed greater access to and control of resources than women. Although few approached the hundreds and thousands of masses that their compatriots in Mexico and Spain ordered, more than half of all wills from 1751 through 1825 did request some masses. In addition to masses, people donated money, bultos and paintings, and other goods to benefit a confraternity or a favorite chapel, in a reflection of personal interests and devotions.

From 1726 through 1825, the souls in purgatory were the most popular destination of pious giving. In paying for masses to help dead relatives and others escape the scalding purgatorial fires, New Mexicans' wills demonstrate at once their extraordinary affection for the dead and the special resonance of the doctrine of purgatory, which allowed people to maintain the connection to dead loved ones and participate in their postmortem fates. Others left money or goods in their wills to pay for masses for a loved one who had preceded them in death. In several cases, women demonstrated greater generosity toward the dead than toward themselves. The widow Juana Roybal, for example, ordered only one novena of high masses for her soul but paid for 150 low masses to benefit her husband, who had preceded her in death two years earlier.[70] Perhaps this bequest fulfilled some unspoken promise she had made, or perhaps she simply believed that he needed more spiritual sustenance to offset an impious life. Regardless, it expressed her ongoing affection. Teodora Gertrudis Ortiz likewise instructed her executors to pay for fifteen masses for her parents and her dead son, José Pablo. Interestingly, Ortiz made no mention of her dead daughter. Perhaps the girl had died in infancy after baptism and did not require masses, destined as she was for heaven. José, however, had died as an adult, and his soul might yet benefit from the masses.[71] Dead spouses, parents, and occasionally children received such postmortem aid. As late as 1840, María Rosa Agustina Chacón left several goats to pay for a mass on behalf of her deceased husband, indicating that these practices and the beliefs that fueled them endured into the Mexican period.[72]

Few testators, male or female, left legacies beyond the immediate masses they wanted the priest to say. Merchant don Antonio José Ortiz, a longtime church benefactor, assigned three hundred pesos for a chaplain to say two weekly masses for his soul and those of his (still living) wife and children (four of ten living at the time). Rather than rely on a single priest, the masses were divided among different parishes so as to allow the masses to be held as soon as possible after death, thereby maximizing their spiritual benefit. Years later, as she made her will, Ortiz's widow, Rosa Bustamante, ordered that the remainder of the money he had bequeathed continue being spent on these weekly masses and on the costs of their chapel. Ortiz and his wife, however, proved exceptional. Reflecting the region's poverty relative to central Mexico and the absence of monasteries, New Mexicans

6. *Christ Crucified and the Souls in Purgatory* by Pedro Fresquís, Harwood Museum of Art, University of New Mexico, gift of Mabel Dodge Luhan, photo by Pat Pollard

did not establish either chaplaincies or chantries. Their pious giving tended to focus on masses in the days after death.

Masses and prayers offered the living the occasion to intervene on behalf of the dead and the dying an opportunity to better their post-mortem fate. They also extended to the sick the chance to rectify any areas in which they had been remiss. Not simply the function of blind faith, these bequests reflected careful thought and provided thorough instructions on the path to salvation. Juan Antonio Ortiz made a somewhat unusual bequest that illustrates the importance of masses to a man on his deathbed, bridging as they did the duty to pay spiritual debts and the desire to reduce one's sentence in purgatory. Having determined that his estate should pay for one hundred low masses for his soul, he proclaimed that ninety of the hundred were to be said,

in case some day I may have taken something that seemed small and was considerable, or if in any dealing I gave less for something that was worth more; in order that God Our

Father might distribute it according to His wishes or deposit
it in the treasury of his church.[73]

In addition to thus ameliorating any offenses, Ortiz left 150 *pesos de la
tierra*, or pesos in locally-produced goods, for the confraternities of the
Holy Sacrament, Our Lady of the Rosary, and Our Lady of Light.
Presumably, these bequests ensured that confraternity members would
offer further prayers on his behalf. Like masses, prayers facilitated salvation. The more people enlisted in prayer—family, priest, and confraternity members—the more quickly one could flee purgatory.

Wills, however, provide an imperfect picture of charitable donations; even those who failed to make pious bequests in their wills
may have extracted verbal commitments from family members for
the same ends. José Viterbo Rivera, a presidial soldier, ordered no
masses in his testament, but at his death, the parish priest received
money for ten masses.[74] Don José Lázaro Trujillo, a vecino of
Cuyamungue, likewise requested no masses as he made his will in
1764. Yet for years after his death, his widow and children paid various priests to perform masses for his benefit.[75] Though masses were
thought most efficacious in the days immediately following death,
family members might defer requests or payments for a loved one's
masses until later. While impossible to quantify what proportion of
New Mexicans actually received more than a funeral mass, the ideal
of saying masses for the dead remained popular well beyond the
nineteenth century.

Like other purchases, people paid for masses in pesos de la tierra—
usually food, wine, or livestock—a local accommodation to the lack of
currency. Parishioners also supplied candles and wine for use during
the funeral mass or for general church use. In addition to the one hundred breeding ewes that Capt. Juan Montes Vigil left for one hundred
masses for his soul, he offered twenty jugs to whichever priest wished
to say masses for his soul.[76] Not all payments were so practical or so
easily made liquid. José Antonio Cruz donated a section of his mother's
house—three vigas' worth—to St. Joaquín while giving the rest to his
daughter.[77] Teresa Fernández de la Pedrera left a burro and a violin to
pay for masses upon her death.[78] Bernardo de Sena, a prominent Santa
Fe vecino, did not ask for a specific number of masses but set aside nine
mules, his weapons, and clothing to cover the costs of his burial in the
San Miguel Chapel, masses, and an offering of bread and wine. A longtime church benefactor and mayordomo of the confraternity dedicated
to Our Lady of the Rosary (commonly referred to as La Conquistadora),

his generous bequest probably included some additional masses for his spiritual well-being.[79]

The shortage of currency necessitated the use of goods to pay for the priest's services, and while both parties might agree on compensation, the practice lent itself to conflict. The value of grain might fluctuate before a parishioner had completed payment on a debt or the priest might determine that a promised mare looked too sickly to pay off a debt's value. Blas Griego, an Albuquerque vecino, in 1824 complained that Cura José Francisco Leyva had overcharged him by exacting ten sacks of corn, a cow, and two mares for a funeral with mass and vigil that should have been valued at twenty-six pesos, four reales.[80] As the complaint wound its way to the bishop in Durango, the complexity of the system surfaced, with questions raised as to the exact size of a sack of corn and the current value of a cow in New Mexico.

Not surprisingly, many religious condemned the custom of payment in kind. Fray Juan Miguel Menchero decried the fact that Spaniards and *gente de razón*—literally "people of reason," used to denote non-Indians—were as guilty of the practice as the Indians. The friar noted that whether for baptism, marriage, or burial, people compensated the priest as they wished; he avowed that the Indians outdid even the Spaniards, making payment only for masses dedicated to the dead or to the saints and neglecting entirely to pay for other services.[81] Complaints over nonpayment, underpayment, and payment in goods remained a favorite theme throughout the colonial and Mexican periods. Bound by their office to minister to those in need, the clergy could often only hope that people would compensate them fairly for funerals and pious bequests.[82] In the case of the latter, the estate's executors ultimately determined the precise nature of the payment.

As noted earlier, the faithful most often allocated their deathbed charity to souls in purgatory or some advocation of the Virgin Mary. Not coincidentally, each of these devotions held powerful associations with death and postmortem intercession. Most people believed themselves destined for a sentence in purgatory upon death, and Mother Mary interceded for individuals before God. Such bequests therefore served a dual function, part Christian charity and part self-interest. Hilario Archuleta, a vecino of Nambé who ran a mill, designated a fruit tree and twenty varas of land in his rancho for the souls in purgatory.[83] Ramón García set aside a cow for masses to benefit the Poor Souls.[84] In theory, these men reaped the rewards of their bequests twice: once in the charity of giving to the Poor Souls and again in the aid they might receive upon joining these same souls in purgatory. While not equivalent to masses for one's soul, they served a similar function in the spiritual equation. The predominance of gifts to the Virgin and to the Poor Souls demonstrates New Mexicans' enduring faith in these devotions' special significance upon death and suggests both an expediency and charity that underscores the pragmatic nature of the faith practiced in New Mexico.

Some made very personal charitable donations. Several women bequeathed jewelry and private trinkets to the Virgin, revealing the intimate connection they felt to the holy Mother. María Guadalupe Sánchez selected a gold chain for Our Lady of the Rosary and two mirrors, a crucifix, and a colcha, or coverlet, for Our Lady of Guadalupe.[85] Perhaps because of the relative scarcity of these luxury items in the province, many New Mexicans preferred to leave a religious icon or santo to embellish a favorite chapel. Juana Roybal, for example, possessed a Virgin of Guadalupe in a *baldoquín*, or enclosure or frame, and a small statue of St. Joseph that she asked be kept in Santa Fe's Chapel of Our Lady of Light.[86] José Manuel Trujillo implored that a silver icon and a bronze Christ belonging to him be placed in the church where he was buried.[87] Juan Antonio Suaso bestowed two pistols and a lance for the defense of the parish church dedicated to San Antonio, in Embudo.[88] During his visitation of New Mexico, Fray Domínguez made note of many such gifts in different chapels and parish churches, suggesting communities' enduring collective memory of donors. Though these gifts may have offered hope of assistance from the saints or the faithful, people just as likely found comfort simply knowing that their treasures would benefit the church where they had worshipped and where their remains awaited the Resurrection.

Gifts to the poor, a common expression of deathbed charity among Mexico's elite, proved less popular in New Mexico. Having suffered on earth, the poor were believed to hold a special place in Roman Catholic thought, and in central Mexico their participation in funerals was essential for those who could afford to compensate them. Mexico City's orphanage, in fact, sustained itself for generations on its residents' earnings as professional mourners. The estate compensated the poor for their participation, supplying clothes and a candle for the occasion.[89] Only a few New Mexicans left bequests for the poor. Rosa Bustamante instructed her executors to make "a small donation for twelve of the poorest modest women," adding—rather disingenuously given her estate's considerable size—that she would like to give the women much more.[90] Her husband, Antonio José Ortiz, left six hundred pesos to be divided among the province's poor.[91] Perhaps because of the less dramatic economic differences characterizing New Mexico, paid mourners did not partake in funerary dramas, and relatively few wills left any charity for the impoverished.

Fulfilling both spiritual and secular objectives, wills combine lofty statements of piety with the collection of petty debts. People often used their testaments to try to collect on debts owed them by neighbors both dead and alive. Santa Fe's Tomás Madrid instructed his executors to collect from the estate of the dead Capt. don Vicente the four pesos owed him.[92] Even one's heirs enjoyed no exemption from postmortem debt collection. Josef Antonio Alarid recorded a long list of things due him, including five goats and their kids, which his son had taken without permission.[93] Priests also had to pay up. Juan Antonio Ortiz noted that he had, since 1788, paid Fray Ignacio Sánchez for twelve masses for his intentions. Reporting that he owed the friar nothing, Ortiz ordered that his executors gather anything due him from the priest upon his death.[94]

The one pious bequest common to almost all colonial New Mexican wills was the *mandas forzosas*, or mandatory legacies, first mentioned in a 1712 will.[95] A sort of death tax, its proceeds went to further various Roman Catholic objectives, including the canonization of Felipe de Jesús, the beatification of Gregorio López, the liberation of Jerusalem's holy sites, and the veneration of the Virgin of Guadalupe. The legacies' various destinations changed somewhat over the years, as the crown eliminated some and established new ones. In 1785, for example, a royal cedula, or decree, eliminated the bequest for Gregorio López's beatification. In central Mexico, only the funds for the Virgin of Guadalupe, the liberation of Jerusalem, and one to provide dowries for orphans and poor women remained by 1806.[96] By the early nineteenth century, the mandas forzosas increasingly addressed secular objectives. During the Napoleonic Wars, for example, the Cortes—the Spanish parliament meeting in the port city of Cadiz—designated a fund to help war prisoners and widows. Rosa Bustamante's will earmarked three pesos for each of the mandatory charities, plus twelve "for the newest one," perhaps referring to the redemption of captives from the Napoleonic Wars.[97] In 1843, the Mexican government instituted a collection for the establishment of public libraries, completing the legacies' transformation into tools of secular government. Though mandatory and indivisible in the sense that one could not opt to leave money for only one objective, among New Mexicans those for the liberation of Jerusalem and for the Virgin of Guadalupe seemed to hold particular resonance, as people occasionally mentioned them by name.

Though the crown and later the Mexican government dictated the tax's destinations, individuals elected the amount they bequeathed to the mandas forzosas. Each archbishopric established which mandas testators had to pay and possessed the authority to fine estates failing to do so. Though little documentation survives on these pious funds, parishes probably assigned special mayordomos to administer them. In one case, Joseph Miguel de la Peña of Nambé identified himself as "syndic of the holy sites" upon receipt of two pairs of stockings, Lázaro Trujillo's contribution to the mandas forzosas upon his death in 1778.[98] Most New Mexicans left the equivalent of one to four pesos for each of the mandas, others as little as one real and as much as one hundred pesos. Those who omitted the tax as they drew up their wills could rest assured that their executors would be called upon to correct this oversight, as Francisco Romero's representatives learned in 1765.[99] Donations after independence kept apace, and even U.S. occupation did not completely end New Mexicans' readiness to give. Long after New Mexicans had become citizens of U.S. territory, Manuel de la Cruz Lucero of Peña Blanca in 1878 left two reales—the equivalent of a fourth of a silver peso—for each of the mandas.[100]

Burial Costume

Beyond their functions as property distributors and debt collectors, testaments compelled even the most worldly to contemplate death. Indeed, composing a will required one to look beyond death and consider the details of one's burial. While striving to negate attachment and focus on temporal goods, the good-death model required that the dying consider the seemingly mundane question of how their cadavers should dress, for example. In marked contrast to residents of Veracruz and Mexico City, 80 percent of New Mexicans from the mid-eighteenth to the mid-nineteenth centuries included instructions on burial attire in their wills.[101] Among those who did, close to 70 percent solicited the habit of St. Francis. In the eighteenth century, these habits were indigo blue, a privilege granted Franciscans serving overseas, and by the mid-nineteenth century, New Mexicans were buried in brown or black habits.[102] The centuries-old tradition of burial in a religious habit was inextricably tied to the ideal of the good death and the conviction that the agonía, or death throes, and the period immediately following played as large a role in one's salvation as the relative merits of one's life on earth.

Since the Middle Ages, popular belief held that burial in a religious habit would lead to special favors in heaven. Pope Leo X (1513–21) had

7. Burial book flyleaf decorated by Fray Manuel de Sopeña, Santa Cruz de la Cañada, 1729, from the Collections of the Archdiocese of Santa Fe

granted a plenary indulgence to anyone who requested burial in a habit or who wore one on his or her deathbed, and other papal bulls affirmed the garment's spiritual benefits.[103] Thomas Aquinas ascribed to the religious habit "a sacramental significance, referring to it as a 'second baptism' that restored sinners to the state of innocence they had enjoyed when baptized."[104] The special blessings endowed by the habit of St. Francis caused the sick to seek its consolation, according to Arbiol. "Frequently, the sick, knowing of the great treasure of indulgences that reside in the Third Order of Our Seraphic Father St. Francis, request the habit and profession in order to die with this great spiritual consolation and comfort for their souls."[105] The habit of St. Francis, who had founded the most humble of the mendicant orders, acted as an outward sign of piety and an added source of blessings. Representing a life of asceticism and dedication to the Lord, the habit signified the meekness and obedience of the deceased before God.

Burial in a habit demonstrated humility and piety before one's neighbors as well as before God and the celestial court. Wearing the habit while dying aided in the transition to the hereafter while affording peers the opportunity to appreciate one's meekness and submission to God. In sharp contrast to the ostentation and pomp of baroque funerals, wherein hundreds of clergy and paid mourners rendered tribute to the dead, people wore the habit to symbolize the rejection of this world and its vanities. In his study of Sevillan deathways, José Antonio Rivas Álvarez suggests that burial in a religious habit served to disguise death and make it more palatable.[106] If correct, this might explain the apparent contradiction in the popularity of this simple garb amid opulent funerals that showcased wealth and privilege for Mexico's nobility.[107] More likely, however, is that contemporaries did not regard this juxtaposition of pomp and poverty as incongruous but accepted it as part of the rich tableau of a hierarchical colonial society.

Although dying Spaniards and Mexicans alike overwhelmingly preferred the Franciscan habit to others, people also requested burial in the habits of the Dominicans, Carmelites, military orders, and others and sometimes wore more than one habit upon death. Reflecting the historical dominance of the Franciscan Order in New Mexico, New Mexicans desiring burial in a habit exclusively requested that of St. Francis in the colonial and Mexican periods. The only deviation is in the Territorial period, when three Santa Fe women on different occasions from 1857 to 1886 requested burial in the habit of St. Rita. As in Spain and New Spain, eighteenth- and nineteenth-century New Mexicans specifically asked for the habit of Nuestro Santo Seráfico Padre San Francisco, or Our Holy Seraphic Father St. Francis, rather than the habit of his order.[108] The semantic difference suggests that beyond the humble garment, people sought a material means of accessing the communion of saints. Bárbara Baca noted that she wished to be buried "with the costume and blessing of the habit of Our Seraphic Father St. Francis," emphasizing the outfit's spiritual significance.[109] Functioning as a sort of mobile sacred space, burial in the habit of this most humble and devoted of Christ's servants held the promise of St. Francis's intervention on behalf of the deceased. Some individuals even wore the habit on the deathbed, hoping thus to ease the transition into the hereafter.

The source of these habits in New Mexico remains open to speculation, though it appears that both the friars and individual entrepreneurs made the garments specifically as burial shrouds. In Mexico, people purchased their habits from the houses of the mendicant orders or from less scrupulous street vendors who fabricated the garments or disinterred and robbed corpses to obtain them. Given the proportionately small number of friars in the region and the absence of friaries, it would have been impossible for all New Mexicans who wanted them to acquire authentic Franciscan habits. New Mexico's friars themselves received only one new garment each year. Though only a few receipts of habits purchased from friars survive, it is likely that friars did make habits for sale.[110] New Mexicans wove locally grown wool into coarse *sayal*, precisely the rough cloth needed to make the humble garb. Notwithstanding his criticisms of Franciscan commercial activity, even Vice-Custos Fray Silvestre Vélez de Escalante approved of the trade in habits, for which he left precise regulations in 1779, including rules for the fabric's production. Vélez de Escalante emphasized that friars had to bless the habit before selling or giving it to anyone. Without consecration, the garment would not grant the wearer the coveted indulgence. To this end, he ordered friars to issue an accompanying note verifying that they had blessed a habit and instructed all clergy who oversaw the burial of a parishioner in a habit to exact proof before interment that the garment had been blessed.[111]

A significant trade in counterfeit habits probably warranted Vélez de Escalante's interest in the matter. In central Mexico, private entrepreneurs engaged in the fabrication and sale of shrouds, taking revenues away from the friars' legitimate sales. This trade in habits placed many souls in jeopardy, since the unauthorized garments did not enjoy the Franciscans' blessing and therefore could not actually facilitate salvation. Though unclear how much contraband New Mexicans purchased in hope of an indulgence, production and sale of habits would have been a logical commercial venture given the garment's high cost relative to other funeral expenses and New Mexicans' easy access to the needed materials. Antonio Ortega, a former presidial soldier, received thirty pesos from one Juan Tafoya for the habit in which he buried his brother in the mid-eighteenth century.[112] When Ortega died two decades later, his family paid Fray Juan Bermejo twenty-three pesos for a Franciscan habit.[113] The enormous cost—more than a month's wages—undoubt-edly placed the garment beyond the reach of many New Mexicans, though given that few New Mexicans worked as wage laborers, it is dif-ficult to get a clear sense of the relative value of money. Presidio soldiers were among the few who collected a salary for their work, which in 1787 was 240 pesos a year.[114] Even among these wage earners, most of their salary was paid not in currency, but in goods. In any event, the habit's cost was great relative to a funeral that cost only one to four pesos. Several men and women requested burial in the habit of St. Francis "if it is available," suggesting too that demand outstripped supply or that cost was indeed prohibitive. For some, the habit may have been reduced to a simple waist cord, which would carry the same connotations of Franciscan humility and demonstrate the desired penitence and piety.

The tradition of burial in a religious habit has led to some confu-sion and misconceptions about the dead and even their places of interment in New Mexico. A 1989 excavation near the base of the bell tower in Santa Fe's Guadalupe Chapel, for example, uncovered a linen cord and several burials in black or brown hooded fabrics with black lace or brown silk lining.[115] Upon finding the remains of these habits and waist cords, some speculated that these represented Third Order or even Penitente burials.[116] The mere presence of these fabrics and the waist cord does not substantiate this argument. Certainly, many New Mexicans belonged to the Third Order of St. Francis, and some even joined after death. The estate of Catalina Durán, for example, in 1752 paid twelve pesos, four reales for her membership in the Third Order of Penitence and dressed her corpse in silk petticoats beneath the coarse habit.[117] Regardless of Third Order or Penitente member-ship, however, women and men alike overwhelmingly requested that their bodies be cloaked in the habit of St. Francis for burial.

Though most men and women dictated how their lifeless bodies should be dressed, this shifted somewhat toward the end of the colonial period, when people increasingly allowed their heirs to take charge of this decision or omitted mention of burial costume entirely. These changes parallel those that took place in eighteenth-century Europe.[118] Of course, even those who left the decision of dress to their heirs or to God, along with those requesting "the most humble" costume, may have been interred in the habit of St. Francis. Yet the move away from specify-ing one's burial dress suggests a gradual shift away from baroque norms, undoubtedly facilitated by the secularization of the missions and the dwindling number of Franciscans relative to the population. The colonial and Mexican periods demonstrate no significant gender differences, but

Figure 1
Burial Dress Requested in Wills, 1700-1899

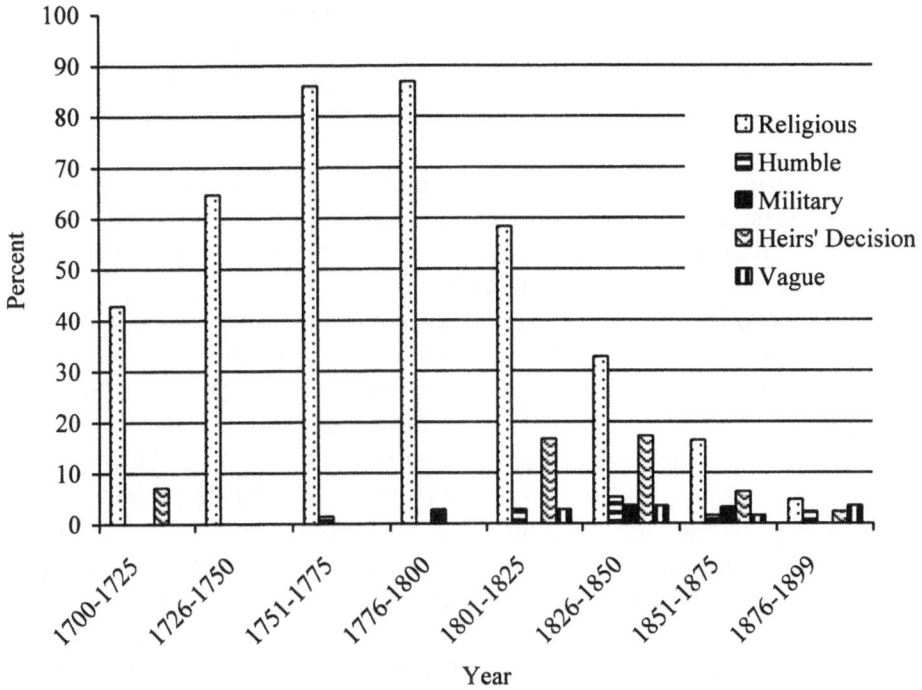

in the last half of the nineteenth century women represent a higher percentage of those choosing a religious habit for burial. In other words, women tended to opt for this more traditional form of dress later than men. Like the resurgence in popularity of some other religious elements found in wills (discussed below), it seems that traditional piety and Roman Catholicism more particularly in this case served as important cultural markers in a period of social change and stress.

On the whole, however, people gradually removed themselves from the decision-making process, suggesting that values shifted in the increasingly competitive and market-oriented culture of the mid-nineteenth century. Even so, one of the first books printed in New Mexico included a blessing for the Franciscan burial costume. Cura Martínez's *Manualito de párrocos, para los autos del ministerio más precisos, y auxiliar a los enfermos* offers the following blessing:

Lord Jesus Christ, originator and inspirer of religious
designs, who willed to don the garment of our flesh for the

salvation of the human race ... be generous and look on the prayers of our humility and deign to bless and sanctify this religious garment and cord of St. Francis, and grant to whoever takes or requests them for wrapping his dead body the remission of sins (granted through the Supreme Pontiffs of your Church), you who live and reign forever and ever.[119]

The prayer—notably, published by a member of the secular clergy—reveals the rather remarkable endurance of an ideal that spanned two continents and at least four centuries, even as fewer and fewer people were actually seeking the habit for burial.

Less commonly seen in New Mexico, the wish for interment in the most humble or poorest of costumes stemmed from the same notion of the good death as burial in the Franciscan habit. Abiquiú's José Manuel Martínez requested that he be dressed as a pauper, which reflected the baroque ideal of humility much as did the habit of St. Francis.[120] Others asked simply for whatever was available, perhaps in a deliberate rejection of material considerations. For some, concern over the burial shroud apparently carried as much temporal as spiritual weight, offering one's neighbors an opportunity to take in the sight of the humbled corpse during the funeral mass. The emphasis on burial costume, which presupposed that the celestial court appraised the fashion in which the cadaver was clad, somewhat ironically affirmed the importance of the physical remains, if only temporarily.

Notwithstanding the spiritual focus of the dying process, temporal as well as spiritual concerns were inherent in the good death. Both the profession of faith and the proper distribution of one's belongings helped ensure a good death. Though they may have already resigned themselves to death, New Mexicans also revealed in their wills how dear life and the things of this world were to them. Along with the fear of death and God's judgment, pious bequests that smack of self-interest and instructions seeking to exert some control over the lives of loved ones make New Mexico's wills at once profoundly spiritual and deeply human documents. Although people wrote their wills to dispose of material goods and make spiritual amends so that they could die well, the documents lay bare people's difficulties in severing all earthly ties. While seeking a serene and fearless death might inspire some to generous bequests, few forgave any debts as a final act of charity. People recalled every peso and sheep that could be collected and added to the bulk of their estates. Despite their aspirations to heavenly bliss, wills demonstrate the great difficulty that people had in letting go of this world.

Like the internal contradictions of many testaments, when viewed as a whole, New Mexican wills demonstrate the complexities of faith and culture and the tensions within New Mexican society. After a notable mid-eighteenth-century decline, the highpoint for both men's and women's pious giving occurred during the last quarter of the eighteenth century, when close to 90 percent of testators paid for masses for themselves in their wills; this figure dropped steadily after the turn of the century, however, and by 1826–50 only 36 percent of wills mentioned masses. Perhaps the crop failures and drought of the 1770s, the devastating smallpox epidemic of 1780–82, and the depredations of Plains Indians groups spurred some to set aside more of their goods for masses and other charity in the late eighteenth century. Hardship and death seemed to besiege New Mexicans and came most disturbingly, without warning. Contemporary thought commonly linked epidemics, natural disasters, and the like to God's disfavor. Logically, the faithful responded by giving more to the church. It is possible that economic and population growth following upon the heels of these troubled times fostered both confidence and a decrease in pious giving.[121]

The contraction in overall pious bequests—both masses and other forms of charity—gained momentum in the 1820s, around the same time that the province experienced rising trade and improving economic conditions. Though for much of the colonial and Mexican periods women's pious giving paralleled men's, men's bequests declined somewhat more rapidly than women's in the nineteenth century, suggesting that not economic necessity but attitudinal change prompted this shift. Requests for intercession in wills decreased in this same period, confirming this assessment. In the increasingly commercial world of the early nineteenth century, greater economic competition, social differentiation, and private ownership may have prompted more people to pass all their resources on to heirs rather than to endow pious bequests.[122] Concurrent with the developing santero industry and the rise in the Penitente Brotherhood in the late eighteenth and early nineteenth centuries, New Mexican society—particularly "urban" centers like Santa Fe—increasingly became concerned with secular pursuits. By the mid-nineteenth century, a detailed profession of faith like Juliana Fernández's became less common, as many testators so abbreviated their professions of faith that they no longer resembled the centuries-old formula. They called less frequently for divine intercession in the hour of their death and when they did, routinely ignored most of the celestial court, counting only on the Virgin Mary's aid. Considered in conjunction with the contemporaneous proliferation of religious art and religious construction around the turn of the century, it seems that the fabric of popular piety itself was changing, replacing old practices with new and perhaps more tangible and less ephemeral expressions.

Against this trend away from matters of the spirit, some New Mexicans framed a powerful and determined conservative reaction in the form of the Penitente Brotherhood and, to a lesser extent, in the Chimayó Rebellion (which will be addressed in chapter 5). Though historians have viewed the emergence of the Penitentes primarily as a byproduct of population growth and the attendant need for ministers, the Brotherhood may have formed in part in response to the ascendance of commercial over spiritual ventures. Even as people would have been more able to afford generous charitable bequests and religious habits for burial, wills suggest a growing indifference to these essential elements of the good death. As some sectors of society gradually moved toward a more secular way of dying and living, others embraced a traditional, baroque religiosity, establishing moradas for communal gathering and group penitence. A generation or two later, the Santa Fe Trail reoriented New Mexico's economy to include trade with the United States. In time, New Mexico gained even greater exposure to powerful outside influences—mass-produced manufactured products, Anglo traders, and French clergy—and people again began requesting intercession in their wills, in numbers that had not been seen for a generation. Just as Roman Catholicism informed nationalist rhetoric during the 1837 Chimayó Rebellion and in the heady 1840s, faith and its more traditional expressions now offered an opportunity for community as well as individual identification in a time of change.[123]

CHAPTER THREE

Rituals to Aid the Soul

I
n the fall of 1800, Lt. don Luis Montoya Cabeza de Vaca lodged a formal complaint against Fray Francisco de Hozio, military chaplain of the royal garrison since July 1787. Montoya described the situation as follows:

> On the fifth of March of this year of 1800 I had someone
> call upon the father that he might administer the holy oils
> to my [since] deceased daughter. He refused to come. They
> returned on the sixth to call upon him, and he refused to
> come. On the seventh day, when he did not agree to come, I
> went to him personally and upon knocking on the door was
> bade to enter. With extremely vulgar and offensive words he
> told me that my daughter was as bad off as he and the oils
> were of no assistance to any Christian.[1]

Notwithstanding the friar's blasphemous words and shocking refusal to perform his duties on this solemn occasion, when a mule injured Montoya a few months later, the lieutenant again called for the chaplain. Hozio demanded that a horse be sent for him. Upon the horse's arrival, however, the chaplain reportedly declared that he would not ride to confess the ailing lieutenant, asserting that he was obligated to hear an individual's confession only once a year. In the end, since Hozio would not leave Santa Fe, Montoya had to implore another priest to administer the sacraments, coming from the capital to his location, an unnamed but rocky eight or nine league distance. To Hozio's detriment, however, the lieutenant survived his injuries and lived to file a complaint against the negligent priest. Other presidial soldiers complained about the friar as well, but Montoya's grievances possessed the most far-reaching repercussions, for in denying the sick the sacraments, Hozio had jeopardized their very salvation.

Though the process of making a will allowed people to settle their spiritual and worldly estates, only a priest could administer the last rites, which were central to the good death. The last rites of the Roman Catholic Church facilitated passage into the afterlife and fortified the soul for the great moral dangers it faced at death. Their importance was such that the Roman rite obligated clergy to attend to the sick with the greatest speed, even if no one had summoned them to the bedside. Upon entering the home of the ailing, the priest was to first ask for the blessing and protection of all who dwelled within the house. He would then proceed to the patient's bedside to administer the three final sacraments of the Roman Catholic faith, collectively known as the last rites. Penitence was the crucial first step, for it opened the door to forgiveness of one's sins. Viaticum—the administration of the Eucharist—eased the spirit's passage into physical death. Extreme unction, or anointing of the sick, benefited the soul while holding the potential to cure the body. Thus the last rites facilitated the patient's spiritual welfare while also extending the possibility of restoring physical health.

Ritual Preparation: The Last Rites

The last rites paved the path for salvation and offered the dying protection against the malevolent forces awaiting them at death. In administering the viaticum, or host, the priest would say "Accept, brother (or sister) the viaticum of the body of the Lord Jesus Christ; may it keep you from the malign enemy and lead you to eternal life."[2] These words reflected the belief in the battle for the soul upon death, signaling that death represented the moment in which one's eternal fate was decided. An eighteenth-century booklet found in New Mexico reiterated the imperative to help the sick in their final hours:

> It is impossible to comprehend the danger that we run
> at the hour of death, the point upon which our eternity
> depends, and the critical moment of eternal sentencing
> or condemnation of our souls; and because it is the most
> decisive moment it is when this infernal monster, whose

power is incomparable . . . uses all of his strength against the dying, who he knows have little time left.[3]

Recounting how the devil deployed all his resources and wiles to ensnare souls at death, the booklet included instructions to empower the soul by exorcising demons. Calling upon the same intercessors implored in wills—the Virgin Mary, Archangel Michael, and the name saints—the exorcising prayer banished demons and their temptations from the dying.

Though certainly aware of individual friars' failings, people must have held the priest's ability to expel evil spirits in high regard. During the witchcraft outbreak in Abiquiú in the 1760s, residents witnessed first-hand the power of exorcism, as Fray Juan José Toledo performed numerous exorcisms on allegedly possessed members of his flock. After treating the sickly Santiago Martín, Toledo asserted, the man's suffering subsided considerably. The episode edified observers, according to the friar, for "we are able to glimpse the torments that take place in the other life if we do not repent." Although "God called on Santiago Martín" shortly thereafter, Toledo remarked that he displayed "a beautiful disposition and good signs of his leaving."[4] Thus, the exorcism allowed Martín to die well while also reminding community members of their own mortality and impending judgment.

Though not everyone could enjoy the enlightening lessons of a neighbor's demonic possession, people accepted that their souls would be a battleground at death. They prepared for the struggle with requests for intercession, prayers, and the last rites. Like many individuals, Albuquerque's alcalde mayor, Miguel Lucero, wanted to resist the devil's last attempts to thwart his salvation. To protect his thoughts, words, and beliefs in his final days, his 1766 will sought not only intercession but protection:

In effect from this point on until the hour of my death, I
invoke as my protector and advocate and defender the most
holy Virgin, my name saint, and guardian angel, all of whom
I love and who will act as my intercessors in the presence
of God and defend me until I am put in the saving presence
of His Divine Majesty.[5]

Likewise aware of the dangers of the final hour, Antonio Sais of Albuquerque revoked anything blasphemous he may have ever said or that he might say, because of either the devil's persuasiveness or the pains of death.[6] Though the moment of death might find one in a corporally or spiritually weak state, requesting assistance beforehand might act as a talisman.

Prayer represented a powerful weapon in the arsenal against the devil. Cura Martínez's nineteenth-century *Manualito de párrocos* included prayers especially formulated to facilitate a good death. According to the manual, the priest could grant a plenary indulgence and the remission of sins to the dying "insofar as I am able and the keys of the church reach, and I absolve you from the pains of purgatory you have merited because of sins committed and derelictions perpetrated in this world."[7] The booklet included prayers to accompany the many ritual steps of dying, which in turn offered succor and guidance to the sick and to the community.

Though in colonial New Mexico a single priest served people living in dispersed ranchos across rough terrain, the church demonstrated considerable flexibility in addressing the challenges of spiritual life on the periphery of Spain's New World empire. The shortage of priests, the distances between settlements, and the possibility of encountering hostile Indians all called for certain precautions in New Mexico, as Domínguez described upon visiting Picurís Pueblo in 1776:

> He [the priest] has taught two Indians in the pueblo how to administer baptism in cases of great urgency, and he has instructed four settlers in his jurisdiction for the same purpose. He has eased his mind by enabling these same settlers to assist the dying to make a good end.[8]

In the absence of a priest and in the danger of death, nonclergy could perform baptism and minister to the dying.[9] Midwives likewise baptized sickly babies at birth rather than risk their death prior to the priest's arrival.[10] At the other end of the continuum, priests often baptized Pueblo or Navajo Indians and the occasional Anglo or French trader on the deathbed, subsequently administering the last rites to ensure the possibility of salvation.

The first of the last rites—penitence—actually included several steps: the dying's confession, the request for absolution, and an act of contrition. While the church only required an annual confession, for those in danger of death, Bishop Márquez de Castañiza asserted, confession represented a "divine precept."[11] Though salvation depended on practicing good works of faith, hope, and charity during one's life, the repose of one's soul necessitated confession. Cognizant of death's imminence, the dying were to be especially contrite in their confessions. Like the will, confession allowed one to resolve any worldly and spiritual obligations. After forgiving the dying person's sins, the priest then questioned him or her in the tenets of the Roman Catholic faith, followed by absolution.

Thus prepared, the priest could next feed the Host, which represented Christ's body, to the dying. Viaticum served quite literally as spiritual food for the soul's pending journey, granting it the necessary sustenance to brave the coming trials. To prevent the Eucharist from falling into the hands of anyone with bad intentions, priests were to keep it in a clean, respectable place under lock and key. Delivering the consecrated bread to the sick itself comprised a ritual, as a small procession of priest and accompaniers assembled to carry the Host, holy oils, and other accouterments for administering this and the other last rites.

Throughout Roman Catholic Europe, the sight of the priest passing with the Eucharist served as an invitation for community members to follow to the house of the dying, where their prayers would aid the soul of kin and stranger alike. The tolling parish bells informed the entire town of the illness. Fourteenth-century Spanish law had dictated that all who saw the priest approaching with the Eucharist en route to minister to the sick either follow the priest or kneel as he passed. If working, one should pause to venerate the Host, and those on horseback had to dismount to show their respect.[12] This tradition continued in the Americas. As late as the 1840s, a visitor in central Mexico observed how when the Eucharist proceeded "slowly along through the crowd, with the mysterious Eye painted on the panels, drawn by piebald horses, and with some priests within carrying the Host...On the balconies, in the shops, in the houses, and on the streets, everyone knelt while it passed."[13] The candlelight leading the procession conveyed that the Host was "the true light," and only a priest or deacon might carry the ornate pyx that guarded the Host like a treasure. Similar scenes transpired in Santa Fe, though the priest had to rely on a vecina's coach and mules to bring viaticum to the dying. While she granted the priest continued use of these items, Rosa Bustamante's will made it clear that they did not belong to him and were strictly for the purpose of conveying viaticum.[14] After the opening of the Santa Fe Trail, an ecclesiastical visitor censured the growing population of North Americans, who disrespected the Eucharist by failing to remove their hats and kneel as the priest passed.[15] This behavior must have scandalized staunch Roman Catholics and heightened the sense of difference between New Mexicans and the foreign population arriving after independence. Welcome as their merchandise was, their impiety and disregard for local values must have been a source of tension for the faithful.

The church itself proved flexible in defining what constituted proper treatment of the Eucharist. Some clergy in Mexico apparently had argued against the administration of viaticum to the poor, contending that it was indecent to bring the Host into the wretched homes of destitute Indians, mestizos, and mulattoes. Perhaps an effort on the part of slothful or avaricious priests to avoid having to administer the sacrament to the poor, ecclesiastical authorities overruled these concerns. Salvation took precedence, and no matter how lowly or miserable the dwelling, clergy should convey the Host where needed. Even in the absence of the requisite light and table on which to place the Eucharist, the priest could administer viaticum by holding onto the Host until the last moment, thereby becoming a living altar, "more acceptable than all the riches, candles, and candelabras of the most sumptuous, brilliant, decorated, and adorned ... altars."[16] New Mexico's religious used portable altars for the express purpose of celebrating mass for distant residents and bringing viaticum to the sick. Individual circumstances dictated how and where the friars administered the viaticum, as Domínguez noted in his report on New Mexico missions:

> When it is necessary to give the Most Holy Viaticum, if the
> place is far from the church, Mass is said on the portable
> altar in the sick person's house. The Most Illustrious [Bishop]
> Tamarón gave permission for this. And meanwhile guards
> and spies are posted in case there might be an attack by
> enemy [Indians]. If it is near the church, Mass is celebrated
> there and afterwards Our Lord goes forth. The Confraternity
> of St. Michael donates the wax for this function.[17]

Though a family member might call the priest with ample time before death, weather, road conditions, distance, and the presence of hostile Indians could still conspire to prevent one from receiving the last rites.

Only when death seemed certain did the priest give extreme unction, the ultimate of the last rites. This sacrament consisted of anointing eyes, ears, nostrils, lips, hands, and feet with oil, in preparation for entrance into heaven. Joseph Martos writes of extreme unction:

> According to Bonaventure the sacramental rite worked by
> helping the dying receive forgiveness for venial sins which

were often left unmentioned in Confession, even in the last Confession which preceded the last anointing. The grace that was offered in the sacrament enabled the recipients to perform supernatural acts of love and devotion which canceled out those sins, thus removing the last obstacles to complete abandonment to God.[18]

Extreme unction was held to have the power to restore one's physical health. Because of the sacrament's great power, the Roman rite forbade its administration more than once within the course of an illness, unless the patient had experienced a marked physical improvement and subsequently relapsed.

Although a patient technically only merited extreme unction when facing certain and imminent death, the bishop, Juan Francisco Márquez, recognized that New Mexican conditions complicated matters. Lamenting that most people died without receiving extreme unction, in 1819 he authorized priests to bestow extreme unction at the same time that they gave viaticum. If an illness prevented administration of viaticum, the bishop permitted priests to confer extreme unction after granting absolution. The bishop also instructed clergy to carry the holy oils whenever they attended to the ailing, so as to anoint them:

> In this manner, you will give the poor sick this most important of comforts; do not wait in its administration until the sick are in such a state that it would be a miracle for the sacrament to have its effect of restoring the body's health.[19]

Like his predecessor, Márquez de Castañiza sought to reduce the burden on New Mexico's clergy in light of local conditions. The bishop and others rightly recognized certain environmental challenges to the priests' work in New Mexico.

ADMINISTERING THE LAST RITES IN NEW MEXICO

Because the last rites represented an intensely private process between a priest and the dying, uncovering the practice and its meanings in New Mexico two hundred years later poses a challenge. Rarely did the rites enter the written record. We do know that even secular officials deemed them significantly important that authorities quickly transferred criminals who had been sentenced to death to the ministrations of a priest, to ensure that the condemned could receive absolution. Gov. Joaquín del

Real Alencaster (1805–8), for example, instructed a friar to immediately inform Antonio Carabajal and Mariano Benavides of their death sentence, so that they might "begin to prepare themselves to suffer death in a Christian manner with the most pious and proper object of directing their souls to Heaven, as the laws and our Holy and Catholic Religion provide."[20] Even—and perhaps especially—convicted murderers merited the comfort and peace that the rites promised.

Material culture offers some evidence of the last rites' importance as well. Parish inventories identify crosses, gold and silver reliquaries, and pyxes dedicated for use in the last rites. Their exclusive use for the last rites suggests something of the sacraments' importance and differentiation from other rituals. To transport these items and other essentials—holy water and holy oils—priests probably used the same wooden carrying cases employed in bringing mass to distant settlements. The second of the Segesser hide paintings, or Segesser II, depicts a battle scene from the 1720 Villasur massacre in which the wounded friar, besieged by six warriors, moves resolutely forward to grant the last rites to dying soldiers. The opposite of Lieutenant Montoya's unhappy experiences with the reluctant military chaplain, in this idealized vision the priest places his duty to administer the last rites before all else, including his own life.

Which image portrays New Mexican reality: the reputedly lazy and hostile Fray Francisco de Hozio of Montoya's indictment or the fearless and dedicated missionary of Segesser II? Though instructed to list in the burial books complete information on the deceased parishioner, including whether he or she died with the sacraments, many priests ignored these directives and made only perfunctory notations in the burial registers. Inconsistent and incomplete parish burial registers make it impossible to reconstruct fully what proportion of the population received the last rites; in only half of the over two thousand entries reviewed did priests make reference to the sacraments at all. A sample of more than one thousand burial entries for which complete information is available, however, reveals that from 1730 to 1850 fully 87 percent of parishioners living in or near the villas of Santa Fe, Santa Cruz, and Albuquerque received some or all of the last rites. Indians living in or near the northern Spanish villas—Santa Fe, Santa Cruz, and Albuquerque—received the last rites as frequently as those identified as Spaniards or vecinos. While few New Mexicans received all the sacraments as they lay dying, most received at least some.

Priests often did not note why they had not given someone the last rites, but when they did, most frequently cited an unexpected or sudden

Figure 2
Population Receiving Last Rites in Albuquerque, Santa Cruz,
and Santa Fe, 1730-1850

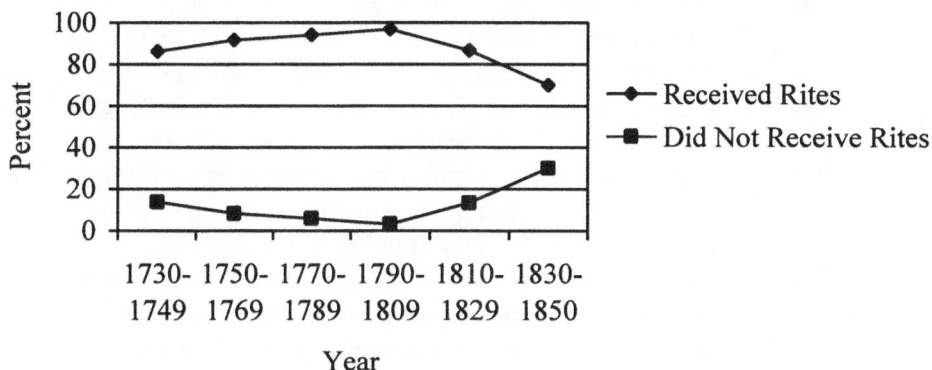

death. Among those who did not receive the last rites, no gender or ethnic pattern emerges; their deaths occurred throughout the seasons and years examined. Friars sometimes indicated that someone had been unable to consume viaticum because of the nature of the illness. According to the burial books, about one-third of those who did not receive the last rites simply had failed to call the priest in time. This fact suggests that family members often waited to call the priest until the last possible moment. Sometimes the friars assigned blame, as in this entry:

> In this mission of Our Lady of Sorrows of Sandia, on March 7, 1788, I, Fray José Mariano Rosete, gave ecclesiastical burial to the dead body of Manuela, Moquina, married to Cristobal, Tigua. She died at about age twenty-five. She received the sacrament of penitence, and because of the bad custom of the Indians, they did not call me to give her extreme unction.[21]

Hoping for the best, perhaps, a family in many cases may have been unaware that a loved one was in fact dying. The insane and the mentally disabled could not receive the sacraments, for all but baptism presupposed the possession of reason and thus the ability to sin.[22] The label *fatuus a nativitate*, or "idiot from birth," kept about 2 percent of parishioners from receiving the last rites.

Suicides, people who by definition died outside the church, by the very nature of their deaths could not receive the last rites and were banned from receiving ecclesiastical burial. In New Mexico, however, even this prohibition might not be absolute. Having slit his throat, Juan Domingo Carache, a native of San Ildefonso Pueblo, appeared to repent and to want to confess his sins to the priest one evening in 1799. Fray Ramón González went to hear the dying man's confession, but a messenger from San Ildefonso met the friar at San Juan and instructed the priest to wait. The wound did not appear too serious, and Carache would be brought to San Juan for confession in the morning. Carache reportedly spent the night praying before the images of the saints in a home altar and subsequently died without benefit of the friar's attention. Despite the ban on Roman Catholic burial for suicides, González argued that Carache should receive an ecclesiastical burial—at the very least in the cemetery—for he had truly repented and therefore deserved interment in consecrated ground.[23]

Murder was far more common than suicide and like other sudden or violent deaths typically prevented receipt of the last rites. Victims of hostile Indians, domestic violence, fights, and reckless behavior frequently died without benefit of the sacraments. Since how one died therefore influenced one's postmortem state, it is understandable why theologians depicted illnesses as gifts from God, for they offered the dying an opportunity to make amends and prepare for death. Childbirth might also prompt someone to call on a priest. Though she had given birth to ten children already, Rosalía Martínez received the sacrament of penitence before the birth of what would have been her eleventh child. A thirty-six-year-old "free Indian" married to "Spaniard" Juan Antonio Casados, she did not survive that final labor and delivery in 1798 but at least had had time to prepare herself spiritually. While she did not obtain all the last rites, Martínez had received the priest's counsel, which in addition to offering her spiritual comfort certainly consoled her husband as he faced the daunting task of raising eight boys and two girls alone.[24]

Notwithstanding the clergy's success in administering at least some of the last rites to their parishioners in the face of substantial obstacles, ecclesiastical visitors felt compelled to remind local religious of the sacraments' crucial nature. After reviewing Albuquerque's burial books, Bishop Tamarón reiterated the importance of swiftly attending to those in danger of death. Recognizing the inherent difficulty of administering the sacraments among New Mexico's scattered population and amid the threat of enemy Indians, Tamarón stated that Fray

Manuel Rojo and his subordinates should bring a portable altar when-ever they visited the sick, thereby allowing them to conduct mass in the home and administer viaticum. Thus, the priest would provide, as Tamarón wrote, "this spiritual consolation and extremely important comfort for the soul so that thus comforted, one is prepared with greater earnestness for a good death."[25]

Comforting the sick and administering the sacraments to the dying across large and often dangerous expanses occasionally led to problems. Subject to scrutiny by the families of the dying as well as other clergy, both the Franciscans and later the secular or diocesan priests became the subjects of criticism. Only a month before he pro-voked Montoya's enmity, Fray Francisco de Hozio himself had lodged a grievance with Bishop Olivares y Benito against Cura José María Bivián de Ortega, in February 1800:

> Recently, sir, on January 11 of the present year, there died
> in the home of the distinguished soldier don Mariano Bernal
> an Indian woman, who by order of the governor, had been
> placed there for already two months, and after I had minis-
> tered to her, having come to see me said Bernal in order to
> bury her, and the grave already open (which even now
> remains awaiting her body), came el Señor Cura Interino
> of this town of Santa Fe, don José María Bivián de Ortega,
> to said house at an inconvenient hour, around one in the
> afternoon, took the body, deposited it in the church, and
> immediately gave it burial in the cemetery, and therefore
> Your Holiness sees the point to which we have arrived.[26]

In Hozio's eyes Bivián de Ortega had neglected to tend to the dying woman in time; notwithstanding his cavalier behavior and tardiness, he had seized the body abruptly for burial without consultation, pre-sumably to collect on the burial fee.

Durango's cathedral chapter received numerous testimonials decrying Bivián de Ortega's inadequate attention to the last rites and disparaging treatment of the poor. The assault on the priest represented part of a larger political battle between him and the Franciscans, whose moral fiber Bivián de Ortega had assailed almost immediately upon his arrival in New Mexico. Bivián de Ortega had, for example, accused one friar of living in concubinage and stated of the Franciscans overall that they were "secret enemies," presumably of the church. He had issued an edict instructing friars and their Indian parishioners on their duties, declaring in part that if a priest left one of his flock unattended at the hour of his or her death, the funeral would be free. Gov. Fernando de Chacón (1794–1805) used words like "tyranny" and "despotism" when describing the vicar's behavior, observing that both the priest's parishioners and the province's Franciscans found him "insufferable." Many people reportedly waited for months to baptize their children rather than face the unpleasant cleric, while others buried their dead in the fields rather than pay his inflated prices.[27]

In his defense, the priest obtained more than a dozen letters from prominent citizens—including one from Montoya—attesting to his unprejudiced and speedy administration of the sacraments. Antonio José Ortiz testified that in the two years since the priest's arrival in Santa Fe, he knew of no incident where Bivián de Ortega had not gone with utmost speed to give spiritual consolation and administer the sacraments to the sick.[28] Juan José Silva noted that the father always had acted with charity and compassion, without regard to a person's status or the distance he had to travel to administer the rites.[29] The testimonials continued in the same vein, reflecting both the esteem in which some people held the priest and the importance they placed on the last rites.

Though emblematic of the tensions between the secular and regular clergy, which we will consider below, the charges that Hozio leveled against Bivián de Ortega were neither new nor restricted to querulous clerics. Such accusations had surfaced throughout the colonial period. Population growth in the late eighteenth and early nineteenth centuries, however, exacerbated the situation as the demands on the Franciscans increased. In San Agustín de Isleta, for example, Fray José Ignacio Sánchez in 1815 defended himself against accusations that he let people die without the sacraments. He counterattacked by charging that the Isletans failed to call him in time but also complained that his flock expected him to be in two places at once, since he oversaw religious life in Tomé as well.[30] In addition to their parish or mission church, priests had to minister to the spiritual needs of the faithful in outlying *visitas*. Whatever their individual failings, in many cases priests simply were spread too thin to meet the growing population's demands.

Certain material deficiencies further complicated matters. Religious officials in the eighteenth century complained about everything from poor vestments to the shortage of holy oils necessary to administer extreme unction.[31] With population growth, the buildings themselves proved inadequate in several parishes. Even before receiving a license to do so, Albuquerque's Cura José Francisco Leyva began organizing the construction of a new chapel at Alameda, having observed that the small existing chapel prevented all from receiving the sacraments and church burial.[32]

Other problems had little to do with demographics and affirm the rather pragmatic popular piety that characterized New Mexico in this period. In 1817, when ecclesiastical visitor don Juan Bautista Ladrón del Niño de Guevara arrived from Durango to examine parish records and assess the state of the faith, his findings corroborated eighteenth-century critiques. Ladrón del Niño de Guevara declared conditions among the Pueblos and Spanish settlers equally dismal, with illiteracy high and knowledge of the catechism low. One of the best-attended churches, that of El Paso del Norte, he characterized as "worse than a Mexican pulqueria," referring to a place where the liquor pulque was sold.[33] Infested with bats and swallows, he found the animals beneath the altar and their excrement in the baptismal font. Of the mission at Picurís Pueblo, the visitor noted that it was "a mortal sin to celebrate mass with these vestments."[34] Only in the capital city of Santa Fe did he locate any cantors, one of whom was so "perverse" that the governor had to banish him. Ladrón del Niño de Guevara concluded his report by stating that it was self-evident how "without pomp or solemnity are celebrated the functions [of the church], divine offices, burials, and other suffrages in this province."[35] This scathing critique of New Mexican religious life would seem to support Michael Carroll's claim of "the golden age that wasn't," but it may also suggest the presence of a piety less attentive to external trappings and more attune to other, more immediate concerns. If we measure popular piety, for example, by the numerous petitions parishioners wrote to ecclesiastical officials—despite paper shortages and a largely illiterate population—New Mexicans in fact appear to have been quite devout as well as wonderfully tenacious.

New Mexicans were perhaps most vociferous and consistent in voicing their concerns to authorities over issues related to religious leadership, which they found wanting both quantitatively and qualitatively. The visitor, Ladrón del Niño de Guevara, and others blamed the Franciscans for New Mexicans' spiritual debility and superstition, but the secular clergy's arrival did not necessarily improve the quality of religious leadership, and complaints persisted. In both Albuquerque and Santa Cruz, the burial registers demonstrate that the percentage of the population receiving some or all of the last rites actually declined from 1790 through 1850, the very period when secularization took place.[36] Some of the incoming priests proved inferior to the outgoing Franciscans. The Spanish-born Cura Gregorio Oliden, appointed by Bishop Francisco Gabriel de Olivares y Benito to lead the parish of Santa Fe in December 1797, had been reprimanded by the Inquisition a decade before his removal to New Mexico's capital. He had confessed to numerous crimes, including heretical blasphemy for denying that at the Last Judgment the dead would rise in restored physical form.[37] Oliden did not reform his profane ways upon arriving in Santa Fe. As early as May 1798 the Inquisition commissary, Fray José de la Prada, heard testimony from parishioners decrying Oliden's farcical masses, negligence in administering the sacraments, and ridicule of extreme unction. The haste with which the faithful attacked the new priest's teachings undermines any claims as to the debility of New Mexican religiosity. However lacking in apparitions, pilgrimage sites, and localized Madonnas, New Mexicans did care deeply about their faith and its leadership, as evidenced by this and numerous other cases. Despite his reputed zeal to extirpate the Franciscans from New Mexico, even Governor Chacón recognized that Oliden was a hopeless case, and the priest soon disappeared from the pages of New Mexico's sacramental records.

Clearly Oliden represented an extreme on the continuum, but to the dismay of many New Mexicans, those appointed to serve their spiritual needs were often at the nadir of their profession. William B. Taylor, in writing of the least desirable parishes in Guadalajara and Mexico in the late colonial period observes that "they were the hardship posts of the diocese, mostly classified as third-class, with some combination of foul climate, meager income, dispersed settlements, uncooperative or ignorant parishioners, bad roads, and great distance from Guadalajara or Mexico City."[38] Taylor's description of rural Guadalajara and Mexico might serve just as well to describe New Mexico, which must have appeared dreadful to priests who could not manage even an assignment to rural Guadalajara. It is clear that some religious opposed their assignments to New Mexico, and some who served the province thought little of their largely uneducated and unsophisticated parishioners.[39] Whether regarding transfer to New Mexico as a challenge or a punishment, few priests clamored to be sent there, though New Mexicans from El Paso to Taos repeatedly petitioned authorities for more clergy to serve their growing parishes.

New Mexicans took an active role in their religious life, not only requesting additional priests but also denouncing clergy—regular and secular alike—they found wanting in some fashion. Disgusted with the state of spiritual affairs, Taos parishioners in 1823 wrote to the bishop complaining of their rheumatic priest's incompetence. Perhaps they could have seen past Fray Sebastián Álvarez's constant bouts with rheumatism and dropsy, but he was also a poor orator. Most troubling, however, was Álvarez's limited availability. The sick routinely died without confession, the letter claimed, for Álvarez would only hear confessions by day. When he did manage to say mass few parishioners could attend because of the excessively early hour. Initially, people had not complained, "in submission to God's will, Who perhaps wished it so, or reasoning that it was the result of our misfortune and sins that were thus being punished."[40] No longer able to suffer Álvarez's religious leadership, however, sixty parishioners wrote to the bishop, beseeching him to send them a priest who could minister to the devout community. Although they failed in their quest to get the recently ordained Cura Antonio José Martínez—a native son—at this point, Taos's faithful succeeded in ridding themselves of Álvarez. His removal probably only served to make another parish miserable, however, for by July 1823, he had become the resident priest of Isleta Pueblo. Here, his ministrations had probably not improved, but it would take some time for residents to build a case against the deficient friar. As in Mexico, the church here shuffled around priests when their actions—or inaction—in a community had worn thin their welcome.

In northern New Mexico, membership in the growing Penitente Brotherhood represented another popular response to the deficiencies of spiritual life. Although virtually no information on its activities before the Territorial period survives, like other lay religious organizations the brotherhood probably did what it could for its dying members. The brothers would regularly say the *sudario*, a prayer to alleviate the suffering of the souls in purgatory.[41] In the absence of a priest, the Penitentes' *rezador*, or prayer leader, would pray at the home of the dying, shouting the name of Jesus three times as he or she died. Upon death, the brotherhood would also assume responsibility for the rosary and the burial, conducting the cadaver to its final resting place with a procession of flagellants whose efforts helped the soul on its path to salvation.[42] Thus, in rural areas, the Penitentes allowed some communities to manage their religious life in those cases where priests proved in short supply relative to the population.

Whether or not a priest tended to the dying, the presence of family and friends ensured that the dying faced death accompanied. They said prayers, comforted the sick, and generally tried to help them die with equanimity. Family and friends watched for the signs that signaled death's approach, including sleeplessness, unwillingness to talk, sensitivity to light, a dry black tongue, the inability to sneeze even with the use of powders, loss of warmth in the extremities, and irregular breathing.[43] Because New Mexico did not share in the rich tradition of diary and journal-keeping so popular in the eastern United States, few descriptive accounts of death survive. Only deaths that deviated from the model—as in the case of murder—merited the paper necessary to record them. In 1825, Pecos's Fray Francisco Bragado reportedly died "in full awareness and very agreeably," suggesting an exemplary death.[44] The most detailed account of a deathbed scene from northern New Spain comes from Nueva Vizcaya's mission of La Junta de los Ríos in the early colonial period. Here, the Indian governor, a man identified only as Francisco, died the good death:

> He made his Confession with the greatest scrupulosity, and on the following day asked for the sacraments of the Viaticum and Extreme Unction; and, taking an image of the holy Christ in his hand, he called his wife and children and exhorted them, saying that the law of God preached by the fathers was the true one, and that they should not believe in the fables [of the Indians], which were all lies, and that there was but one God, the creator of the universe, and that they ought to serve him and keep his holy commands. Having said this, he continued to give expression to these words and acts of the love of God, saying, "I believe in God, I love God, I have faith that God will save me, God's will must be done in all," until he died, to the great edification of all those present, who had been moved to tears by his behavior.[45]

Reflecting the age-old idea that the dying enjoyed exceptional wisdom, Francisco's death proved instructive. His beliefs did not falter, and indeed, he strengthened the faith of others. Francisco's story adheres so closely to the ideal death that the friar recording it undoubtedly did so with an eye to echoing the prescriptive literature, embellishing the events in La Junta de los Ríos to conform to the model death. The extent to which tranquility and submission characterized death for most New Mexicans, however, remains a mystery.

CONCEPTIONS OF DEATH

Regardless of how they died, most people received burial within twenty-four hours. Fearing burial alive, many nineteenth-century Europeans and Americans asked that their interment be postponed for at least twenty-four hours. No such belief preoccupied New Mexicans, who requested burial on the day of death, provided that they died "at a reasonable hour." When the hour of death prohibited immediate burial, the funeral mass and burial would take place on the following day. Since many communities shared their parish priest with other settlements, in the absence of a priest, residents buried the dead themselves. When the priest returned, people would remember whom they had buried in his absence and request his blessing for the dead. There might be a gap of several months, as in the May 1777 burial of Indian curandero Miguel de Arias, buried in San José de las Trampas without the assistance of the ailing Fray Sebastián Fernández. When a new friar arrived two months later, residents simply asked him to bless the dead healer's grave.[46] If more than a day elapsed between death and burial, contemporaries attributed the lapse to the unusual circumstances of the death. Albuquerque's Gerónimo Antonio, for example, drowned in the river, and two days therefore passed before his burial.[47] It presumably took a day to discover the missing man and retrieve his body. The priest likewise interred Manuel Sánchez, killed by a horse, two days after his death in 1819.[48] Rather the priest interred the "cadaver" of Manuel Sánchez—for this is how he recorded it in the burial book.

Those persons who had occasion to write about death generally eschewed euphemisms. Priests did not linguistically shroud the corpse but unequivocally noted whose "cadaver" or "dead body" they buried in the parish church. Even as they enjoyed the prayers of the living, the dead were already rhetorically distinguished from the living community of believers. The few surviving condolence letters do not refer to a sick relative who "passed away" or a beloved child who had been "lost." The excessive, self-indulgent sentimentality that emerged in the northeastern United States in the late eighteenth and early nineteenth centuries bypassed New Mexico. The dead did not "go home" to be among the angels; they simply died, to purge their sins in purgatory and await resurrection. The absence of florid language suggests a very different approach to death than that seen in the Protestant Northeast, where mourning manuals, consolation literature, and the rural cemetery movement conspired to promote an optimistic view of death and a culture that emphasized the art of bereavement. In identifying the dead individual from the start as the "cadaver" rather than the "dearly beloved," New Mexicans already distinguished between the corpse and the person who had once animated the body, presaging the more radical distinction they would make between the corpse and the skeleton.

New Mexicans' matter-of-factness stemmed from a view of death that stressed both indebtedness to God and the quest for salvation that endured beyond death. As noted earlier, wills frequently echoed Roman Catholic teachings, articulating the notion that death represented the debt humanity owed God for life. Correspondence reveals that beyond mere formula or dogma, New Mexicans viewed life as a debt they had to repay with death. José Antonio Casados stoically remarked of his son Nicolás's death, for example, that "this is how the people of this world pay for the good."[49] After suffering terrible pain, at two o'clock one morning in 1820, Josef Mariano de la Peña's daughter "delivered her soul to her Creator," suggesting death's reciprocity.[50] Though his statement borders on euphemism, it reflected the deepest truth for de la Peña. Offering the governor his condolences on the occasion of his wife's death, one friar stated in part that "God has given you understanding of what a debt is, fundamental to all mortals and without knowing the time of its exaction."[51] This knowledge perhaps tempered grief somewhat, but on the whole less optimism characterized New Mexicans' references to death when compared to contemporaries in the Northeast, who in poetry, journals, and even music conceptualized death as sleep and emphasized reunion in the afterlife. In the early nineteenth century, in contrast, New Mexicans frequently used words like "justice" and "judgment" in referring to death. Toribio González, for one, wrote of his wife's death by observing, "God has seen fit to call to justice my wife Luz."[52] These words aptly described what New Mexicans believed actually happened at death.

Though less sanguine than the Protestant vision of death, the doctrine of purgatory allowed Roman Catholics to maintain a meaningful relationship with the dead, in part negating the need for the elaborate mourning rituals their northeastern contemporaries embraced. New Mexicans certainly grieved, but instead of investing in black crepe and lockets that memorialized the dead, they spent their earnings on masses to alleviate the dead's suffering in purgatory. Masses and other pious acts allowed the bereaved to channel their grief in a meaningful way. Purgatory ensured that the living were not helpless before death but could decisively act to hasten the dead's repose. Since the church in this manner actually empowered the faithful, New Mexicans logically concentrated their postmortem attentions on the spirit rather than the body, which at this time in Protestant America become the nexus of people's care, resulting in painted, casketed, and eventually, embalmed corpses. The Protestant emphasis on the deceased's carnal aspects found a corollary in consolation literature that discussed heaven in physical terms, going so far as to contemplate what the dear departed ate in heaven. This exaggerated emphasis on bereavement in the antebellum United States stemmed from a combination of causes, including early industrialization, the growth of market capitalism, urbanization, and the resultant undermining of liberal ministers' authority. The radically different conditions in New Mexico in this same period likewise explain the absence of a similar impulse in New Mexican deathways.

THE PRICE OF DEATH

A single arancel, or standard list of fees, governed the cost of funerals in New Mexico. Notwithstanding the fact that the arancel itemized the costs for different funeral expenses in an effort to ensure uniformity across parishes, funeral costs varied greatly, determined in part by individual preferences, parish priests' inclinations, and the means of exchange. A single silver peso, or *peso de plata*, was valued at eight reales. The salary paid presidial soldiers, and the goods and services purchased for the presidio and its Indian allies, provided the chief source of specie in New Mexico, which saw a marked increase in hard currency in the late eighteenth century as a result of the Bourbons' interest in securing the frontier. Presidial soldiers received annual salaries, offering a sense of the peso's relative worth: 700 pesos for a lieutenant; 350 pesos for a sergeant; and 290 pesos for a soldier.[53] Still, most New Mexicans did not engage in wage labor. Those employed as seasonal laborers might earn only between two reales and one peso for a day's work. Since silver pesos only occasionally made their way into New Mexicans' hands, people relied on a system of imaginary coins to discuss the prices of goods and services.

Spaniards and Indians alike typically paid for goods or services in goods or services, relying chiefly on the peso de la tierra in their transactions. This system of currency might grow complicated as the value of the goods fluctuated according to the season, the quality of the harvest, and other conditions. Ross Frank demonstrates how in the late colonial period, for example, the value of some products rose and fell in response to changing export demands. Though cattle and oxen retained the same value in pesos de la tierra in 1791 that they had had in 1776, export goods such as sheep, wool, tobacco, and chile gained in value relative to silver.[54] Many noted the resulting confusion. Fray José Mariano Rosete observed widespread puzzlement regarding the imaginary peso, contending in 1801 that:

> For the spiritual and temporal good of the inhabitants of
> this province, it would do good to employ coinage and
> forget about the pesos de la tierra, which not even those
> who invented them understood, and even less those today.
> I call these imaginary pesos. As I see it, there are silver pesos
> that are valued at 1/4 of a real, others 1/2 a real, others one
> real, and others two Spanish reales. This is why there is no
> understanding or agreement, and as a result there are
> frauds, profits and deceptions, in prejudice to consciences
> and the eternal perdition of souls.[55]

Some of the disputes between clergy and their parishioners, discussed below, probably stemmed in part from confusion or disagreement over the pesos de la tierra. The expansion of commercial trade with Chihuahua exacerbated tensions, as in the case of Albuquerque vecino Blas Griego. Griego, who described himself as "an impoverished old man burdened with family," felt that Cura José Francisco Leyva had overcharged him for a funeral mass, vigil, and burial in 1824.[56] Although at times perhaps in disagreement over the value of goods, the stream of complaints like Griego's reveals that New Mexicans possessed a keen awareness of the costs priests were entitled to charge under the arancel—a fact remarkable not only because much of the population was illiterate, but also because some parishes appear not to have maintained a copy of the document in their records.

The arancel, in effect since Bishop Crespo's 1730 visit, determined priests' fees—in specie—for all manner of services, including funerals. Prices varied according to the dead's ethnicity, the number of attendants, the degree of pomp, and burial location. According to the arancel, for example, a high mass and burial for a Spaniard within his or her own parish cost sixteen pesos, four reales. In-kind contributions of bread, wine, and wax had to be provided as well but at the discretion of the executors or the family. The same funeral for a mulatto or free black cost eight silver pesos—and the price decreased to six pesos for a low mass. Mission Indians were exempt from paying obventions.[57] Like the different racial admixtures, the church assigned different costs for children's funerals. A Spanish child's burial that included a high cross and cope cost eight pesos, with a low cross six silver pesos. The cope, a hooded cape worn in solemn functions by priests, would have added an air of stateliness. The families of blacks, mulattoes, and Indians who worked in the missions or in a Spanish household (*indios de servicio*) were charged three pesos for a child's funeral with a low cross and five for a high cross.

The arancel established the minimum cost for goods and services the priest provided, but individuals might elect costlier and showier services, for which they likewise paid in goods rather than hard currency. The estate of Juana Galvana, a coyota from Zia who had been held captive by the Navajos as a child, paid an extraordinary 220 pesos in livestock and blankets to cover the costs of her funeral mass, burial, and novenario in 1753.[58] Manuel Olguín, a vecino from Bernalillo, left an estate valued at 5,709 pesos, of which his executors paid 380 pesos in funeral expenses, including a mass with the body present, a humble burial in the church at Sandia, dozens of masses for his soul, fifty masses for specific devotions, and 100 pesos in cows, sheep, or oxen to pay for adorning the church at Sandia.[59] Most funerals of pomp in New Mexico cost only a fraction of what Galvana's and Olguín's estates paid. More typical was Viviana Silva's thirty-six-peso funeral, which included a vigil (four pesos, paid in reales), mass with the body present (six pesos), a six-peso offering, the personal participation of the parish priest (two pesos), and one pound of wax (two pesos) to illuminate the wake at the home and the bier in the church.[60] Though some people elected to pay for lavish funerals, most New Mexican funerals did not approach even the muted display of Silva's service. In fact, an enormous gulf existed between the ideal, as presented in the schedule of fees, and New Mexican reality.

New Mexicans customarily paid considerably less than the arancel dictated. The detailed accounts the friars left indicate that only rarely did anyone pay sixteen pesos for a funeral, and when they did, the priests accepted fees in pesos de la tierra, which were only worth two reales each. Domínguez summed up obventions in Santa Fe thus:

> Although this [the arancel left by Bishop Crespo] is prescriptive, the settlers do not abide by it, but expect the missionary to accept what they are willing to give, not paying in accordance with the dispositions of the schedule. For not only do many say, *I bet according to my hand,* but some *show their hands as willingly as they bet,* not paying their pledges (this custom of pledging the obvention is usual in these parts, and it leads perniciously to other things that are obvious to the discerning) or not paying them when they fall due, or paying a smaller amount.[61]

Responding to a detailed complaint Santa Cruz residents lodged against him, Fray Diego Muñoz Jurado in 1781 left a remarkable if rather long-winded portrait of the state of affairs in the villa, where he had been

accused of a number of abuses, including fleecing parishioners for burials. His often scathing missive includes a description of each interment
he had conducted since his arrival in June the previous year, along with
the form of payment he received, or had been promised. As a relative
newcomer to New Mexico, the Spanish-born friar naturally expected
adherence to the schedule of fees. His recounting of burials and fees collected—typically in the form of livestock, grain, or both—reveals his vig-
ilant observation of the arancel, including consideration of the
deceased's caste, which other clergy ignored entirely.[62] The grieving parents of Spanish infant María de Jesús Trujillo, for example, promised to
pay eight pesos for her burial, per the arancel. They paid the priest with
corn valued at four pesos and owed him the remainder. The vecinos'
unhappiness therefore originated in the difference between custom and
practice, a discontent that would be repeated in other communities with
the secular clergy's arrival in the early nineteenth century.

While Muñoz Jurado and Domínguez recognized the gap between
prescription and practice, Gov. Fernando de la Concha (1788–94) a few
years later painted a pathetic picture, lamenting that orphans sold
their meager inheritances to pay for their parents' burials. Funeral
costs, he contended, were exorbitant, and "it is the commonly held
opinion in this country that whatever individuals work for and
acquire is absorbed by the religious for baptisms, marriages, and the
burials they perform; the arancel that has been in effect for more than
fifty years in this region is summarily high."[63] He recommended a new
schedule of fees that would correlate services to costs in livestock and
other goods, rather than specie, which remained in short supply. Ross
Frank notes that in fact, "a more money-conscious society, and the
effect of a dose of inflation on New Mexican produce, altered the per-
ception of the vecinos, who found themselves paying for the sacraments in more valuable commodities."[64]

Priests' avarice remained a favorite topic throughout the colonial,
Mexican, and Territorial periods. Echoing the words of Mexican visitors, secular officials, and some vecinos, Anglo newcomers picked up
on this theme and likewise demonized the clergy. More than half a century after the governor's indictment, one Anglo writer asserted that:

Poor parents have been known to abandon their dead
children because they could not afford to pay the cost of
interment by the Church. The regular fees for burial service
have in some instances been known to be as high as $400
and $500, the price always being regulated by the length and

kind of ceremony, and in the case of burial, by the number
of masses said for the repose of the soul.[65]

What outsiders failed to understand was that masses, like many of the
other available accouterments, were optional. Though abuses certainly occurred, these gross exaggerations frequently stemmed from
anti–Roman Catholic or, in the case of some visitors from the cathedral chapter, anti-Franciscan bias. They acquired the air of truth in
the retelling.

In fact, based on the surviving evidence, Domínguez and other friars most approximated the truth in their observations that few paid
the price dictated for a burial. Cura Bivián de Ortega concluded at the
turn of the century that the churches were impoverished "because the
vecinos are buried in the same manner as the Indians."[66] The reasons
become clear when delving into account books and funeral receipts.
Notwithstanding the arancel, parish burial registers indicate Santa Fe's
residents in the 1770s and 1780s paid on average only five pesos for the
cheapest interment inside the church, near the entrance. By 1801 the
average amount for a burial had fallen to twelve reales, or three pesos
for burial in the first section of the church, closest to the doorway. The
parish of San Felipe de Neri in Albuquerque accepted as little as a bot-
tle of wine or a pound of wax for the interment of a parishioner, and in
1818, most burials recorded there yielded only a single peso. Within a
few years of his arrival, Albuquerque's new secular priest Cura Leyva
complained that "neither in burials, nor in marriages does one find the
distinction among castes that the schedule of fees dictates."[67] He
stated that the parish did not even possess a complete copy of the
arancel, though he felt certain that people underpaid for burials. In El
Paso, Indians and soldiers reportedly paid nothing for burial, except in
those rare cases when someone requested a high mass or the office of
the dead. In 1814–17, people there generally paid six pesos for a child's
burial and fourteen for that of an adult.[68] Though nearing what the
schedule of fees dictated, the price still fell short. Thus, while costs
varied throughout New Mexico, the price parish priests normally
exacted was consistently lower—in most cases considerably so—
regardless of the service, than that dictated by the arancel.

Santa Cruz de la Cañada in northern New Mexico's Río Arriba district offers a snapshot of funeral costs and how little they changed over
time. Fray Andrés García's drawing of the church shows the prices for
burial in 1768; at some point, someone noted an increase in fees in a
lighter hand on the same plan. For merely two pesos, one could receive

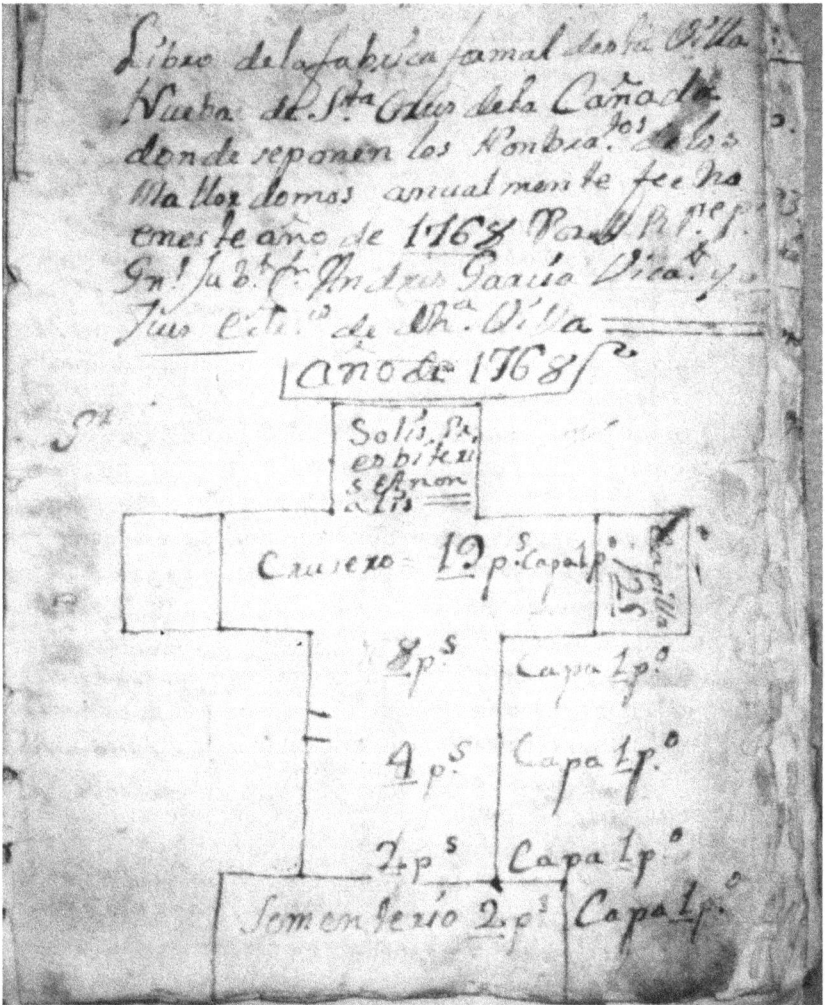

8. Plan of the parish church, Santa Cruz de la Cañada, 1768, from the Collections of the Archdiocese of Santa Fe

interment in the graveyard before the church entrance or just within the church doors. The nave itself was divided into thirds, with burial costs ranging from two to eight pesos, depending on how close to the altar one wished to rest. A diagram for the Belén chapel shows a similar division, with the area around the doorway marked "1" and sections 2 and 3 on either side of the transept. In the Santa Cruz drawing, a notation indicates that burial in the sanctuary, the space immediately around the main altar, was reserved for priests. In 1776, Santa Cruz's

9. Plan of the chapel at Belén, 1797, from the Archivo Histórico del Arzobispado de Durango, photo by José de la Cruz Pacheco

mayordomo informed Domínguez that burial in the nave cost four pesos, sixteen in the transept, and twenty-five in the chapel dedicated to Our Lady of Carmel, reflecting a modest change in some prices.[69] All this was prescriptive, however, for the burial registers indicate that in the 1790s people still paid an average of four pesos de la tierra—the equivalent of two strings of chile—for burial; thirty years later, the cost remained the same and included the high processional cross, a mass with the body present, the office of the dead, the priest's use of the cope, and interment inside the church.

While this system had the sanction of tradition, it did not please the new vicar. Almost immediately upon settling into his post at Santa Cruz, don Manuel Rada sent a detailed report to the bishop decrying the sad state of record keeping and complete lack of funds in the parish coffers. He protested that mismanagement combined with the fact that none of the parishioners paid in cash had placed the parish in financial straits. Everyone wanted to bury their dead in the church, yet even this cost a maximum of four pesos.[70] Rada had arrived recently from Sonora, and his discontent with the status quo in Santa Cruz indicates that even as far removed from the viceregal capital as Sonora, funerary customs were more in keeping with the Spanish norm. Probably in response to the vicar's efforts, at some point before 1831, the costs for burial in the nave doubled, as is faintly visible in the church plan. Though the erstwhile governor, visitors, and in time even Anglo traders criticized the schedule of fees and accused the clergy of avarice, the evidence all points to the fact that New Mexicans actually underpaid for funerals and burials. A regression analysis of Albuquerque, Santa Fe, and Santa Cruz burial records furthermore shows that over the years 1730–1850, people actually were spending less and less on burial.[71]

Despite the disparity between the arancel and the actual costs charged, the priests' fees frequently provoked discord in the late eighteenth and early nineteenth centuries. In the wake of the devastating smallpox epidemic of 1780–81, the resultant loss of Pueblo lives, and the end of Indian labor and obventions, missionaries became increasingly dependent on the vecino population for their economic support.[72] The secular clergy's arrival exacerbated the situation, as the newcomers tried to undermine customary practices. While parishioners had always found reason to grumble about their religious, their grievances with the Franciscans most commonly had centered on an individual's incompetence or failure to say masses or administer the last rites. The criticism presented by Juan Armijo of Cochití Pueblo was typical of these complaints. In 1821, Armijo wrote of Fray Manuel Bellido in part that "it is true, what the blessed father says, that he gives mass every day, but he gives it for himself alone, because he makes no signal with the bells, since he does not expect anyone," and so no one knew when to attend mass.[73] In contrast, the diocesan clergy who arrived in New Mexico in the early nineteenth century more commonly earned people's enmity for trying to adhere to a schedule of fees that for much of the colonial period largely had been ignored. As in the case of Santa Cruz cited above, only with the arrival of Vicar Rada did burial prices—which had remained fairly constant for half a century—show a marked increase. Even before his arrival, however, parishioners had cause to lodge a complaint against their first secular priest, Cura Juan José Lombide, whom they accused of shamelessly extorting goods in payment for burial of the town's most destitute. In one instance, the priest had wrested twelve pesos from a poor widow; on another occasion, he exacted a colcha in payment for his burial of a little girl.[74] Conversely, Belén's ayuntamiento in the 1820s sought to keep Fray Juan Bruno González in the community precisely because he only charged them half the mandated obventions.[75] Thus parishioners took issue with the diocesan clergy more often than not because of the priests' adherence to the arancel, rather than true avarice. Not surprisingly, the secular clergy in turn objected to their flock's or the Franciscans' dogged adherence to custom.

Although officially secularized in 1797, Albuquerque, El Paso del Norte, Santa Cruz de la Cañada, and Santa Fe saw their disgruntled secular priests leave the province after only a few years of service. From the end of 1803 until early 1816, no diocesan clergy served New Mexico. After 1816, the secular clergy who arrived did not confine their attentions to their own parishes but considered the affairs of outlying communities as well. A by-product of their zeal survives as a stream of complaints against the allegedly wayward Franciscans, whom the priests accused of everything from celebrating Holy Week without the proper decorum to cohabiting with women.[76] Though undoubtedly motivated at times by personal as well as political considerations, like similar denunciations of the secular clergy by later arrivals to New Mexico, enough of these reports survive to suggest their foundation in some truth. Indeed, one can easily imagine that some veteran Franciscans had grown complacent in their handling of religious affairs, especially after decades in the province with relatively little support or oversight.

In the 1820s, with the death of several Franciscans, more secular clergy came to New Mexico. In 1821 five secular priests served the province; this number increased to eight by 1829 and eleven in 1846.[77] Although they did not confine themselves to criticizing the Franciscans, they were aghast at the perceived physical and moral deterioration of many communities and assumed responsibility for revitalizing their new parishes. They commissioned artisans to create more acceptable representations of the saints, instituted needed building repairs, and improved on things the Franciscans perhaps had not thought to correct—such as putting doors on the confessionals. Of course, they did not confine their restorative efforts to physical structures. They also demonstrated concern with what they perceived as New Mexicans' moral debility, which they corrected in some cases through more careful oversight and instruction, establishing primary schools or becoming involved in politics.[78]

The secular clergy had served for some time in New Mexico before the energetic Bishop Zubiría replaced the old arancel with a new one in 1833, part of an ongoing process of institutional centralization. Perhaps because the reform-minded diocesan priests had already endured their share of complaints in the preceding years, the new fees did not cause much of a stir. The new arancel actually seems to have more accurately reflected New Mexican realities than the previous schedule of fees.

Though still pegged to the silver peso, costs fell from those listed in the one-hundred-year-old arancel implemented under Bishop Crespo, and Bishop Zubiría recognized the right of parishioners to pay either in cash or the equivalent. The bishop fixed the price of burials at one to six pesos, depending on location. One would incur additional charges for frills like the use of a high cross (four reales), a cope (one peso), an incensory (four reales), and a table in any funeral of pomp (one peso). The bishop valued the ringing of bells at four reales per bell for burials with a high cross and two reales for those with a low cross, with a limit of one bell in the latter type of burial.[79] Even with the reduction in fees the 1833 arancel codified, however, only rarely did New Mexican priests exact the full payment allowed. As late as 1848, adult parishioners in Albuquerque paid an average of only one peso for burial, with burials of eight pesos or more exceptional.

In the late eighteenth century, the Bourbons had sought to regulate public life by curtailing some of the excesses of baroque funerals. Some of these changes held the promise of democratizing deathways by eliminating some of the "extras" that nurtured social distinctions among the dead. A royal pragmatic had banned funerals of pomp and excessive ringing of bells in the late eighteenth century. The crown also banned the practice of *posas*, the stops in the funeral procession where the priest sang a response. Priests had been paid for each posa they made, and people measured the social standing of the deceased in part by the number of stops. Despite the crown's efforts to rationalize deathways, ample opportunity to maintain social distinction remained. The 1833 schedule of fees ensured that both the idea of pomp and the actual use of the term endured. It included costs for the tolling of church bells, the use of incensories and high processional crosses, as well as paid mourners. An abundance of candles might still convey social status.[80] Yet much of this remained theoretical, for as in the colonial period, only rarely did the priest extract the requisite fee for burial listed in the arancel.

In New Mexico, of course, a funeral of pomp did not carry the same connotations as it did in central Mexico. Instead of paid mourners or dozens of mendicants, a stately funeral in New Mexico signified a high mass with the body present, a table with candles, the priest's use of the cope, and a high processional cross. From the extant if sometimes cryptic receipts, we can piece together what such a service might have included. The funeral of Corp. Antonio Ortega in 1785 cost his estate sixty-one pesos, plus twenty-three pesos for the habit of St. Francis in which his corpse was dressed. The expenditures included the priest's retrieval of the body (six pesos), candles (three pesos), sung masses and office of the dead (sixteen pesos), and two novenas with response (thirty-six pesos).[81] Santa Fe's pious benefactor, Antonio José Ortiz, enjoyed one of the most expensive colonial funerals. In 1806, his estate spent almost six hundred pesos for his funeral and associated costs.[82] The itemized receipt lists the expenses:

Burial	70 pesos
Two hundred masses	200
Two spoken novenas with response	24
Attendance of six priests	34
Sung novena of masses with response	54
Funeral honors	40
Attendance of three priests	18
Cantor	19 pesos, 4 reales
Sacristan and acolytes	15 pesos, 2 reales
Mandatory charities	12
Masses said from Christmas through Aug. 14	65
Masses paid Father Bragado	29
Six low masses, day of burial	6
Total	586 pesos, 6 reales

Though death was in one sense the great leveler of humanity, clearly some maintained positions of privilege even in death.

The tradition of funerary excess had been transferred seamlessly from Spain to New Spain, where baroque ostentation transformed funerals into gaudy public spectacles of social standing. In Santa Catarina, outside of Mexico City, the wealthy typically had between sixteen and thirty attendants, a high processional cross, an offering, a mass with the body present and burial inside the church. Secular and regular clergy accompanied funerals in large numbers, their presence and their prayers a show of social rank and conspicuous piety. Like the hundreds of masses said for the dead, attending funerals provided a vital source of income for the religious. While the parish of Santa Catarina interred most of its dead in the parish cemetery, the rich received burial plots within the church, near the altar of one of the confraternities. Those at the very top of the economic ladder bypassed the parish church entirely and found rest in one of the city's large monasteries. Their funerals easily included more than one hundred attendants. By the first half of the eighteenth century, the growing popularity of confraternities ensured that more people had access to burial within the church.[83]

Certainly, New Mexico's social hierarchy remained far more elastic than that of Bourbon Spain or central Mexico, where only elites and confraternity members in good standing could hope for interment within the church. Although the higher costs associated with burial in a chapel or in the section closest to the main altar kept these spots out of reach for many New Mexicans, burial somewhere within the parish church was a prerogative for most throughout the colonial period. Made relatively affordable by a barter economy and sympathetic friars, almost 90 percent of people specifically requested burial within the church in their testaments, a phenomenon that will be considered more closely in chapter 5. Parish burial books corroborate the wills, revealing that for most of the colonial period, approximately 95 percent of the dead did indeed repose beneath the church.[84] In the first decade of the nineteenth century, for example, Fray Teodoro Alcina did not bury a single Santa Clara Pueblo resident, Chama vecino, or Ute captive outside the church, notwithstanding a deadly 1805 measles epidemic.[85] Lacking the family crypts found in many Roman Catholic churches, wealthy vecinos, the indigent, Indian servants, and foundlings shared the space beneath the church.

To be sure, social status and ethnicity played some role in mortuary practices in some areas. In some parishes, those laid to rest in the cemetery during the colonial period tended to be Ute or Navajo captives or the indigent. Even so, in the three Spanish villas, from 1730 through 1850, 68 percent of Native Americans—primarily Apaches, Navajos, and Utes—found a final resting spot within a church or chapel, compared with 73 percent of those identified as Spaniards. Priests only occasionally recorded the dead's ethnicity, but these figures are based on analysis of the approximately six hundred cases (of more than two thousand considered) where the burial registers identified ethnicity. A good number of the poor likewise found a final resting place within the church floors. New Mexican funerary rituals on the whole tended to be far less elaborate and less entangled with reinforcing social hierarchies than those in central Mexico. In Mexico, the most coveted church burial cost upward of one hundred times an artisan's daily wage, making it prohibitively expensive for most Spanish subjects.[86] Recall, however, that in Santa Cruz de la Cañada, residents paid only four pesos for a burial from the 1760s and as late as the 1820s, despite the mayordomo's report to Domínguez in 1776. As a result, the population beneath the church floors was representative of the settlements themselves, a mixture of Spaniards, Indians, and mestizos. Even though New Mexico developed its own elite, colonial mortuary practices support scholarship that shows that people on the northern frontier lived in more egalitarian and more socially mobile societies than their peers residing in central Mexico.[87]

Wealth and membership in a confraternity were not prerequisites for church burial, but those receiving charitable burials certainly had little hope of a coveted spot in a chapel or near the altar, the pinnacle of the church's sacred geography. Though the friars routinely buried within the church those who had left no will because of their poverty, they understandably did not typically relinquish the most desirable plots for the indigent. Ignacia López, a "genízara vecina" of Santa Fe, received a charitable burial within the San Miguel chapel in 1780.[88] Though he died intestate, Estanislado Chávez was buried in the second section of Albuquerque's parish church in 1819.[89] Despite the reference to his poverty, Chávez's funeral included a high cross, cope, office of the dead, mass with the body present, and two tables of pomp. Though the poor typically had only simple funerals, as in this case, some charitable burials were far more elaborate.

Although each parish provided charitable burials to the indigent, most people paid something for interment, even if on credit. In the parish of Albuquerque, approximately 94 percent of parishioners could pay the average of two to four pesos de la tierra for an adult's interment within the church; a child's burial might cost only a single peso. Even the poor could usually string together enough chiles or onions to pay for a parent's or child's burial. Furthermore, account books make it clear that many parishioners paid only part of the fee at the time of burial and owed the remainder to the parish coffers; thus, those with few resources during a hard winter could wait until the springtime to pay the friar or hope that the debt might be forgotten.

Confraternities' Funerary Roles

Though funerals in New Mexico were inexpensive relative to the arancel and practices elsewhere in New Spain, masses could elevate considerably the costs associated with death. Many people arranged for their own masses by leaving cash or goods to cover these costs. Family members might also assume responsibility for additional masses, particularly on prescribed days following death. Antonio Severino Martínez's dutiful sons Antonio José and José Manuel, for example, paid for masses on the seventh and thirteenth days following their father's death.[90] An anniversary mass with the office of the dead cost ten pesos and might also be paid for by survivors, who routinely made an offering of bread and wine in addition to paying for the mass.[91] Rosa Bustamante, in addition to her humble burial, mass with the body present, and funeral honors, instructed that she receive the *cabo de año*, the service performed on the one-year anniversary of death.[92]

In Spain and much of Latin America, confraternities assumed responsibility for anniversary masses along with funerals. Allowing people of modest means a respectable funeral and burial within the confraternity's section of the church, they ensured their members a good funeral and prayers upon death. Paying into the confraternity over a lifetime of membership helped to alleviate both material and spiritual concerns for the dead and their survivors. Notwithstanding lengthy membership lists suggesting their popularity, their role in New Mexican life remains somewhat shrouded because of the paucity of surviving documentation. Perhaps the affordability of New Mexican funerals negated some of the need for these organizations, making them less critical in popular religious life. While the Third Order of St. Francis possessed its own graveyard adjacent to Santa Fe's parish church (Illustration 13), presumably for the exclusive burial of its members, the sacramental records and accounts books do not indicate what role, if any, the confraternities played at funerals. No evidence has surfaced to indicate that New Mexican confraternities provided their members with coffins, burial attire, and other essentials typically included among their responsibilities. Though these were perhaps implicit and therefore warranted no documentation, the silence of the historical record may be significant and is certainly noteworthy.

What New Mexico's confraternities did provide was a mass at the death of a member and another on the one-year anniversary of death. They also supported weekly or annual masses dedicated to their namesakes. Santa Fe's "devotion" to the Poor Souls—Domínguez refused to call it a confraternity because it had no brothers or other elements of a confraternity—each November 6 or 7 celebrated the office of the dead with a mass and responsorial. "On the evening of the same day there is a sermon on the poor souls, after which a procession of the Rosary goes forth with vested celebrant. While the procession reciting the Rosary goes through the street, the passing bell tolls."[93] This anniversary celebration cost fifteen pesos plus bread, wine, and wax (an estimated four pesos), three pesos for the cantor, twenty-five pesos for the sermon, and sixteen for the rosary procession. For a high mass, the priest received six more pesos, and if this included the office of the dead or vespers the cost increased to ten pesos. In addition to the annual services, the confraternity took responsibility for each Monday's mass dedicated to the souls in purgatory.

The growth of the confraternities appears to have been uneven over the course of the eighteenth century. Ecclesiastical visitors and resident priests alike deplored the absence of records, underpayment for devotions, and inactive membership characterizing these organizations. Both Santa Fe and Santa Cruz supported an increasing number of confraternities by the late eighteenth century, while Albuquerque continued to house only the ones dedicated to the Poor Souls and the Third Order of St. Francis.[94] Santa Cruz sustained confraternities dedicated to the Blessed Sacrament, Our Lady of Carmen, and St. Michael. In addition to its Third Order of St. Francis, Santa Fe supported confraternities dedicated to the Blessed Sacrament, Our Lady of the Rosary, and the Poor Souls in Purgatory.[95] Despite a fair number of confraternities, they seem to have lacked both funds and vigor—or, as Cura José Bivián de Ortega complained in 1799, Santa Fe's confraternities were impoverished "materially and devotionally."[96] Ross Frank, however, suggests the confraternities' growing wealth in the years after the Domínguez visitation, citing not increased membership but the concentration of wealth in the wake of the smallpox epidemic.[97]

Notwithstanding the variable state of lay activity, the devotion to the Poor Souls at least appears to have been popular. Its Albuquerque membership included most parishioners, and in 1807 Belén residents established their own confraternity for the Poor Souls.[98] The confraternity's November masses to the Poor Souls did not approximate the lively Day of the Dead traditions developing in central Mexico. Perhaps because New Mexicans relied almost exclusively on burials within the church, there is no documentary evidence for a tradition of leaving offerings at the grave. The dead were always present, and the community had regular contact with them through the ritual of the mass. Only one community showed some signs of similarity with those Day of the Dead traditions developing in central Mexico.[99] In Nuestra Señora de Guadalupe del Paso del Norte, in 1814–17, parishioners said the rosary in memory of the dead on the first of November. The following day, they left offerings of chickens, eggs, apples, squash, guayava, lighted candles, and coins on the tombs. The priest divided the offerings among the sacristans and acolytes, but kept the cash offerings—which thievery reduced from approximately thirty pesos to ten—for the church. The ritual celebration began with the priest ordering a tomb covered with eight or twelve candles. Once lighted, the priest

10. "Child's remains excavated at Santa Rosa de Lima de Abiquiú, 1977," photo courtesy of Charlie Carrillo

would sing the office of the dead and a mass. The ceremony concluded with three sung responses in the church and one in the campo santo. On November 8, the Indians would celebrate the same event in a similar fashion, with offerings, and the priest would again sing the office of the dead and the mass. In addition to the perishable offerings, the Indians would leave about six pesos on the graves.[100] This form of the Day of the Dead tradition may have migrated to southern New Mexico as trade along the Camino Real grew in the late eighteenth and early nineteenth centuries. In any event, it appears that the custom reached northern New Mexico only after the mid-nineteenth century, based on the limited written evidence.

THE FUNERAL

New Mexicans did share the tradition of festive children's funerals with their contemporaries in central Mexico. The death of a baptized child held a special place in Roman Catholic thought. Freed from the stain of original sin through their baptism, children lived in the state of grace until reaching the age of reason, generally held to be around age eight. While the unbaptized were doomed to spend eternity in limbo, people believed that baptized children became *angelitos* upon

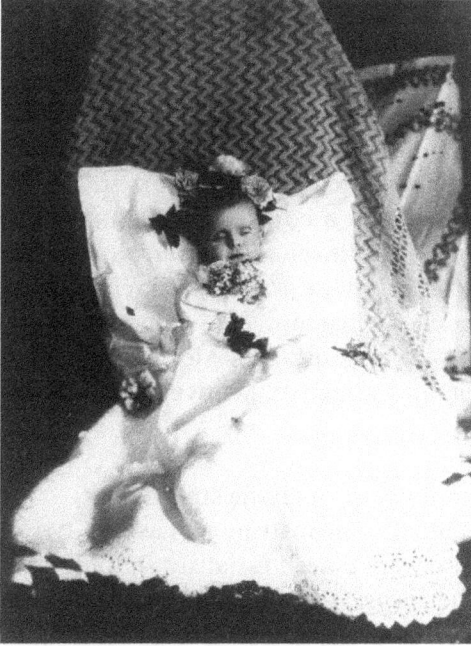

11. "Dead infant propped in draped chair, ca. 1885–92," Museum of New Mexico, photo by J. C. Burge, courtesy Palace of the Governors (MNM/DCA), 76429

death, ascending directly to heaven. Still, for much of the colonial period, children were slightly more likely than adults to receive burial within the church. Only after 1810 is a decline evident, and in some churches at some times the parish priest interred all children—regardless of parentage and ethnicity—within the church. In the 1970s, for example, archaeologists working in the eighteenth-century church of Santa Rosa de Lima in Abiquiú uncovered the remains of eight children, ranging in age from a believed miscarriage to eight years. Wrapped in cloth, all the children had been buried in the area around the altar.[101]

The community celebrated the funeral of an angelito with a lively, music-filled funeral. Bells did not toll, but pealed joyously. Custom dictated that people dress in white; even the priest wore a white stole at the burial. Crowned with flowers in an affirmation of the life after death, the dead child might wear an outfit imitative of St. Joseph or the Virgin Mary. The dig in Abiquiú revealed mica chips around the craniums of male children and wildflower pollen around the female skulls.[102] More recently, excavations in nineteenth-century cemeteries in Santa Fe and Alameda found children's craniums with mica flecks and/or iron crowns, silent testimony to the endurance of this practice well after the colonial period.[103] In Mexico, a whole genre of painting and later photography grew out of this tradition, as parents sought remembrances of their flower-bedecked dead children dressed as a saint, a little lady or gentleman, or in the simple frock of a priest.[104]

The celebratory nature of children's funerals shocked, amused, or fascinated Anglo visitors to New Mexico, depending on their inclinations. Trader Josiah Gregg described a corpse "gaudily bedecked with fanciful attire and ornaments of tinsel and flowers; and being placed upon a small bier, it is carried to the grave by four children as gaily dressed as their circumstances will allow."[105] Lt. James W. Abert, who accompanied Stephen Watts Kearny into New Mexico, witnessed such a procession in Santa Fe and effectively conveyed the occasion's merriment:

> They marched with great rapidity through the streets near the church, with a band of music. The instruments were principally violins, and these were played furiously, sending forth wild raging music. The corpse, that of a child, was exposed to view, decked with rosettes, and flaunting ribands of various brilliant hues, and the mourners talked and laughed gaily, which seemed to me most strange. I was told, too, that the tunes played were the same as those which sounded at the fandangoes.[106]

Clara Fergusson as an adult recalled how family members surrounded the pink-cambric decorated coffin, "and in their midst a fiddler played bright and carefree tunes."[107]

Festive as these funerals were, people did not forget the death of a child, nor were the children anonymous. As noted earlier, priests almost always recorded dead children's names in New Mexico, ensuring that even foundlings received the requisite María or José. For legal purposes, men and women alike identified their dead children in their wills, often recalling their names and ages. In Mexican popular Roman Catholicism, a family's angelitos served a role akin to favorite saints, with postmortem portraits serving as a visual focal point in private devotions. Absent the survival of painted postmortem portraits, we cannot know the role the dead child played in family piety; perhaps a locket of hair or a child's trinket would have served the same purpose as a portrait.

The mirth of children's funerals contrasted greatly with the somber funerals of adult community members. No matter how well one had prepared for death—leading an honest life, studiously reflecting on death, carefully crafting a will, and receiving the last rites—none of these measures guaranteed admittance into heaven. Most expected to spend time being cleansed in purgatory after death. Grieving their loss and acutely aware of the soul's jeopardy immediately after death, family members and friends marked the solemnity of a death with prayers and candles. Decorum and respect marked the occasion. According to Domínguez, at Jémez's church the choirboys and sacristans:

> Have the burial service for adults written down on boards, and that for children on a card. On the aforesaid they also have the responses for the Day of the Dead, and the manner of receiving the prelate. When there is a burial, whether of an adult or a child, the Office for the Dead is performed at the door of the church, and from there to the grave.[108]

The cortege, like so many elements of Spanish Roman Catholic funerary ritual, presented another opportunity for the living to intercede on the dead's behalf. In baroque piety, the presence of community members distributed the spiritual burdens of the dead among the group, which implored God's mercy for the dead. Spanish theologian Alejo Venegas had calculated that the greater the assemblage in the funeral cortege, the more prayers one received. An inflated crowd therefore signified not only one's standing in the community but also lessened the time one's soul was condemned to spend in purgatory. Charitable acts performed in life might pay off, as those held in popular esteem would enjoy large numbers of mourners at their funerals. Given the small size of most settlements, and the failure of wills and burial books to make mention of accompaniers, paid mourners were not likely a common sight in New Mexico. The parish priest probably presided over a small crowd, performing the requested prayers and offices with the aid of a sacristan. If the hour of one's death dictated a burial deferred until the day after death, people sat with the body in the home through the night, praying the rosary and singing hymns, practices that continued in rural New Mexico well into the twentieth century.[109]

In the morning, the processional cross would lead the priest and those carrying the corpse from the home to the church for the funeral mass. The pungent smell of putrefying bodies greeted mourners inside the sanctuary. Since existing burials had been disturbed in the

12. "Funeral procession, Mora, NM, ca. 1885," photo by Tom Walton, courtesy Palace of the Governors (MNM/DCA), 14757

process of making room for the newly departed, there might even be bone fragments visible on the church floor, near the new grave. If the estate had paid for the use of an incensory, the fragrance of incense masked the worst of these odors. The church, illuminated by the natural light entering through the clerestory window, candles carried by mourners, and tapers placed on the table and altar, felt appropriately sober for the occasion. The corpse rested upon a candlelit bier, a table, or carpenter's horse draped in coarse black sayal cloth and decorated with black tassels.[110]

Surviving documents provide only glimpses of these solemn occasions, but one in particular sheds light on many aspects of the funeral, including how people negotiated the payment and what New Mexicans deemed appropriate behavior. At his father's funeral in 1789, Francisco Olbín [Olguín], or el Lindón—"the pretty one"—as he was known, horrified the friar by his scandalous actions. Young Francisco's misdeeds began even before his father's death, when instead of coming himself to get the friar, he sent another to call the priest. Fray José Mariano Rosete contended that by this point he had rushed twice to the side of the dying man to hear his confession. He refused to go on this third occasion because the ailing man had been moved to Santa Ana, which fell outside the friar's jurisdiction.

Furthermore, Olbín had failed to provide a guard to escort the friar along the road, which was beset with hostile Indians. According to Rosete, the son's oversight on this point undermined the call's urgency, as did the fact that the messenger sent to retrieve the friar spent a good two days dancing and merry-making in Sandia Pueblo. Rosete concluded that "if they had called me according to custom, I would have gone. In such a case no priest would ignore his duty."[111]

Notwithstanding the friar's failure to attend to the dying man on this critical occasion, Olbín enlisted Fray Rosete to officiate at the funeral, for the price of thirty-three pesos. From the outset, el Lindón lacked the proper disposition:

> Mr. Lindón arrived in high spirits, smiling as though not his father but some dog had died. He arrived, I say, not to arrange the funeral but to lie, posing as the most unhappy, impoverished, and unfortunate person, who could only pay with an old but serviceable horse. To this, I agreed. He told me that he would like the burial with a sung mass. I responded that if he wanted a sung mass, he would have to pay me an additional two serapes ... To this we agreed.[112]

An obscene display of disrespect followed, worth quoting in detail for the richness of the friar's description:

> The dead body was carried through the cemetery into the church, but not by el Lindón. Perhaps it would have been an affront for him to carry his dead father on his shoulders. They placed candles around the body of the deceased, but these gave no light because of the wind entering the church ... Then, the referred to Lindón had the audacity to enter the church, roll a cigarette, and light it using one of these same candles around the corpse, and begin to smoke. He would have continued in this manner had an indignant Indian sacristan not thrown him out of the church. How improved we are. Already the Indians show more respect (at least on this occasion) for the house of God than the children of old Christians. At his indignities, I remained as though made of marble.[113]

Whether the scandalized priest allowed the son to return to the church for the remainder of the funeral mass remains unclear.

Although his antics at the funeral were reprehensible, the son's subsequent behavior motivated Padre Rosete's letter in defense of his own reputation. When the time came to pay the friar, the promised horse turned out to be nothing but "hair and bones." While Rosete likened the horse to don Quixote's Clavileño—the wooden horse filled with firecrackers that finally explodes—the brazen Olbín contended that the horse more accurately resembled don Quixote's horse Rosinante. To this, the friar responded that he would have preferred Rosinante, who could at least gallop. In contrast, the nag received in payment for the funeral could scarcely go a quarter of a league carrying a rider. After complaining to Olbín, the friar received another worthless piece of livestock: a cow that resembled a skeleton more than an actual living bovine. Feeling himself mocked by the impertinent Lindón, who, it turned out, had the money to pay, Rosete grew even more incensed upon learning that el Lindón had besmirched the friar's good name by complaining to the vice-custos.

The literary and comedic qualities of Rosete's account notwithstanding, the conflict with Francisco Olbín reveals a great deal about New Mexican funerary customs. No coffin shielded the corpse, which lay exposed on a table or bier lighted by candles during the funeral mass. The funeral arrangements had been made verbally, with the acceptable goods for payment negotiated and agreed upon in advance. The condition of livestock, the quantity of materials, and the needs and abilities of both parties determined suitable payment. Although the friar did not customarily adhere to the arancel given local conditions, in light of the son's miserliness and numerous transgressions and after repeated attempts to extract payment, Rosete in this case felt impelled to invoke the schedule of fees. Having died intestate, by law the friar could charge the dead man's estate double what the arancel dictated. Rosete implored the vice-custos to determine what the son should pay the priest. Thus, Padre Rosete, like so many other clergy, used local custom in making decisions. Rather than rigidly following church mandates in exacting payments for services, the priest allowed New Mexican conditions and his parishioners' circumstances to guide his actions.

Essential to the good death, Roman Catholic rituals from the last rites to the funeral mass gave the dying and the surviving community the spiritual sustenance necessary for the soul's salvation. People recognized the last rites' importance, but when someone did not receive them in time, priest and parishioner alike routinely assigned blame elsewhere. Priests faulted members of their flock for not notifying

them in time while parishioners bitterly cited failed spiritual leadership for their loved ones' unprepared deaths. Almost as soon as secularization began in the late eighteenth century, a third party—the
secular clergy—joined the list of culprits. As important as the last rites
were, life frequently interfered with the model death.

The Roman Catholic Church proved highly adaptable, and ecclesiastical officials worked within the dictates of the New Mexican environment. Just as the local civil leadership validated wills in the
absence of a notary and substituted ordinary paper for the requisite
stamped paper, the bishop in distant Durango sanctioned modifica-
tions to Roman Catholic rites to meet local needs. Thus the sick might
receive extreme unction before death was imminent, and priests
allowed midwives to administer baptism when death appeared close
at hand. Priest, sacristan, acolytes, and others all accepted payment
for their services in goods, their compensation frequently lower than
what the schedule of fees dictated. The arancel meant little to the
average person, for whom custom dictated prices. People completed
the trajectory of the good death with their burial in the parish church,
and after burial, survivors paid for masses in memory of the dead,
thereby maintaining a vital spiritual connection to family members.

CHAPTER FOUR

Treating the Physical Remains

A fter strangling his wife with a cord one winter evening in 1834, Manuel Gallego passed the night with her corpse in their conjugal home in San Antonio del Rancho, near San Ildefonso Pueblo. The following morning, the forty-seven-year-old farmer fled to his father's house. Investigators from Santa Cruz de la Cañada learned of the crime from an unnamed third party and arrived later that morning to find the murder weapon still coiled around María Espíritu Santo Roybal's cold neck. After questioning the cadaver and receiving no reply, authorities declared her dead.

The criminal proceedings left relatively little room for dispute or argument, for Gallego had freely confessed to killing his wife. Several witnesses testified, furthermore, that Gallego had given Roybal *la mala vida*, a marriage characterized by domestic abuse. Notwithstanding the overwhelming evidence against Gallego, his defender, Alonso Martín, argued against capital punishment. Gallego had spent the night with the corpse, Martín argued, and thus though a murderer, he had shown himself to be more humane than the heartless, cold-blooded killer portrayed by the prosecutor. Martín agreed that Gallego should be punished, but his night-long vigil with his wife's cadaver demonstrated remorse; he clearly warranted a sentence other than death.[1]

Though Martín admittedly was hard pressed to provide a defense for Gallego, who had made no attempt to conceal his crime and had confessed upon questioning, the case is suggestive of values and beliefs about the dead body in New Mexico at the time. Martín's reasoning reflected defense arguments common throughout colonial Spanish America, where the murderer's attitude and behavior after the crime might have an effect on the sentence. In Peru, for example, repentance could mean the difference between death by burning and death by strangling.[2] Although archival records do not reveal Gallego's fate, Martín's argument indicates that contemporaries would have recognized some redeeming social value in Gallego's loyalty to the corpse of his slain wife. Gallego's decision to pass the night with his murdered spouse suggested regret, which warranted consideration in sentencing.

Gallego's decision to stay with the corpse during the night had a much deeper significance than remorse, however. Few people in the late eighteenth or early nineteenth centuries would have situated death in a single, fixed moment in time. The standard dictionary of eighteenth-century Spanish, the *Diccionario de Autoridades*, defined death not primarily in physiological terms but as "the division and separation of body and soul."[3] Clearly, this was not measurable. Death represented not merely the end of the present state of existence but the onset of a regenerative process entailing the temporary separation of the body and soul and the body's return to its original state. In Roman Catholic ritual, this idea appeared in the biblical commendation of "ashes to ashes and dust to dust."[4] Before burial, when the priest spoke these words over the corpse, people believed that the cadaver retained some sensibility and that the dead thus remained in a liminal state.[5] The dormant and the dead appeared so similar that only the cadaver's decomposition offered irrefutable evidence that death indeed had occurred. In one instance, an Alameda woman believed her very elderly, deaf husband asleep when in fact, the priest later observed, "his soul was already in eternity."[6] Not all people would have shared the friar's insight so soon after death, however. In the case of the unhappily married María Espíritu Santo Roybal, her body probably remained relatively warm for several hours, and her skin would not have lost its suppleness. Even after cooling and rigor mortis began, many people would have viewed Roybal as existing in a liminal state, her soul present near the body.

APPARENT DEATH AND THE BODY'S LIMINALITY

Before death became apparent by clear physiological processes such as desiccation, some semblance of the living person was thought to endure even after rigor mortis set in. Eighteenth- and nineteenth-century folk beliefs attested to the enduring vitality of the corpse. Dating from at least the Middle Ages, it was widely held, for example, that the body of a murder victim would react in the presence of its murderer, revealing the killer to all. A variety of traditional techniques helped determine when death had occurred. Those in attendance might call the person's name three times, prick the body with a needle, or try to find a pulse. In New Mexico murder cases, the investigating authorities posed three questions to the corpse—asking the person's name, for example. Receiving no reply, they could safely pronounce death. The difficulty in measuring death muted the boundaries between life and death, and for every scientifically minded individual who might oppose these notions, countless stories of revived cadavers and rapping coffins testified to the enduring life of the physical remains, particularly in the days following death.

Popular belief only reinforced the findings of the single greatest proponent of incorruptible bodies: the Roman Catholic Church. The church provided countless examples of saintly corpses that retained their elasticity, emitted floral rather than putrid odors, and refused to undergo the usual process of decomposition. In baroque theology, the body and the senses provided the essential means to communicate the divine, especially for the average person, who could only begin to grasp the greatness of God through the excitation of the senses. Saintly corpses were disinterred and examined, sometimes in response to the activities of the cadaver, which might make noises or emit fragrant odors that impelled the living to revisit the grave. Ironically, as in the case of St. Teresa of Ávila, the very extraordinary properties of the dead body might be its real undoing. As Carlos Eire explains, St. Teresa's incorruptible flesh "prompted a very different kind of disintegration. Little by little, the saint would be carved up, and pieces of her would be distributed throughout the globe."[7] Spiritual leaders like Puebla's Bishop Juan de Palafox y Mendoza instructed that their internal organs—in his case the heart and the eyes—be deposited in places of special devotion. People figuratively and literally embraced miraculous physical remains as evidence of virtue and holiness; popular beliefs and folklore echoed these ideas even in the wake of the Enlightenment. In this very corporal piety, the body offered an opportunity to access the divine.

Science served theology, as doctors and other experts employed scientific instruments to probe, measure, and explore these remains. Central Mexico sheltered the sacred bodies and body parts of many bishops, friars, and *beatos*, or pious lay people. While making floor repairs in the cathedral of Michoacán in 1744, workers unearthed the entrails of Bishop Joseph de Escalona y Calatayud, buried there some seven years earlier. The bishop's remains had been divided for burial among different religious houses and churches, at his request.[8] Ecclesiastical officials and medical professionals together examined the bishop's entrails, observing that the blood, while discolored, remained fluid and fragrant. Employing microscopes for more careful examination, the experts noted the most remarkable occurrence: where they had expected to find insects and unpleasant organisms invisible to the naked eye, they instead discovered rosemary and cinnamon. Though Roman Catholic authorities commonly moved such relics to visible, glassed enclosures for public veneration and edification, in this particular case, after studying the precious entrails, officials again interred them in the cathedral floor with the requisite ritual and public ceremony. Tales such as this punctuate hagiographies and other colonial texts, promoting their diffusion in popular culture.

Although New Mexico lacked microscopes to examine the dead, the province had its own sacred corpses and popular mythology about the dead. For example, Fray Francisco Bragado died one January evening in 1825, "fully aware and in an agreeable state," after having served in northern New Mexico for fifteen years. As one Juan José Salazar cleaned the cadaver's face with vinegar, a common means of conservation, he noticed that "from a razor cut there flowed blood so fresh it was as though he were still alive, the blood running down to the point of his beard."[9] Surely, this signaled the good friar's virtue. Fray Teodoro Alcina deemed the occurrence sufficiently noteworthy that he not only recorded the presence of several witnesses, but also had the alcalde mayor sign the parish burial book to give the event the civil authority's imprimatur.

Fray Juan José de Padilla's levitating corpse remains the most powerful and recurrent symbol of postmortem sanctity in New Mexico's history. The rising remains of the Laguna Pueblo missionary had to be unearthed and reinterred repeatedly over a one hundred year period. Notable among the Franciscans serving in New Mexico for his fluency in the native Keresan of his flock, he had labored among the Indians of Laguna Pueblo for more than half of his twenty-three year tenure when unknown assailants beat and stabbed him to death. Fray Pasqual Sospedra first buried Padilla in 1756 in the church of Isleta Pueblo, close to the high altar in the presbytery. Nineteen years later, the cadaver, remarkably incorrupt, mysteriously had risen to the surface of the church. The dead friar's remains seemed to demand exhumation; officials complied and probably studied them in an effort to understand the phenomenon. The corpse remained outside the grave for about two weeks, suggesting that after examining the body, authorities perhaps allowed access to the cadaver for public veneration. To contain the corpse and prevent a recurrence, Fray José Eleutherio Junco y Jungera sealed the body in a coffin before reinterring it.[10]

The cottonwood box, however, did not contain Padilla's remains for long. The body rested only forty-four years before again requiring exhumation in 1819. At this time, Custos Francisco de Hozio carefully examined the cadaver and wrote a detailed report of the event. Fray José Ignacio Sánchez had reported to Hozio that the coffin "has been rising from the depths where it was buried to above the church floor, on the gospel side of the presbytery."[11] When Hozio went to see for himself, he determined that the coffin should be opened and its contents examined. After retrieving the cadaver, Hozio and the other ecclesiastical and civil officials who had gathered found the body dressed in the blue wool serge habit worn by the Franciscan order. Suspended from the neck hung a rosary adorned with St. Francis and St. John Nepomuk and a bone that resembled a saint's relic. Custos Hozio marveled at the cadaver's integrity and flexibility:

> The body having been cleaned of the dust into which the
> habit was reduced, I approached closer... beginning to
> inspect the body, I found it whole, with the exception of
> the toe-bones of the right foot, the eyes, and the tongue;
> the flesh dried up: but so flexible that on being dressed with
> a habit it lent itself to the action of extending the arms for
> the sleeves to go on, and in the same manner and without
> difficulty [its arms] were crossed.[12]

Hozio had found what seemed to be a remarkably well-preserved corpse.

This examination of Padilla's body reveals a fascination with death untempered by disgust for the dead body. The dry corpse was all the more compelling for the circumstances that warranted its study. Hozio poked and prodded the cadaver from head to toe in an effort to establish the cause of its mysterious and tenacious resurfacing. Though he did not liken the remains' aroma to rosemary and cinnamon, Hozio did declare that the now sixty-three-year-old corpse emitted a pleasant odor, "as the earth smells when it is watered."[13] As with the remains of saints and religious leaders, death and its effects on the body were hardly repugnant. Instead, Hozio described the cadaver with a mixture of awe and delight. Witnessing the corpse's spiritual significance, Hozio wrote, "even the women and children look on it and admire it without terror, and it fills all with reverence."[14] Echoing the themes of numerous theological tracts, death here proved enlightening, informative, and spiritually rewarding.

The edified observers who admired the pious man's relics reinforced the cadaver's sanctity. For a two-month period after the initial examination, the church left the corpse "exposed with religious decency" to public viewing, suggesting that the mission church at Isleta had become a pilgrimage site, though its identification as such does not seem to have lasted beyond Padilla's reburial. The church facilitated a mutually reinforcing relationship between the public that came to see the corpse and the blessedness of the remains; the reverent gaze of the faithful validated the body's sanctity. Finally, the bells pealed again for Padilla on the day of his third funeral, in July 1819. After a solemn high mass and vigil with responsorial, officials again interred his remains in Isleta's church.

By 1895, at the time of the next exhumation, folklore had transformed the story into one of epic proportions. People now claimed that Padilla had arrived with the Coronado expedition to New Mexico in 1540 and blamed his death on the Quivira Indians. The myth transformed what Fray Angélico Chávez contends was murder at the hands of Spaniards into martyrdom. Indeed, if these stories had been true, Padilla would have been New Mexico's first martyr. Although Chávez effectively discredits these elements of the legend, the mythic qualities ascribed to Padilla in the late nineteenth century indicate that New Mexicans had made the leap from the corpse's saintly appearance to martyrdom. A medical doctor who examined the remains in the company of several religious in the late nineteenth century seemed far less impressed with the condition of the corpse than previous examiners. Doctor Rivera noted that the corpse was missing a foot, perhaps the result of a relic seeker from an earlier exhumation. The doctor's tone was blasé as he recorded the testimony of several Isletans, who reported having heard noises emanating from the friar's burial as recently as 1889. Evidence of the growing medicalization of society and changing ideas of death, the 1895 examination of Padilla's remains took less than twenty-four hours, and reburial took place on the same day as disinterment.[15]

The enduring lifelike qualities of saintly corpses highlighted the difficulty in measuring death while underscoring the liminality of apparent death. This imprecision meant that the dead and the living coexisted on the same plane at least until burial, when the recently deceased more clearly joined the camp of the unequivocally dead. Ordinary bodies would decay, providing definitive proof of death and an unambiguous conclusion to the body's liminality. The notion of a state between life and death and the attendant uncertainties led some testators in Europe and North America to request an interval of twenty-four to seventy-two hours between apparent death and burial. Motivated by a fear of being buried alive, they might also instruct that a physician open the body, an incision without response serving as conclusive proof of expiration. More commonly, people kept vigil with the body to ensure the presence of witnesses should the corpse exhibit signs of life. Having a servant or family member stand watch at the graveside also ensured that medical students or mercenary resurrectionists would not steal the corpse for anatomical dissection. Concern for premature burial only emerges in one New Mexican document. An 1833 *bando*, or proclamation, in Santa Fe mandated the burial of all cadavers within twenty-four hours, excepting those cases—e.g., childbirth, drowning—in which more time was warranted to ascertain that death was certain.[16]

Once established, physical death, people knew, was only temporary; they were confident that Christ would return to resurrect the dead. In a sense, theology at once denigrated and elevated the body. As a vessel for the soul, it frequently proved imperfect, subject to urges and temptations that made the path to salvation quite rocky. The body might, in extraordinary circumstances, however, prove the site of pious manifestations, as in the case of stigmatics.[17] The church likewise asserted that the resurrection of the dead meant the physical reconstitution of the body, granting the humble vessel—like the miraculous remains of the saints—a preternatural significance. The insistence on separate burial grounds for Roman Catholics, like the exclusion of suicides from sacred ground, underscored the importance of the physical remains. Presumably, Padilla's violent death meant that his remains could find no rest and caused the altar to shake and his corpse to rise. His imagined martyrdom would have been a potent reference point for New Mexicans, a reminder of the early Franciscans and settlers killed during the Pueblo Revolt of 1680. Not just those martyred and presumed martyred captured the imagination, however.

In the mid-seventeenth century, Fray Asencio Zárate and Fray Gerónimo de la Llana had been buried in the churches of Picurís and

Quarac, respectively. Although neither had died a martyr, the friars were remembered for their extreme virtue and bodily mortifications.[18] Agustín de Vetancourt noted in his description of Fray Ascensio Zárate that twenty-five years after his death, "his body was found whole, pliable, and fragrant, by which God manifested the sanctity of his Servant."[19] When the churches fell into ruin, people forgot about their abandoned remains for nearly a century. In 1759, the centennial of de la Llana's death, Gov. and Capt. Gen. don Francisco Antonio Marín del Valle (1754–60) ordered the two holy men's bodies exhumed and brought to Santa Fe. Marín del Valle had the men's remains interred in an impressive stone sarcophagus within the parish church. Again, the dead here were men of virtue, whose physical remains held spiritual significance among the community of believers. Though the governor's motives may have been political as well as religious, the fact that he conceived of the rescue of the bones as a public act of piety suggests the physical remains' importance.

New Mexicans commonly retrieved the bones of those who had died violently to provide a proper burial. People recovered and interred the remains of military and religious leaders as well as anonymous men and women. These cases underscore the importance of burial within the church and, more generally, within consecrated ground. The physical remains' collocation in sacred ground might itself facilitate the soul's exit from purgatory. Whether or not people believed in the material continuity of body and soul in the afterlife, the idea informed the popular ethos.

THE COHABITATION OF THE LIVING AND THE DEAD

Popular piety held that the location of burial was crucial to the afterlife and the resurrection of the dead. The practice of burying the dead inside churches had been customary in Roman Catholic Europe for centuries, based on the belief that interment in proximity to the sacred—whether relics of the saints or images of the Virgin Mary—facilitated salvation and reduced the time a soul had to spend in purgatory. As João José Reis observes in his study of nineteenth-century Brazil, "the physical proximity of the corpse and sacred images on earth represented a model for the spiritual contiguity desired in heaven between the soul and the divinities. The church was a gateway to paradise."[20] The Council of Trent had affirmed the primacy of burial in clarifying that the physical body would indeed be resurrected with

Christ's Second Coming.[21] Therefore, despite its inevitable decomposition, the body in a sense endured beyond this life. The physical and the spiritual awaited reunion and reanimation at the Resurrection.

Churches exemplified the integration of the spiritual and the material. Here, the priest transformed the host into Christ's body, and the dead mingled with the living. The church's exterior mirrored this convergence, with the graveyard situated right outside the principal entrance. One eighteenth-century Franciscan visitor described Albuquerque's San Felipe de Neri church as actually being located inside the cemetery.[22] However one situates church and graveyard, people routinely walked through the space allocated to the dead each time they entered and left the church. Thus the cemetery was neither physically nor conceptually removed from the world of the living.

In fact, the graveyard served many social functions, some sanctioned and others not. The land doubled as pasturage for livestock. Priests read announcements. Vendors hawked food and beverages, encouraged by the crowds drawn to theatrical productions and other events held in the graveyard.[23] In Mexico City's Hospital Real de Indios a hospital annex housed the sick in the cemetery during a 1761 epidemic. In this same period the archbishop found a blacksmith's shop located in the graveyard of the hospital at the former Colegio de San Andrés. In one extraordinary Santa Fe case, a house actually rested almost on top of the cemetery, the result of Gov. Fernando de la Concha's gift of parish lands to three servants in 1793. In constructing houses on the land, fences were moved, and bodies that had rested within the cemetery's consecrated grounds now lay outside the cemetery.[24] Whether used for sacred or profane purposes, the cemetery constituted an integral part of the community's landscape.

Around the mid-eighteenth century elites began to question the propriety of such cemetery uses. Increasingly, they conceived of the cemetery as a space meriting decorum. Those who embraced the new rational piety tried to convey these modern values to the masses, banning all manner of activities in hopes that they could transform the cemetery into a place reserved for burial and somber reflection.[25] In the unhurried transition from the old ways of thinking to the new, these different meanings often clashed. The shift in thinking became apparent in El Paso when the town's first secular priest, Cura José Ignacio Suárez, in 1800 complained to the bishop of theatrical productions being performed in the cemetery.[26] Though Suárez clearly considered such performances in the cemetery scandalous, some clergy—and clearly, El Paso's citizenry—still deemed public functions acceptable.

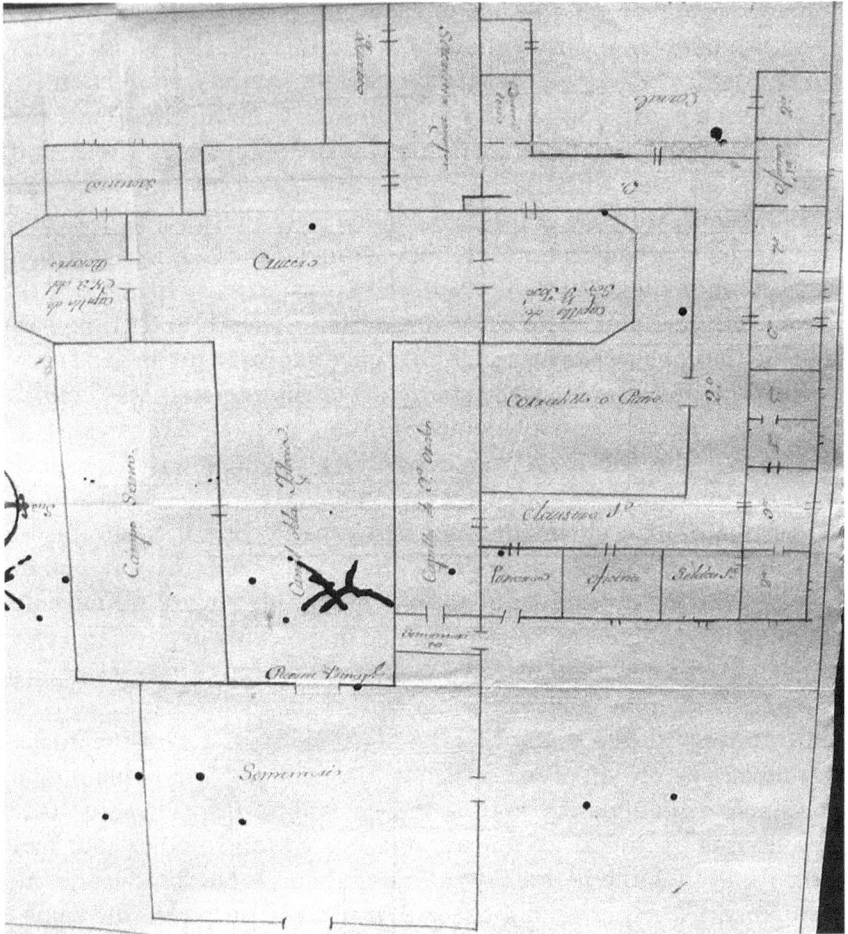

13. Plan of the parish church of Santa Fe, 1814, from the Archivo Histórico del Arzobispado de Durango, photo by José de la Cruz Pacheco

Inside the church, the dead and the living commingled in an even more pronounced way. Despite the availability and use of graveyards, people preferred burial within the church, which was considered most spiritually advantageous.[27] Antonio Urban Montaño, for example, in 1772 sought a final resting place in the transept of the Rosario Chapel in Santa Fe's parish church, likely hoping that his corpse's proximity to the statue of Our Lady of the Rosary would cause Our Lady to mediate on behalf of his soul.[28] Others requested that their remains be placed in a particular spot in the church, such as an altar, station of the cross, or occasionally near a deceased family member. Some asked for burial locations that promised to offer more than just intercession. Capt. Francisco Ortiz Niño Ladrón de Guevara in his 1749 will asked that that he be interred in the doorway to Santa Fe's parish church, precisely because it represented the most humble place in the church.[29] Though he could have paid for a more exalted spot, the captain knew that this modest location meant that generations of the faithful would trample his grave. He undoubtedly believed that this act of humility would yield great rewards for his soul. Capt. Joseph Baca of Albuquerque likewise solicited interment beneath the baptismal font in Isleta's San Agustín church.[30] This site extended the possibility that the occasional stray drop of holy water might reach his decomposing corpse, offering untold benefits to his soul. Thus the dead lay near the sacred, and the living—according to the ideal of the good death—acknowledged their own mortality as they trod on the undistinguished, unmarked graves of family and neighbors.

The absence of grave markers within the churches reinforces the idea that New Mexican mortuary practices were much less entangled with reinforcing social hierarchies than those of contemporaries in central Mexico and elsewhere. Yet this is not to say that burial patterns were completely egalitarian. Were it possible to map the burial locations of individual parishioners in the eighteenth century, a clear social hierarchy would emerge in the burial geography. We would find the remains of many of society's wealthiest members situated in chapels whereas the most impoverished would have been relegated to the areas near the churches' entrances. Many exceptions would emerge as well, however, such as the socially prominent women and men who received burials in conspicuously humble locations. The map would be imperfect, too, as it would not tell us the role individual priests—and presumably, sacristans—played in determining burial location. Though many adult Indians found a final resting place inside the parish church, some clergy demonstrated a greater propensity to bury adult Indians or the poor in the graveyard rather than the church. Still, the contrast with central Mexico would be great. In Mexico, the most coveted church burial cost upward of one hundred times an artisan's daily wage, making it prohibitively expensive for most people.[31] Whereas the rising merchant classes and the popular classes in Veracruz would embrace the new suburban cemeteries' more egalitarian nature, no such democratic incentive existed for New Mexicans, who paid only a fraction of the sixteen pesos for burial the official schedule of fees required. As a result, the population beneath the church floor remained fairly representative of the settlements themselves, a mixture of Spaniards, Indians, and mestizos.

People worshipped surrounded by the bones of their ancestors and friends and enjoyed a symbiotic relationship with the dead. Ideally, their presence within the church induced the living to pray for them, thereby hastening release from purgatory. According to the spiritual economics of the day, the more popular a church or the more populated, the more prayers would be heard on behalf of the dead. Subfloor burials therefore served as a potent mnemonic device, reminding the living of their own inevitable fate. The dead, who remained a part of the community of the faithful by virtue of their interment in the church, comprised a vital element of baroque faith, which promoted a communal and participatory piety.

The logical corollary to the popular belief that linked burial location with salvation was the mistreatment of corpses as punishment. Authorities meted out additional punishment by leaving the cadavers of their vanquished enemies exposed. Fray Carlos Delgado complained about one particularly cruel and capricious Spanish military leader, who killed three Suma Indians who had failed to keep pace in a forced march. He ordered their corpses abandoned and left unburied.[32] Although Delgado found the officer's behavior reprehensible, his account leaves one wondering which he found more blameworthy—the senseless murders or the neglect shown the corpses, which left exposed would become food for wild animals. Ultimately, the same principle informed both the vindictive military leader and the institutionalized forms of punishment enacted under the crown, in which the ignominy exacted upon the cadaver was integral to the death sentences passed down in criminal cases.

Authorities throughout Europe and the Americas routinely sanctioned the abuse of the dead body, including but not limited to giving cadavers over to anatomists for dissection. For generations, authorities had exerted social control by condemning criminals and the socially marginalized not only to physical death, but also to social death through public display, mutilation, and even dissection of the corpse. Even in cases where the state did not sanction an individual's death, funerary rites and disposal of the body gave those in power a final opportunity to assert their authority. Like the public ritual of noble funerals and "fictitious funerals"—those without the presence of the cadaver—public executions and the treatment of the corpse that followed affirmed and maintained the social order.[33] Beyond the execution itself, the punishment inflicted on the corpse after the death sentence had been carried out reminded the public that the state exercised its authority and meted out justice to both the living and the dead.

On the few occasions when the Audiencia of Guadalajara condemned someone to death in New Mexico, the sentence mandated
not only the person's execution but also public display of the body
after death; postmortem dishonor was integral to the punishment
itself. In 1779, Spanish officials ordered the cadavers of two Cochití
Pueblo women, María Josefa and her daughter María Francesca, suspended from poles for days as an example to the community after
their execution for the murder of María Francesca's abusive husband.[34] Likewise, along the well-traveled Camino Real, authorities
exposed the corpses of Antonio Carabajal and Mariano Benavídes,
executed in 1809 for murder.[35] Such postmortem humiliation served
as an especially harsh penalty in the critical days after death, when
prayer most benefited the soul. Although eventually receiving ecclesiastical burial, these convicted murderers found themselves at a
decided disadvantage in the postmortem quest for salvation at the
same time that their bodies reinforced the state's authority, which
thus extended even beyond death. Of course, the community might
have other notions of authority and justice, as reflected in the burial
of María Josefa and María Francesca in the transept of Santa Fe's
parish church within a few hours of their execution.[36]

The liminality of death cut both ways. Just as the dead were not
completely dead and might be subjected to rituals of public veneration or state punishment, the living might not be completely alive.
One case illustrates how people equated the loss of reason with the
absence of the soul in the same way that sleep suggested the temporary concentration of the soul outside the body. The case of María
Márquez de Ayala v. Juan Rafael Ortiz, heard in the jurisdiction of
Pojoaque in 1811, demonstrates the intersection between social death
and bodily death. Testimony in the surviving court records indicates
that María Márquez de Ayala suffered from some kind of *locura* (mad-
ness) or that her son, Mariano Trujillo, had labeled her insane with
the tacit or formal concurrence of the community. At some point,
Trujillo had mortgaged his mother's house and land in Cuyamungue
to pay his own debts. In the wake of her son's death, Márquez asserted
that she had not authorized the sale of her lands and sought retribu-
tion. The case pivoted on whether Trujillo had legally sold the property belonging to his mother. The answer rested on the issue of
whether the mother had died before the deceased son's transaction.
The new owner, don Juan Rafael Ortiz, contended that no tribunal
should even hear Márquez for "she lacks the natural understanding
that God gave her. For this reason it should be considered that her son,

Mariano, outlived her and not she her son."[37] By this logic, losing her reason made Márquez legally dead and the sale valid. Márquez contested Ortiz's interpretation of her state. She argued:

> Although Señor Juan Ortiz says that my son Mariano out-
> lived me, on account of my illness, that does not prove my
> death, because only God who placed me in this condition
> can subject me to death, because he is the author of my life.
> I can prove that it is not as the said Señor don Juan Ortiz has
> said, because I find myself in the world with my soul in my
> body and my son is now in his grave.[38]

The measure of death, in Márquez's view, was the soul's abandonment of the body. The repose of her son's body in the grave proved his very real death as opposed to her continued fleshly existence.

Granted a power of attorney by Ortiz, and legally representing him, José García de la Mora agreed that Márquez had outlived her son but quickly contradicted himself. In his opinion, Márquez was "dead and without the mental faculties enabling her to argue in her defense," for she had not received the sacraments in a quarter century, clear proof that she was "dead" and that her son had "outlived her."[39] In the 1811 judgment, the alcalde of Santa Cruz de la Cañada, Manuel García, concluded that Márquez was indeed "partly dead," ruling that she had no rights to the property, but "as a kind of charity and recompense for having been deprived of her son ... and looking upon her as ready to die, she shall be supported by don Juan Ortiz, who shall bury her and furnish her with a shroud and standard funeral."[40] Despite her vociferous protests, Márquez was declared socially dead and at least "partly dead" in body. The still very much biologically alive Márquez appealed the decision, demanding fifty pesos for her future silence on the matter. In September 1811, García determined that she receive—in addition to the Franciscan habit for burial and the funeral—four candles and fifty pesos. This case illustrates the fluid definition of death, which remained contested ground. Although all witnesses agreed that the soul's absence from the body equaled death, not all concurred on how to measure the soul's departure.

Just as death existed on a continuum rather than in a fixed moment, the dead body itself resided in an indeterminate realm neither completely of this world nor the next. New Mexicans differentiated between the dead but still-intact body and the reduced version of that body, the skeleton. The sinewy corpse enjoyed the ministrations of the living, who prepared it for burial with a final bath, shave, hair-cut, and even new garb. At this stage of death, the cadaver still resem-bled the person whose soul had animated its limbs. The physical form remained fleshy and lifelike, and even hair and nails were thought to grow in this liminal state. It is no coincidence that this was also the time when the dead faced the greatest spiritual danger and suffrages proved most efficacious. The soul, while absent, might linger and was therefore still within reach of the living, whose postmortem offerings could make the difference between purgatory's extended torments and heaven's immediate rewards.

Corresponding to this indeterminate state between the here and the hereafter, the treatment of the newly dead body was intertwined with the soul's transition. The surviving community had to take spe-cific ritual steps to ensure the successful journey between the two states of being. New Mexican practices are reminiscent of those Mircea Eliade describes:

> It is well known among traditional societies that death is not considered real until the funerary ceremonies are duly completed. In other words, the onset of physiological death is only the signal that a new set of ritual operations must be accomplished in order to create the new identity of the deceased. The body has to be treated in such a way that it will not be magically reanimated and become an instrument of mischievous performances. Even more important, the soul must be guided to her new abode and ritually inte-grated in the community of its inhabitants.[41]

In New Mexico, the succession of rituals—bedside prayers, last rites, cleaning and dressing the corpse, wake, and funeral mass—centered on the body and culminated in interment in sacred ground.

Insofar as it served as a physical reminder of the deceased, and with the soul presumably lurking nearby, the corpse merited careful attention before burial. Once the requisite rituals had prepared it for interment, however, its disintegration was both expected and accepted—those saintly cases noted above the recognized exceptions to the rule. On the whole, New Mexicans seem to have been uncon-cerned about shielding the cadaver from the ravages of the elements after burial. A blanket or a winding-sheet may have provided a thin barrier between the body and the earth, but New Mexicans made no obvious effort to slow the process of decay or protect the corpse from

14. Cross made of metal studs on a child's coffin (burial 20) found beneath burial 16 in the excavation of the Santuario de Guadalupe narthex, 1989, courtesy Edward E. Crocker, Crocker Collection, CSWR, University Libraries, University of New Mexico

insects through either embalming or a coffin. In fact, people may have used lime both to disinfect and hasten decomposition.[42] Though the additional two pesos for a coffin may have discouraged some from using one, it appears that colonial New Mexicans simply did not value coffining and relied instead on a litter to carry the corpse to the church for burial.[43] Among the hundreds of New Mexicans who left wills from 1750 to 1850, the well-off, twice-widowed Bárbara Baca alone asked in 1838 that her corpse be coffined prior to burial in Santa Fe's parish church.[44] It would be the 1850s before more wills started to include such requests.

Among the wealthy, in late baroque fashion, piety—conspicuous or otherwise—may have provided people who could afford them a reason to reject coffins. Just as one might don the coarse Franciscan habit for burial in a show of humility, so might one opt for interment without a coffin, thus rejecting all illusions of permanence and embracing a sanctity made visible to the world. Like other paradoxical elements of baroque piety, both display and the rejection of display could serve as indicators of personal virtue. Rosa Bustamante, who along with her husband had expended considerable amounts in support of the church, specified that her body be buried without a coffin in her 1814 will.[45] Since she could have afforded a coffin, Bustamante's gesture almost certainly represents an act of conspicuous humility. Pamela Voekel argues that this "flamboyant modesty" was part of the move to a more interior piety in late eighteenth-century Mexico.[46] In New Mexico, however, requests for humble burials or humble burial dress are consistent throughout the colonial and Mexican periods, suggesting no apparent shift similar to what Voekel documents.

In terms of coffins, Rosa Bustamante's and Bárbara Baca's wills are the exceptions that prove the rule. Although New Mexicans invested meticulous detail in their wills—planning funerals, specifying burial location, and itemizing debts—only twice in one hundred years did they mention coffins. Wills and funeral receipts in New Mexican archives confirm archaeological findings, which affirm that coffins were not used with any frequency until about the 1860s. A 1989 excavation of the narthex of Santa Fe's Santuario de Guadalupe found that only seventeen of sixty-three burials had coffins. According to Edward Crocker, the absence of coffins was not the result of their disintegration but indicates that most of these burials never had been coffined. Significantly, the coffins were from the most recent burials, believed to be mid- to late nineteenth century in origin.[47] It is likely that most if not all these burials took place before 1881, when the church began to serve Santa Fe's English-speaking Roman Catholics. At the site of the old Alameda cemetery, believed to have been in use from about 1832 to 1904, excavations in 2003 and 2005 found that only approximately 40 percent of burials were in coffins.[48] A number of these coffins had been superimposed on earlier burials; further investigation of the hardware and other material culture found at the site will help archaeologists better determine the likely dates of the burials.[49] Thus, all the evidence indicates that coffins were unusual in colonial and independent New Mexico, as they were in Mexico City at the time.[50] Not until the late nineteenth century would coffins become customary among New Mexico's Hispanic population.

Of far greater interest than coffins was burial location. Fixated on the goal of Christian salvation, families sought a choice resting place within the church floors for their loved ones. The Roman rite instructed that all Roman Catholics be interred in consecrated ground; once safely buried, their remains joined the anonymous community of the dead. This emphasis on community seems to have been the preeminent concern. Beyond this concern for burial location, however, people showed little regard for the body after consigning it to the earth. Paradoxically, as the family left the cadaver of a loved one in the hallowed ground of their parish church, any number of indecencies might befall the dead. In one sense, New Mexicans affirmed the temporary character of the burial by breaking bones and disturbing earlier burials, practices that may have been common elsewhere in New Spain.

Once New Mexicans surrendered the groomed, lamented, and blessed corpse to the earth, their view of the dead changed dramatically. In a sense, after burial in sacred ground, New Mexicans literally rejected attachment to the body itself, symbolically rejecting the temporal world. Although no calendar could measure the soul's progress, the evidence suggests that people believed the soul definitively absented itself from the body and moved on to purgatory upon interment. Thus, relative indifference was shown the physical remains once the funeral had ended, for the body had served its purpose. The Resurrection would presumably take care of the rest.

INTERRING AND DISINTERRING THE DEAD

New Mexicans found it important to optimally situate the corpse within the church floor. Based on limited archaeological evidence, it seems that this generally meant that adults' heads faced east, as people believed that Christ would come from the east. The dead were to await the Resurrection in this posture, their corpses recumbent beneath the church floor until Christ reanimated their decayed bodies. Early twentieth-century folklore dictated that placing the corpse with its head toward the east ensured that the dead would not return.[51] Thus this ritual placement also directed the soul's progression to purgatory—or heaven, if especially fortunate.

Far from being a final resting place, however, the grave proved at best chaotic and impermanent. Though a small population probably allowed New Mexico's dead a quiet repose for much of the colonial period, by the early nineteenth century population growth and limited burial space resulted in the regular disturbance of graves. A single plot might include the remains of literally a dozen individuals, with children and adults mixed indiscriminately, in defiance of the Roman rite.[52] Lacking coffins, each time the community dug a new grave in the church, the existing remains were displaced and scattered. Whereas the same challenges of limited burial space in Europe led to the use of ossuaries, only a single document of unknown New Mexican provenance indicates that a parish priest wanted to construct an ossuary.[53] Apparently his suggestion went no further, and so, in nineteenth-century New Mexico, people interred the newly dead on top of existing burials, dislodging skulls and other skeletal remnants as they did so.

While the burial books might occasionally mention a burial near the baptismal font, the confessional, or in a particular section of the church, New Mexicans used neither grave markers nor any type of diagram to indicate the precise location of burials within the church.[54] The church structure itself served as the only marker that family and friends needed to identify a loved one's final resting place. It is likely that survivors would remember that a parent had been buried in a particular chapel or near the principal doorway. Parishioners likewise relied on human memory to determine where to dig a new grave. Knowing that approximately three years had passed since the interment of a parishioner near the chancel, for example, the same plot could be reused without encroaching on the space of the recently dead. In practice, however, people habitually unearthed cadavers and human remains interred only a short time before in the quest for new burial plots. As Josiah Gregg, an American merchant who spent considerable time in Santa Fe in the 1830s, observed:

> There being nothing to indicate the place of the previous graves, it not infrequently happens that the partially decayed relics of a corpse are dug up and forced to give place to the more recently deceased, when they are thrown again with the earth into the new earth with perfect indifference.[55]

Though Gregg was far from objective in his observations on New Mexican life, the findings in Santa Fe's Santuario de Guadalupe corroborate his early nineteenth-century description. Here, the dead had been stacked like cordwood up to four deep, and subsequent to burial, bones were moved, femurs broken, and skulls tossed pell-mell. In one case, someone charged with burying the cadaver broke its neck rather than dig a bigger grave. The skulls of decapitated skeletons even served as chinks to support new burials.[56] The Guadalupe burials, which probably date from the mid- to late nineteenth century, show that New Mexicans made no effort to retain even the semblance of skeletal integrity, freely breaking and scattering bones. The Alameda dig suggests similar activities, as just under half of the seventy-four disinterred burials had been disturbed after burial.[57] It appears clear, therefore, that the limited archaeological record agrees

15. Dissociated skulls found with Burial 8, Santuario de Guadalupe, Santa Fe, 1989, courtesy Edward E. Crocker, Crocker Collection, CSWR, University Libraries, University of New Mexico

with travelers' observations. In fact, the breaking of bones at or soon after burial appears inevitable when reading Gregg's account. According to him, the very manner in which people filled in the new grave probably damaged the corpse, "the earth being pounded down with a large maul, as fast as it is thrown in upon the unprotected corpse, with a force sufficient to crush a delicate frame to atoms."[58] Gregg's comments echo those of John Stephens, who traveled extensively through Chiapas and Yucatán in southern Mexico in this same period. Stephens wrote that his "blood ran cold," so heavy was the force of the sexton's blows as he buried a child in the floors of the parish church.[59] Though shocking to foreigners, New Mexican practices, like those of Palenque and probably other communities, reflected a traditional conceptualization of the dead body that differed from the emergent sentimentalized view in the northeastern United States and Europe's urban centers.

New Mexicans did not find solace in ornate funerary monuments, sentimental literature, and embalmed, painted corpses. Their conception of the cadaver remained closer to the more pragmatic approach that had historically characterized Roman Catholic Europe. The most extreme example was the Cemetery des Saints-Innocents in Paris, which had for centuries overflowed with corpses in mass graves,

16. Coffin fill found in Burial 19, Santuario de Guadalupe, Santa Fe, 1989, courtesy Edward E. Crocker, Crocker Collection, CSWR, University Libraries, University of New Mexico

bodies barely covered with a thin layer of soil. According to Philippe Ariès, only in the late seventeenth century did Parisians begin to express disgust at the cemetery's indecorous treatment of the dead. Yet little changed until the end of the eighteenth century, when intellectuals increasingly challenged deeply engrained customs by tendering public-health arguments against the poisonous miasmas that the cemetery emitted. Others framed their opposition not against the cavalier treatment of the dead but the implicit disrespect that church burials showed the house of God. The practice of disturbing graves—not exclusively for the removal of bones to ossuaries but also as a result of overcrowding and the many social uses of the cemetery—was widespread in Western Europe through at least the eighteenth century. Thus, New Mexican practices remained in keeping with traditional views of the dead, a mixture of piety and seeming irreverence confounding to modern sensibilities.

Even within the hallowed safety of the church walls, folk beliefs and superstitions on occasion led to disinterment of the dead. The international Roman Catholic traffic in relics paralleled popular beliefs shared in Europe and Spanish America, which attributed special qualities to soil, bones, and other objects that one could obtain only from a grave. Spanish, Pueblo, and Mexican cultures ascribed magical and healing powers to the remains of the dead.[60] Believing that it would prevent fatigue, for example, one individual in central Mexico wore a bag of human bones harvested from a cemetery.[61] Closer to home, in Abiquiú, New Mexico, Fray Juan José Toledo reported that witches used the rope of a hanged person as well as teeth and the bones of the dead to practice their craft.[62]

Because of popular associations of curative and magical powers with remains, graves might be subject to any number of invasive deeds. Some people employed human remains for medicinal purposes, and penitential groups might use skulls for meditation, while the less piously minded raided graves for personal gain. One Mexico City resident added a bone fragment retrieved from a hospital's ossuary to beverages to boost sales.[63] Entrepreneurs unearthed cadavers to salvage burial shrouds for resale and sold the human remains to a saltpeter refinery for powder production. Others let their pigs graze in graveyards, feeding on the cadavers that had not been buried deeply enough to discourage the practice.[64] In New Mexico, Fray Pedro Montaño accused Pedro de Chávez of numerous heresies in 1729, among them entering the church and digging up a criada of Chávez's so as to retrieve the wool sheet in which she had been buried.[65] As in central Mexico, animals grazed in New Mexico's burial grounds. Inspector Agustín Fernández de San Vicente complained in 1826 that Santa Fe's graveyard not only lacked the requisite cross in its center, but the cemetery's ruined walls and lack of doors invited animals to foul themselves and disrespectfully violate the graves, destroying these remnants of the former "living temples of God."[66] The violability of the grave and the relative irreverence accorded the dead probably characterized much of Mexico in the colonial period. Fernández de San Vicente's concern, however, reflects how the old sensibility was giving way in an age that afforded the body a new status, even after death.

New Mexicans' treatment of the body—both dead and living— became increasingly anomalous as Spanish and Mexican elites followed the lead of French intellectuals in redefining the body in society. Bourbon notions of the body differed radically from those of the baroque period, when corporal mortifications and the senses both had served as gateways to the divine. Deeply engrained in Spanish Roman Catholicism, these views came under fire in the late eighteenth century as a new enlightened sensibility redefined ideas about the body. In tandem with the growing medicalization of society, which afforded the body a distinct social space, the body now required personal hygiene, perfuming, and behavioral control. Those who deviated from modern conceptions might find themselves in any one of the institutions—asylums, hospitals, and prisons—that would proliferate in urban areas.

The increasing incongruity of New Mexican corporal practices surfaced in visitors' reactions to local customs. The Pentitentes' communal self-flagellation offered bloody evidence of the old baroque view of the body and society. While private mortifications remained acceptable, the public and communal nature of New Mexicans' folk Roman Catholic rituals troubled Mexican church authorities.[67] During their inspections of churches and parish finances, visiting religious leaders censured not just the Penitentes but also local clerics. Almost a decade before Fernández de San Vicente's critique of Santa Fe's cemetery, ecclesiastical inspector don Juan Bautista Ladrón del Niño de Guevara had expressed horror at the presence of seven skulls in a room next to the church, where they perhaps served as memento mori. He ordered their immediate interment and forbade exhumations without the express permission of the bishop of Durango.[68] Of course, the skulls may not have been the product of intentional exhumations but the byproduct of routine exhumations that occurred as the population grew and the burial space beneath the church remained finite. Evidently, bodies continued to surface in ensuing years, for Lt. James W. Abert, who came with the conquering Kearny expedition in 1846, recorded:

> This morning I visited the "Capella [sic] de los Soldados,"
> or military chapel. I was told that this chapel was in use
> some fourteen years ago, and was the richest church in
> New Mexico... One here finds human bones and sculls [sic]
> scattered about the church... [69]

Even beneath the church, however, the dead were dislocated as a matter of course. The archaeologist's map of the excavation in the Guadalupe church's narthex demonstrates the somewhat haphazard method of burial, the persistent superimposition of new burials atop existing graves, and the overwhelming displacement of skulls, indicated throughout.

Reusing graves had been customary in Roman Catholic Europe for centuries, and the custom continued in New Mexico. The idea of occupying a grave exclusively and in perpetuity was most certainly foreign to New Mexicans in this period. Funeral attendees certainly observed that old burials made way for new ones within a few years. In 1819 Fernando VII codified the practice through a royal decree sent

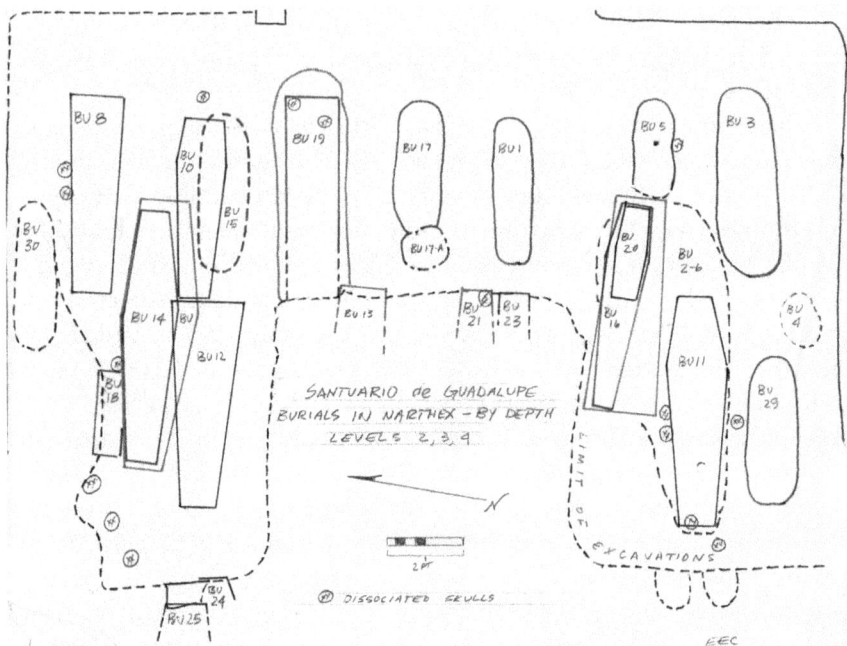

17. Diagram of the excavation at the Santuario de Guadalupe, 1989.
Coffined burials are outlined in straight lines and uncoffined burials are
indicated with rounded corners. Individual, dissociated skulls appear as circles with xx. Courtesy Edward E. Crocker, Crocker Collection, CSWR,
University Libraries, University of New Mexico

to the colonies wherein he ordered a three-year interval between
burials in the same plot.[70] In reality, no mandatory waiting period
existed before New Mexicans might share their graves with the more
recently departed. Any number of circumstances might result in a
single grave containing multiple burials. If two people died on the
same day in the same parish, the priest might deposit their corpses in
the same plot. Those who had been joined in matrimony and died at
the same time likewise might be buried together. Triplets who died
within days of each other shared a grave in the transept of Sandia's
church.[71] Even if the dead were unrelated, the priest might inter their
bodies in the same plot. In 1818, for example, Cura Juan Tomás
Terrazas recorded in the burial book of Santa Fe:

> Ecclesiastical burial was given in this parish church to the
> cadaver of Cristóbal Segura, Spaniard and resident of this
> place, widower of Juana Brito. He did not leave a will

because he did not have to [because of poverty]. He received no sacraments as a result of his sudden death. On the same day and in the same grave José Florentino, infant child of unknown parents, was buried.[72]

Thus, stranger and kin shared the plot. The cohabitation of the dead was the logical and pragmatic culmination to lives based on communal ties rather than individualism.

Mass graves were, above all, practical. During times of pestilence, mass burials not only proved expedient but also promised to reduce the risks of contagion. Violent mass death—for example, the killing of twenty-one Tomé residents at the hands of Comanches in 1777—appears to have resulted in a common grave for all the victims as well.[73] During the late eighteenth-century remodeling of Santa Fe's parish church, laborers removed burials and reinterred the dead in a mass grave.[74] Clearly, colonial New Mexicans felt none of the modern need to confine and isolate the dead in an individual tract in perpetuity.

Once the dead were no longer identifiable and once they were safely outside of the liminal phase, their anonymous remains mingled with those of their desiccated neighbors. New Mexicans' treatment of the dead proves consonant with baroque practices, which attached little importance to the dead body, the cadavers of the nobility and the saints representing exceptional cases.[75] People distinguished, however unconsciously, between the cadaver—which was the logical locus of attention—and the skeleton, which had lost its identity but remained, for all its anonymity, a member of the community and therefore warranted ongoing shelter in consecrated ground until the Resurrection.

Postmortem Cesarean Sections

One piece of Spanish legislation sheds light on ideas of the body in this period. Although Spanish law prohibited burying the dead with valuables to avert grave robbing, social order as well as the integrity of burials concerned the crown. One law, however, which was on the books in New Mexico, mandated not only the exhumation of the dead but also the performance of a cesarean section on the cadaver. Thus, not just the grave but the very integrity of the corpse was to be disrupted.

In April 1804 Carlos IV issued a royal cedula, or royal order, on postmortem cesarean sections. His legal measure, responding to an initiative from the canon of the cathedral of Bogotá, dictated the removal of the fetus from any woman who died during any stage of pregnancy.[76]

The legislation offered an enlightened response to a problem that had perplexed theologians for centuries. Rather than doom the unborn to spending eternity in limbo, the cedula promised baptism and with it the removal of the stain of original sin, ensuring a place in heaven for those who died before the age of reason. With the cooperation of family members, the medical and spiritual team would descend on the house of the dead woman and perform the operation.[77]

Not the first of its kind in Spain, the 1804 law repeated the message of an earlier decree, placing renewed energy into enforcement.[78] These laws and the growing literature on postmortem cesarean sections reached the Americas by the mid- to late eighteenth century. In 1772, New Spain's viceroy, Antonio María de Bucareli y Ursúa, and Archbishop Alfonso Núñez de Haro ordered the procedure performed throughout the viceroyalty.[79] The viceroy threatened anyone who interfered with its performance with a fine of five hundred pesos, and all relatives found obstructing the law were to be reported to the authorities. Those who notified "the priest or authorities of any pregnant woman in danger of death with the purpose of saving the offspring by means of the operation and its subsequent baptism," would receive an eighty-day indulgence for their efforts.[80]

Roman Catholic theologians had published a number of volumes testifying to the operation's utility, which informed the crown's legislation. A Spanish Cistercian monk, Fray Antonio José Rodríguez, published *Nuevo aspecto de teología médico moral* in Spain in 1742 and again in 1787. Sicilian Fray Francesco Cangiamila published his *Embriología sacra* in 1745. Cangiamila's work proved influential in the Spanish legislation, and in 1772 a Mexico City publisher printed an abbreviated translation of Cangiamila by the Franciscan Fray José Manuel Rodríguez. Bucareli's 1772 circular referred specifically to Rodríguez's publication, *La caridad del sacerdote para con los niños encerrados en el vientre de sus madres difuntas, y documentos de la utilidad y necesidad de su práctica* as the impetus for this law.[81] Theology mandated performing this operation, but the state elected to codify the procedure, lent its authority to ensuring obedience, and punished those who disobeyed or undermined its precepts with fines and other sanctions.[82] Fray Francisco González Laguna enthusiastically promoted the practice in Lima and the Andean highlands, writing his own treatise on the subject.[83] By 1795 the operation had been performed on a cadaver in Mexico City, and within four years a friar undertook the surgery in the mission at Santa Clara, California.[84]

The authors of these texts demonstrated scant interest in extending the physical life of the extracted fetus, which might only survive for a few hours after removal. Eternal life rather than mortal life concerned theologians and doctors alike. Once it was certain that the woman was indeed dead, the operation, which required only two scalpels, a razor, or a penknife, could begin. According to the 1804 legislation:

> The incision will be made on the side where the belly is
> most bulging, or where the creature best shows ... If the
> creature should give no signs of life, it will not be extracted
> before it is baptized conditionally. It if is alive and seemingly
> robust, it will be extracted holding it by the feet, or in the
> least laborious way, and will then be baptized pouring the
> sacramental water on its head. ... In the case of a miscar-
> riage, the amnion must be opened with great care, and the
> creature being in view, even if it were like a grain of barley, if
> it has movement, will be baptized, and if it has not, the
> same will also be done, conditionally.[85]

Even with its physical existence extinguished, the operation guaranteed the fetus the higher reward of eternal life.

Conditional baptism stemmed from the same concern with the moment of death that caused the dead woman to be poked and prodded before the operation. Since only a living person could receive baptism according to the rites of the Roman Catholic Church, the priest would baptize the fetus conditionally in the absence of any obvious signs of life. The difficulty in ascertaining physical death allowed at least this conditional welcome into the Roman Catholic faith, thereby extending the promise of heaven to those otherwise condemned to an eternity in limbo. Although conditional, baptism was nonetheless deemed so important that the decree forbade priests from burying any pregnant women who had died without undergoing the procedure, thus denying them ecclesiastical burial. Carlos IV's cedula did not equate the failure to perform the cesarean section with murder as his father's decree apparently had a half-century earlier, but denying these women an ecclesiastical burial essentially sanctioned the dead for the livings' negligence. Despite this penalty, priests and parishioners alike had reason to resist the law, and New Mexicans probably had little fear of exhumation for the purposes of postmortem cesarean section.

Although the late eighteenth-century mandate does not survive in New Mexican archives, we know that this circular reached as far north as California, where between 1769 and 1833, priests performed at least fourteen postmortem cesareans throughout the mission system. Christianized Indians proved the most frequent subjects of the surgery, which resulted in the removal of fetuses at an estimated seven to eight months of gestation. One fetus reportedly lived for two days, and some survived for a few minutes, but most probably had died already when the friars conditionally baptized them. After conferring the sacrament, the priests buried the infants with their incised mothers. Fray Isidoro Barcenilla, who would become custos of New Mexico soon thereafter, himself performed one of these fourteen procedures, extracting an eight-month-old fetus at the Mission of San Gabriel Arcángel in March 1803.[86] Perhaps emboldened by his successful completion of the operation, Barcenilla actively promoted adherence to the 1804 cedula when he arrived in New Mexico in 1815.

Carlos IV's order arrived in Chihuahua by August 1804 and probably reached New Mexican parishes soon thereafter.[87] Although New Mexican archives offer no proof of postmortem cesareans performed in New Mexico, the idea clearly reached the northern frontier. In one of myriad mid-nineteenth-century efforts to demonstrate the supposed barbarity of the Mexican people—and hence their need for U.S. dominion—Lt. James W. Abert cited an incident from Chihuahua. Abert claimed that, after murdering an Apache woman in an ambush, the Mexicans had ripped the "living child" from her and then mockingly baptized the fetus.[88] While perhaps apocryphal, the anecdote reveals the general diffusion of knowledge of the postmortem cesarean and conditional baptism.

By empowering doctors, the new authorities of the day, the decree relied on the authorities of the baroque age, priests, to apply science to two age-old theological problems: how to ensure the salvation of the unborn and how to measure death. Doctors and clergymen were instructed to cooperate to ensure that any woman who died during any stage of pregnancy undergo a postmortem cesarean section. Regardless of how small the fetus, the procedure promised to extend the possibility of salvation to the unborn child who would otherwise be denied liberation from original sin. Once safely extracted, a priest would baptize it and through baptism free the child from an eternity that would otherwise have been spent in limbo.

The law on postmortem cesarean sections privileged the spiritual over the secular, while at the same time validating doctors' and the state's social authority over the dead. As has been well documented elsewhere, medical professionals would in time loosen the clergy's grip on matters of life and death. Pamela Voekel argues that Mexico's enlightened elites deliberately excluded women practitioners from their program of medical reform. The 1804 cedula codified this exclusion while also enacting upon women's bodies the same type of ignominious procedure previously reserved for executed criminals. Warning of the procedure's difficulty, the decree summoned not midwives but licensed male surgeons and doctors to perform the cesarean section. In the absence of a surgeon, another *facultativo*, or degreed medical professional, had to undertake the cesarean section. Only if no professional physician were on hand could the priest and local magistrate designate:

> the person who they believed to be possessed of the best talent, dexterity, and aptitude to execute the cesarean operation in precise and exact accordance with the instruction, which will be at hand in the act, and to which perfect execution the priest will collaborate, if necessary, with his advice and knowledge.[89]

For just such an event, the cedula provided step-by-step instructions on how to perform the operation.

Custos Fray Isidoro Barcenilla omitted these careful instructions in his 1815 circular to New Mexico's parishes but did request that any priest with a copy of "the great Cangiamila's" book on the topic lend him the volume so he could issue precise directions to New Mexico's clergy. In the meantime, recognizing the operation's complexity, Barcenilla ordered priests to determine who in their parish might be capable of performing a cesarean section. In the absence of a competent local practitioner, he declared that the priest should himself perform the operation. Barcenilla anticipated resistance from his priests over the potential for contact with even dead females to sully priestly chastity. He admonished the clergy, however, that "the apparent temptations do not exempt us from this most strict duty."[90] If careful to guard his modesty and that of the dead woman, a priest could safely perform the cesarean section. Finally, the custos directed New Mexico's religious leaders to educate their parishioners on the procedure's importance and warn them of the serious—but notably unspecified—penalties resulting from disobedience.

Barcenilla construed performing a cesarean section on the dead as a religious duty of the highest order. The operation offered hope of salvation where before none had existed. While ignorant families might seek to avoid the operation for their dead daughters, sisters, and wives, the clergy must not waver from their calling to save the souls of these "children, not extracted from the belly of their dead mothers."[91] Although Barcenilla despaired at finding these "children" alive upon their extraction, he based his directive, as had his superiors in Spain and New Spain, on the notion that life could briefly dwell within a dead mother. After all, had not San Román Nonato (St. Raymond Nonnatus) himself—the patron saint of pregnant women, midwives, and the unborn—thus come into the world? Surely, the moment of death was imprecise and difficult if not impossible to measure.

The decree on postmortem cesareans implicitly and explicitly spoke to the difficulty in ascertaining death. The clear-cut medical science of the operation did not eliminate the considerable gray area in establishing death. Although death mocked precise measurement, the law instructed that the mother's death be established to the degree possible before rescuing the trapped fetus. Did applying ammonia at the woman's mouth, nose, and eyes revive her? Did she react when someone inserted a pin beneath her nails? Once death had been established, the king's instructions emphasized the importance of undertaking the operation as soon as possible to increase the potential for extirpating a living fetus; however, the procedure reportedly had been performed successfully on women who had been dead for days.

New Mexicans frequently disinterred the dead and relocated entire skeletons, but violating the integrity of the corpse would have troubled many individuals, families, and communities. Just as the corpse's similarity to the living body blurred the distinction between apparent death and actual death, the resemblance of the corpse to the living person served as a powerful disincentive to cutting it open, even for spiritual ends. When investigators arrived on the murder scene that morning in 1834 in San Antonio del Rancho, they established the death of María Espíritu Santo Roybal not by some invasive procedure or even so much as a pinprick, but through verbal inquiry. The authorities asked the strangled woman questions and when she failed to respond, pronounced her dead.[92]

Modern notions of interment—confining a body to a coffin, the need for individual burial plots, perpetual care—would have seemed foreign to people of the late eighteenth and early nineteenth centuries and perhaps especially so to New Mexicans. Certainly, burial practices for royalty and other persons of high standing were exceptional, and these modern attributes of death would have been reserved for elites. New Mexicans found comfort in the knowledge that they had met their spiritual duties by providing burial in consecrated ground and Roman Catholic masses for their loved ones. In their minds, the Resurrection promised that the dead would reinhabit their decayed bodies at Christ's coming. Although people accorded desiccated skeletons a status different from fresh cadavers, all persons reposing beneath the church would ultimately join the same ranks. A communal and corporate world view rather than Protestant notions of individualism directed the treatment of the dead body, as reflected in the indiscriminate mingling of remains, with no clear boundaries and no identifying markers. New Mexicans demonstrated little concern for how the "clean" bones were treated, but they agreed on the importance of keeping them within the parish church.

CHAPTER FIVE

Exiling the Dead

P roclaiming their faith in God and their devotion to Christ, rebels
in northern New Mexico violently threatened their parish priests
as the summer of 1837 drew to a close. In Santa Cruz de la
Cañada, the pious insurgents jabbed a gun in Cura Fernando Ortiz's
back and ordered him to inter a corpse underneath the parish
church's floors. Taos rebels pledged to kill Cura Antonio José Martínez
if he tried to prevent their burying a body near the chancel steps in
the chapel of St. Francis.[1] Martínez later recounted to the bishop that
the rebels had said that "they will pay neither obventions nor contributions to church building funds, and they would be buried in the
churches."[2] Though Cura Martínez dutifully continued to administer
the sacraments to his flock, after performing numerous baptisms,
marriages, and burials he reported that only one couple had offered
to pay him for his services. While human nature rather than political
ideology may have motivated some to cheat the priest of his compensation, the fact that even parishioners not actively participating in the
rebellion took advantage of the situation suggests that the insurgency
sweeping northern New Mexico in August 1837 articulated a more
general discontent in the region.

Although not strictly about burials, like contemporaneous
cemetery rebellions in Guatemala and Brazil, the uprising in New
Mexico's Río Arriba, the district including Santa Fe northward, con-
flated political, economic, and religious grievances.[3] The uprising
reflected the same political cleavages evident throughout Mexico in

this period, namely, the debate over a federalist versus a centralist system of government. During the rebellion, three to six thousand people united in their opposition to "godlessness," taxation, the recent centralist constitution or "Departmental Plan," and the 1835 arrival of a new governor and military commander from Mexico, Col. Albino Pérez.[4] Some New Mexicans resented Pérez's lavish lifestyle and suspected him of immoral behavior, while others— especially Indians and the poor—felt burdened by mandatory militia service.[5] Enjoying widespread support among New Mexico's economically disadvantaged populations, the bloody insurrection resulted in the murder of the governor and his entire cabinet— eighteen people in all—before the rebels' final defeat in January of the following year. A clear racial component informed these events, as Andrés Reséndez observes that the governor and his cabinet "were all white Hispanics of the highest social standing, . . . whereas the men carrying out the executions were overwhelmingly Indian."[6] "More than anything else," argues Reséndez, "the specter of such a caste war galvanized a powerful counterrevolutionary movement," resulting in exceptional unity on the part of civil and religious authorities, who invoked nationalist and Roman Catholic rhetoric as they squashed the revolt.[7]

While existing scholarship on the Chimayó Rebellion highlights its political and social dimensions, consigning the burial issue to historical footnote, tensions over burial location in fact had simmered for decades, anticipating some of the grievances expressed in the 1837 revolt. By the time of the rebellion, priests in many communities had been burying the dead in cemeteries instead of under the church floors for almost two decades, despite popular opposition. It was no coincidence that the heart of the rebellion resided in Santa Cruz, where the issue of burial location had festered for years. The Chimayó Rebellion represented the most radical—and, as it would turn out, the final—overt challenge in the battle over where to bury the dead. Only by exploring the burial controversy does the apparent contradiction in the rebels' high-minded religious discourse and their violence against priests begin to make sense. The ongoing dispute over interment also elucidates the social and economic transformations taking place in New Mexico during the late eighteenth and early nineteenth centuries. Though less sanguinary and less tangible than the violence of 1837, these changes had disrupted both life and death for many New Mexicans and ultimately would prove more enduring than the short-lived rebellion.

To understand fully what impelled people to bully their parish priests in 1837, we must first turn to the final decades of Spanish rule and consider the reasons and meanings behind the crown's burial reforms, as well as the persistent but halting efforts to implement them in the colonies. It was in the last quarter of the eighteenth century that the Spanish crown attempted to undermine the long, comfortable coexistence of the living and the dead by banning the burial of cadavers inside and adjacent to churches by ordering the construction of cemeteries outside of towns. Contending that subfloor burials endangered public health, the king instructed his subjects through a series of royal cedulas and orders to bury cadavers only in *cementerios ventilados*, or ventilated cemeteries, to be established at a distance from population centers.

THE BOURBONS AND PUBLIC HEALTH

Though this discussion focuses on the movement to create these extramural or suburban cemeteries, burial reform represented only one in a series of reforms the Bourbons promulgated in their effort to modernize and secularize Spanish-American society. Spain's Bourbon monarchy, heavily influenced by ideas of the Enlightenment, restructured elements of economic, political, and social life in Spain and the colonies. Some of these changes meant to bolster military strength or strengthen the royal treasury while others sought to reduce the influence of the Roman Catholic Church. Though seeking administrative control and wealth, reformers were also genuinely enamored with science, reason, progress, and modernity. Beginning in the mid-eighteenth century, reformers began to secularize American parishes, establish standard fees for ecclesiastical services, and restrict the role of priests in judicial and financial matters. Priests lost cherished privileges as well as their immunity from prosecution in the royal courts. The reasons for these reforms were manifold. "Bourbon administrators," William B. Taylor observes, "were inclined to regard priests as usurpers of royal authority and the church as an obstacle to material progress, a bastion of entailed, unproductive wealth, and the agent of revelation and tradition rather than reason and efficiency."[8] In the pursuit of hygiene, conceptions of science, progress, and modernity converged. Rather than merely react to periodic epidemics, enlightened governments promoted prophylactic measures against disease.[9] Once reform-minded officials took up their appointments, new hospitals confined the sick, aqueducts brought clean water to urban residents, lanterns graced city streets, and paved roads led the way to those same cities.

In the case of burial reform, public-health legislation dovetailed nicely with efforts to reduce church power. None of the legislation promised any resources to construct cemeteries. In order to implement the reforms, parishes had to dip into existing financial resources to pay for the construction of new cemeteries. These costs might include clearing the land, building a wall around the cemetery, and creating a road to allow public access. Despite the additional costs to the church, priests could not reasonably charge parishioners for burial at the old rates; the suburban cemeteries by definition were too far removed from the altars and the relics to compel parishioners to pay the established fees. Since funerals comprised one of the principal sources of parish income, burial reform undermined the churches' already precarious financial situations, especially in many rural communities.[10]

While New Mexico's already strapped parishes found themselves financially compromised as the result of the reforms, society as a whole remained somewhat insulated from their social and political implications relative to other areas of Mexico. The reforms created deep social fissures in the city of Veracruz, for example, where they "directly and explicitly threatened their [traditional elites'] principal idiom of distinction and technique of rule."[11] The reforms' implicit egalitarianism led to considerable tensions when, in 1790, Veracruz's enlightened leadership began constructing a cemetery on the outskirts of town. The project initiated an intense debate, pitting the procemetery *sensatos*, or enlightened, and the poor against confraternities, the regular orders, hospital orders, and church benefactors. The sensatos came from Veracruz's rapidly expanding merchant class and advocated an interiorized, nominally egalitarian piety, rejecting all the showy trappings of the mediated and corporate baroque piety. Some clerics embraced these new ideas as well, promoting a theology that emphasized self-examination rather than priestly intercessors. Together with the poor, who embraced the cemetery's more democratic spirit, they faced off against traditional elites and traditionally minded individuals within Veracruz's Bourbon state. Pamela Voekel observes:

> Passionately involved in guiding others to moral improvement, the enlightened found the dead's presence in the center of the city an affront, a statement of their power's limited parameters, their inability to transcend mortality. In stark contrast to the ancien régime pattern of fixed social

identities, enlightened identity depended on the desire to improve one's own life—and the ability to do so. Thus, the dead's presence served the enlightened less as a prod to pray for others' eternal life than as a reminder of their ultimate mortality, their inability to prolong their own and others' worldly existence.[12]

Concern for public health fueled burial reforms across Spanish America. One of the period's most influential intellectuals, Baltasar Melchor Gaspar María de Jovellanos, pondered the potential dangers of burials in a lengthy discourse first published by the Royal Academy of History in 1786. The essay combined a detailed legal history of ancient and modern burial practices with modern ideas of public health to make the case for reform. Jovellanos expounded on the ideal location of cemeteries and discussed how to retain cherished social privileges despite the removal of burials from churches. Understandably, this adviser to the crown did not deem all the ancient practices desirable. Although applauding the Roman custom of burying the dead on the outskirts of cities, Jovellanos disapproved of burials lining the roads into the cities or their proximity to water sources and towns generally, "for while this may serve to remind us of our mortality, it may not avoid the damage of infection which is to be prevented."[13] And it was, after all, disease that most concerned Jovellanos. Citing examples from around Spain, he noted that even in Madrid, the church of San Sebastián had had to cancel mass for eight consecutive days because the cadaver of architect don Juan Durán, "who was a man full of humors, released an insufferable stench."[14]

Though employing the findings of prominent French doctors to prove the pernicious nature of decomposing corpses, Jovellanos did not confine himself to medical science to make his case in "Informe sobre la disciplina eclesiástica antigua y moderna relativa al lugar de las sepulturas." As its title suggests, the report relied heavily on the writings of different saints and medieval church councils to make the case against existing Spanish burial practices. Jovellanos traced contemporary practices to the ancient church, which had permitted the burial of exceptional civil and religious leaders within the church. During the Middle Ages, it became customary to inter saints and martyrs within churches, and in time even the impious sought church burial for the presumed benefits it would bring their souls. Throughout this long history, however, many church councils had inveighed against this practice that placed the profane so close to the sacred.

Although precisely calculating the damage done by the proximity of burials to the living proved difficult, Jovellanos agreed with the French Faculty of Medicine's conclusion that the coexistence of the living and the dead could only lead to the spread of epidemic disease.

The public-health argument, propelled by an ascendant group of doctors and anatomists, drove the crown to take definitive action. The crown's burial reforms, set down in the last third of the eighteenth century, were the product of enlightened thinking, scientific inquiry, and changing conceptions of medical practitioners' status. Though still lacking the tools to diagnosis and treat most diseases, the increasingly popular science of anatomy emboldened doctors and surgeons, whose privileged access to the body set them apart even from priests, as holding the keys to life's mysteries.[15] The lessons thus acquired radiated beyond these learned men of science. As Michael Sappol notes, "Anatomy was an exemplary science, featured in the court philosophy of middling and high aristocratic circles."[16] The knowledge gained through anatomical dissection buttressed cameralist principles, drawing a connection between state wealth and population growth. The body in turn served as the model for larger ideas about society, resulting in numerous reform campaigns, innovative ways of organizing and regulating urban life, and the development of new institutions designed especially to treat society's infirm and undesirable.

Having conferred on doctors the capacity not only to treat infirmities but also prevent disease, reform-minded urban administrators and medical experts seized upon air and related environmental and climatic conditions (such as excessive cold or heat) as among the most crucial means of preventing sickness. In particular, the circulation and purity of air and water became increasingly important to safeguarding public health. Miasmic theories of disease warned that contagion spread through the sluggish movement of air and water.[17] Likewise, poor air circulation transmitted pestilence because it did not permit the dissipation of dangerous smells. Fetid humors offered tangible evidence of the risks to public health, and people reasonably drew a connection between stench and disease.[18] Although miasmic theories prevailed across Europe from the Middle Ages until the last quarter of the nineteenth century, the Enlightenment had infused the old paradigm with new energy. According to Carlo M. Cipolla:

> Not even men of high intellectual calibre ever dared to question the humoral-miasmatic paradigm whose clarity, logic and consistency were sanctioned by antiquity and tradition.

Time after time correct factual observations were made
and recorded but, by some perverse mechanism, what was
correctly observed did not cast doubt on the validity of the
prevailing paradigm but was dialectically adapted to that
very paradigm to serve as further proof.[19]

As late as the mid-nineteenth century, medical experts in England
"acted and behaved not only as if all 'smell' was disease but also as if
all disease was 'smell.'"[20]

During summer months and in warm climates, the heat exaggerated
the odors dominating urban areas—garbage-polluted rivers and
manure-littered streets—which authorities increasingly deemed responsible for epidemics. In Spain, experts instructed young women confined
in convents to walk regularly in verdant gardens and advised all citizens
to open windows three times a day to expel the dangerous odors that
accumulated indoors.[21] Authorities focused special attention on urban
areas, which they believed particularly susceptible to assaults on public
health because of narrow streets, tall buildings, and high population
density, all of which impeded the free circulation of air and water.[22]

These intellectual currents quickly crossed the Atlantic and
slowly gained disciples in the colonies. To improve hygiene, Mexican
reformers initiated ambitious sanitation campaigns and public-
works projects in the last third of the eighteenth century. Viceroy
Carlos Francisco de Croix promulgated an edict that forbade "dumping of all manner of refuse in the streets, plazas, and canals."[23]
Although largely ignored, the decree demonstrates growing elite
awareness of the connection between waste and public health.[24] Of
course, public health was not an exact science. Scenting bonfires with
herbs and firing cannons to purify the air possessed dubious value,
even during an epidemic.[25] Planned sewer systems and regular
garbage collection correspond more to modern sensibilities. The city
of Veracruz required residents to sweep in front of their homes twice
a week, installed lanterns, and collected rubbish for disposal in the
ocean.[26] Viceroy Conde de Revillagigedo (the younger) stepped up the
pace of reform in Mexico City, and two decades after Viceroy de
Croix's decree, Mexican authorities ascribed the city's lower illness
and mortality rates to improved sanitation measures and the resultant purity of the air and water.[27]

By the 1830s many of the issues troubling reformers in central
Mexico also worried New Mexico's leadership. Filthy streets, roaming
dogs, dirty irrigation ditches, wandering livestock, vagabonds, and

public drunkenness all plagued Santa Fe. In 1832, the ayuntamiento hired two men to remove unattended animals from the streets and fine their owners.[28] The following year, a bando banned dumping garbage and dead animals in the acequias and rivers, ordered that streets and plazas be swept and kept clean, promoted the dissemination of the smallpox inoculation, required the licensing of all midwives, and instructed that all dog owners keep their animals leashed or risk their dog's death in the campaign to eliminate strays.[29] New Mexico's leadership clearly participated in the intellectual dialogue of the day and supported its tenets, as reflected by the fact that many of the decree's thirty-seven provisions focus on miasmas. While the council named the creation of a public-health council as crucial to the promotion and enforcement of sanitation, many of the measures mandated changes in individual behavior as essential to the public welfare.[30]

The dangerous miasmas cadavers emitted represented a special problem for reformers, and the dead came to bear responsibility for many of the worst public-health offenses. Just as the free flow and circulation of vital elements like blood and oxygen in the body and air and water in the city was accountable for health and well-being, the converse was also true: the inactivity of vital bodily fluids caused cadavers to decay. Spanish physician Joseph de Aranda y Marzo argued that "it is evident from experience that pestilence is born of the decay of cadavers, or intensely fetid putrefaction of some ponds, which because of ventilation cause the rise of poisonous, corrupting vapors that take the resources of the living."[31] Another doctor, Sebastián José López Ruiz, argued that candles and closed doors only exacerbated the poor ventilation in churches. He recommended the use of incense, Gregorian chants, and bells to clear the air and restore its elasticity but above all advocated outdoor burials removed from population centers.[32] Spanish military physician Mauricio de Echandi warned that miasmas entered the body not just through the nostrils but through one's very pores. He also found churches exceptionally dangerous, not only because human corpses released more deadly exhalations than animal cadavers, but because "in temples the holy spirit enters the body... activating all of the internal powers of the soul... so that corporal forces relax and the body becomes more vulnerable to dangerous air."[33]

BURIAL REFORM

Medical authorities' and intellectuals' dire warnings found a receptive audience in Carlos III (1759–88). Impelled by recent epidemics, he banned the practice of subfloor burials with a royal cedula in 1787. Reasoning that burials inside churches and towns jeopardized public health, the decree ordered the construction of cemeteries away from population centers to eliminate the public-health risks of corpses decomposing in proximity to the living. Clergy were to enforce the new legislation first in those areas of the country that had suffered epidemics and in densely populated urban areas, where burials were more frequent and more crowded than in the countryside. Far from universal, the law allowed some to maintain existing privileges. This exemption pertained chiefly to clergy and persons of "virtue or saint-liness," who retained the right to burial within the church. In a concession to traditional elites, the decree also allowed elites and confraternities who had acquired rights to a burial crypt to maintain subfloor burials. Thus, while burial reform democratized and sanitized death for some, the legislation's numerous caveats ensured that some members of society would receive interment in coveted proximity to saintly intercession.[34]

Though the decree did not specify how far from population centers the new cemeteries had to be situated, it did require that they be in "well-ventilated areas," away from the homes of residents so as to prevent contagion. That same year, a priest resident at the court celebrated the reforms with a poem extolling their reform's virtues:

Long live healthy providence/which gives worship to God
and life to men/flees abominable corruption/of His sacred
illustrious house/In the temple, breathe the pleasant/
aromatic odor that invites to prayer, triumphant now
the/primitive incenses/and the dead do not kill the living.[35]

Remarkably, the poem held the dead accountable for the welfare of the living. As such, segregation of the living and the dead was the only rational response to centuries of dangerous cohabitation.

Citing concerns expressed by the governor of Cuba, don José de Ezpeleta, and the archbishop of Mexico, Carlos IV (1788–1808) in 1789 ordered detailed reports on burial practices from throughout the colonies.[36] The Cuban governor had reported to the king that most of the island's illnesses and epidemics originated in the cadavers putrefying within churches. Ezpeleta had contended that "in certain seasons there were so many buried that in some churches one could scarcely tread without touching fresh and fetid burials."[37] While the particulars of disease transmission remained a mystery, miasmic theory confidently correlated exposed corpses with disease. In reality, buried corpses did not in and of themselves pose much threat. Disinterment of old burials as new graves were dug could indeed, however, have exposed people to microscopic fluids that may have infected them with any number of viruses, including smallpox, cholera, and yellow fever. Once airborne, these particles can live up to seventy-two hours.[38] Therefore, the fears were not entirely unfounded, but extremely exaggerated. Rather than simply impose his will on the colonies without regard for local conditions, the king contextualized his concern using the Cuban example and solicited further information from his subjects.

Although the situation in Cuba was exceptionally grim, the solution to these grave public-health dangers would ultimately be the same throughout Spain and its colonies: eliminate indoor burials and establish "ventilated" cemeteries a good distance from population centers. Assuring his subjects that he enjoyed the support of the church, the king instructed parishes throughout Spain's possessions to report on the number of cemeteries they needed in proportion to the population, the associated costs, and financing for the new cemeteries. Anxious for the well-being of his subjects, the king also expressed concern for the royal treasury, dictating that any changes be implemented with the least possible impact on the treasury. Thus the king relied on an American problem—Cuba's epidemics—to explain the need for the reforms. Careful contextualization of the problem and its solutions, however, could not impel his subjects to embrace the changes or even reply to the request for information. Despite New Mexico's recent smallpox epidemic, the wills and burial books demonstrate that the custom of burying the dead within the church endured. New Mexico's parishes ignored the call for reports on the topic and did not copy the royal order into parish records.[39] In fact, in much of New Spain, priests and communities likewise disregarded the cedula. As a result, the crown issued an edict reiterating the earlier instructions.[40]

IMPLEMENTING THE REFORMS IN NEW MEXICO

The bishop of Durango, Francisco Gabriel de Olivares y Benito (1796–1812), also pursued the matter, instructing parishes in 1799 to send him a detailed report on their burial practices. Reflecting his beliefs in prevailing medical theories, Olivares inquired about the location of cemeteries in relation to settlements, the nature of cemetery and church ventilation, and the quality of the soil on which the churches stood. Since the crown would not underwrite construction costs, the bishop also solicited suggestions from each parish to learn how they might pay for the new cemeteries.[41] Several of New Mexico's parishes responded to the bishop's request. The priest of the recently secularized (1797) parish of Santa Fe, Cura José María Bivián de Ortega, assured the bishop that the parish church, along with Santa Fe's chapels dedicated to Our Lady of Guadalupe, Our Lady of Light, and San Miguel, would be more than adequate to bury cadavers even during an epidemic. Praising the quality of the soil on which these churches had been built, the priest guaranteed the bishop that these buildings all enjoyed superior ventilation.[42] Fray José Mariano Rosete's reply from Santa Cruz de la Cañada had a less optimistic tone. Although the church's transept enjoyed "ordinary" ventilation, Rosete asserted that "even if the building had superior air circulation, this would be worthless, for the church floor is so covered with bones that one could nowhere dig open a space without releasing an abominable stench."[43] Rosete proposed the construction of an adobe pantheon in the campo santo but immediately dismissed this solution because of the community's tremendous poverty. Noteworthy is the assumption implicit in his reply that burying the dead outside the church represented an adequate solution to the problem. In fact, of course, the legislation called for extramural cemeteries. As it turns out, neither innovation would occur anytime soon in Santa Cruz or Santa Fe.

Albuquerque's Fray Ambrosio Guerra, who had served for more than two decades in different New Mexican communities, responded to the bishop's request for information with an equally pessimistic report. Noting that the parish had few financial resources, Guerra reported that Albuquerque's parish church and campo santo, along with the chapels in outlying Tomé and Alameda, adequately met the annual burial needs of the jurisdiction's 1,467 residents. Guerra estimated that it would cost between fifty and one hundred pesos to construct a new graveyard, should the bishop deem it necessary and order it done.[44] While professing obedience, the tenor of Guerra's letter suggests a lukewarm reception to the reforms. His actions in the years following the ban on indoor burials confirm this view. In fact, parish burial books demonstrate that until his removal from Albuquerque more than seventeen years later, Guerra continued to bury almost all parishioners within the church floors.

Not content to dismiss the issue as easily as the clergy had, Carlos IV in 1804 issued precise instructions on the construction of suburban cemeteries in the form of another royal cedula banning subfloor burials.[45] The cedula stated that disobedience defiled God's house and jeopardized public health and underscored the importance of "making the priests understand the merit they will gain in contributing to this laudable end, my only objective being the greater decorum and decency of the churches, and the public health, which so concerns me."[46] Again, the king gave an American endorsement in an effort to legitimate the decree in the colonies, praising Cuzco's governor, bishop, and audiencia for their progress in "this noble cause." Attached was a detailed diagram for the model layout of the suburban cemeteries. Resembling a city for the dead, the ideal suburban cemetery was a model of balance, harmony, and well-proportioned planning. Carefully spaced trees (M) enclosed the neatly laid-out burial grounds while allowing superior ventilation. A chapel (C) for masses and contemplation, meticulously plotted graves (Y), and an orderly walkway for visitors (H) completed the diagram. Reflecting the best of modern thought and rational urban planning, the model provided for the well-being of the dead without endangering the health of the living. Its design struck a careful balance between faith and hygiene, the here and the hereafter.[47]

In forwarding the cedula, Bishop Olivares included an edict of his own, along with a lengthy discourse reinforcing each of the points that the cedula raised. Olivares offered as a model the newly constructed cemetery of Durango's Santa Ana Cathedral and drew a portrait of a king who was paternalistic and concerned for the welfare of his charges. The bishop himself provided a litany of reasons to endorse the reforms: respect for God, hygiene, and respect for the king. In addition to describing the king's great personal concern for his subjects, Olivares emphasized that the king's decree was completely in keeping with canonical dispositions. Unlike the earlier legislation, which had exempted some social groups, all subjects regardless of state, status, or gender had to obey the present decree.

Bishop Olivares described in great detail how the people of Durango had followed the king's mandate by constructing a ventilated cemetery with adequate space for burials that also took into consideration anticipated population growth and possible epidemics. Despite the scarcity of resources, the new cemetery, adjacent to the church of Santa Ana, included space for 180 burials in stone vaults, 200 underground burials with stone slabs, and a central space for common burial. The community had constructed another cemetery measuring eighty-by-thirty varas, situated in front of the Santa Ana

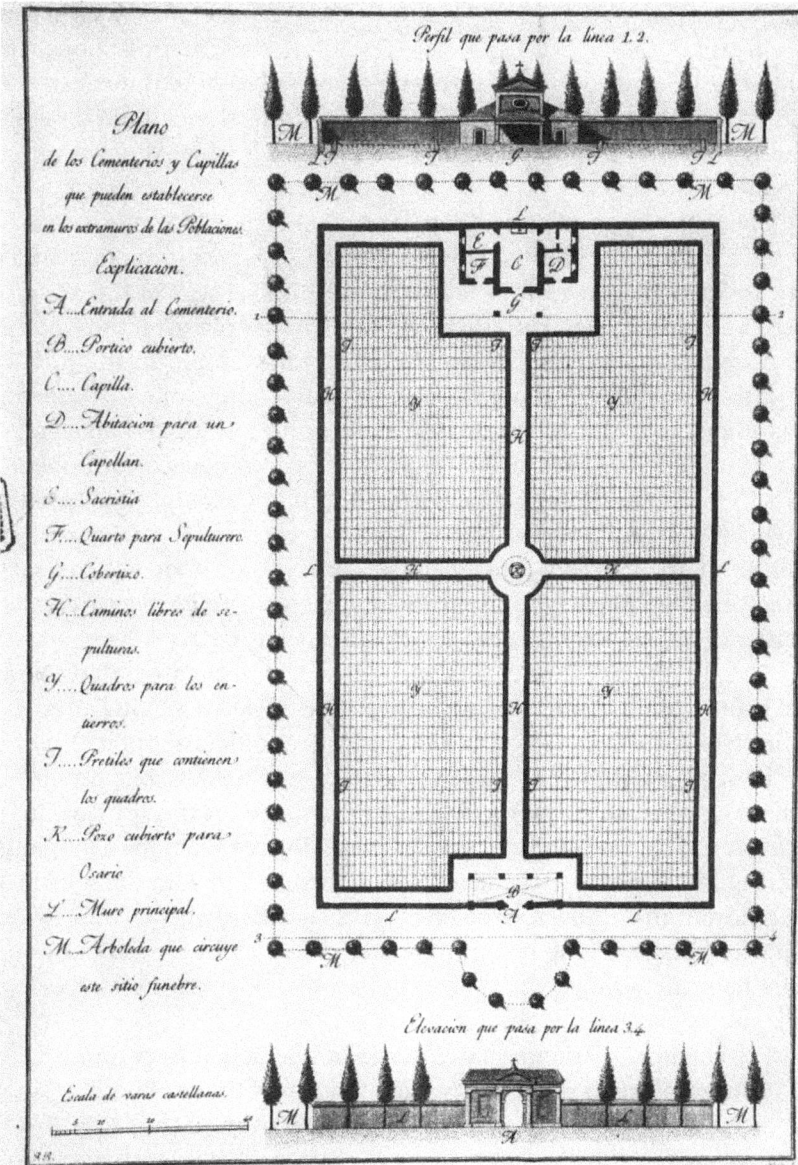

18. Model plan of a ventilated cemetery, 1804, Spain, Ministerio de la Cultura, Archivo Histórico Nacional, ES.28079.AHN/4/CONSEJOS, libro 1502, fol. 161

cemetery, in case of an epidemic.[48] Ironically, while the bishop cited the new cemeteries as evidence of his adherence to the king's wishes, technically they did not comply with the letter of the law. Although

149

removed from the cathedral, burials would still take place within the very heart of the city of Durango. Instead of constructing suburban cemeteries as called for, the bishop merely had seen to the construction of cemeteries adjacent to and across from the cathedral. Even among reformers, then, different interpretations of what constituted obedience prevailed.

The bishop hoped parishioners would embrace the new cemeteries on a number of counts. The cost for burial in the cemetery adjacent to the cathedral fell to half of what a burial within the church cost. If economic considerations did not win people over, the bishop suggested that cemetery burial would be an example to the public "how to conclude the course of this miserable life with a disposition so laudably in support of humanity and for the health and conservation of one's fellow creatures."[49] Thus the bishop constructed obedience to the legislation as a final act of Roman Catholic charity. This powerful message should have resonated with those making their wills on their deathbeds. The bishop did not rely on good will to guarantee obedience, though, and threatened to suspend any priests or sacristans found burying corpses within any church.

The bishop's lengthy discourse clearly indicates that New Mexicans alone did not cling to the traditional ways. Even in Durango, under closer scrutiny of lay and ecclesiastical officials, opposition to the reforms must have been significant to warrant the bishop's protracted commentary. In an effort to compensate for the spiritual loss engendered by the cemetery regulations, Olivares seemed to bargain, offering indulgences to those who readily complied with the reforms. He granted an indulgence of forty days to those who in their wills requested burial in the new campo santo, as well as for a number of other acts, including:

For each Our Father and Ave Maria of the Holy Rosary and other prayers of the Church said, and for all those of both sexes who assist in saying prayers for the souls of the faithful departed in the church of Santa Ana where the funerals are to be held, in conformity with the distinct regulation, and in the chapel of the cemetery, and similarly for all who contemplate the Sacred Mysteries of the Passion of Our Lord Jesus Christ by each of the Stations of the Cross in the mentioned portico and also for those who, while passing by said cemeteries, lift their hearts to God, asking His Holy Majesty to give benediction and peace to the souls of the dead, and

finally we give the same favor [forty days indulgence] to all
people who in the expressed places bring to mind even if for
a brief moment, the certainty of death, in whose recollection
one must scorn the moments of the present and place one's
attention on the eternity of the future.[50]

Having upset the spiritual equation with the removal of burials from
churches, the indulgences promised to restore balance.

While the bishop's language echoed seventeenth- and eighteenth-
century theological treatises and manuals on the good death, his
emphasis on contemplation and reflection suggested an affinity for the
reformed piety that some in Mexico's and Spain's ecclesiastical hierarchy had begun promoting in the second half of the eighteenth century.[51] Though this interiorized piety rejected the baroque dependence
on external, sensual means to incite the faithful, Olivares suggested
that the cemeteries themselves serve as visual spurs to piety, much like
the dead in the church floors had. In the bishop's estimation, the expul-
sion of burials to cemeteries should not strip the living of their connection to the dead. In fact, the cemeteries presented new opportunities to
contemplate death and assist the souls of the dead. Significantly,
Bishop Olivares encouraged both contemplation and ironically—given
the concern over putrid exhalations—physical proximity to the cemeteries. Expelling burials did not mean that death lost its spiritual place
in the community. Death still instructed and gave sober pause to the
most modern of Spain's subjects, who, rejecting the vanity of baroque
deathways, encountered new inducements to pious meditation in the
cemeteries. Olivares insisted that traditional spiritual values could
accommodate the new world view and the new burial sites.

RESISTING REFORM

Far from the cathedral chapter in Durango, New Mexicans adhered to
their traditional spiritual values by continuing in their former practices. The Franciscans, who retained their leadership in New Mexican
religious life until the second decade of the nineteenth century,
ignored the reforms. Their failure to comply with the law reveals itself
in the burial registers; when indicating burial location, none of the
friars observed a shift to cemetery burials. Burial preferences
expressed in wills remained constant throughout this period of repe-
titious royal decrees and orders. While making a will did not guarantee observance of one's wishes, wills do provide strong evidence of

popular opinion. Even in the capital city of Santa Fe, where one might expect greater adherence to the law, wealthy and poor testators alike disregarded the new cemetery regulations. A few individuals charged their heirs or the officiating priest with choosing the exact burial location, but even those who entrusted the living to make this all-important decision indicated in which church they wished to be interred. Despite their prohibition, burials continued apace beneath the floors of New Mexico's church and chapels.

With the exception of the new piety's promoters in Veracruz, non-compliance and resistance seem to have been common in much of Mexico. During an 1825 epidemic, for example, Chihuahuan authorities worried about the safety of burying the dead inside the city's churches, indicating that little had changed there since the ban. Even before the 1804 decree, residents in Mexico City had protested the reforms with petitions, protests, and flight to outlying towns to secure a church burial. A royal order in 1791 had tried to reduce tensions by permitting those with acquired burial privileges in churches and convents to maintain these rights. Notwithstanding this concession, Mexico City's ayuntamiento opposed the construction of cemeteries for financial reasons. Not until the 1830s did the metropolis construct the much-discussed general cemetery on the city's outskirts.[52] Before this, despite the efforts of enlightened elites, only during epidemics did cemeteries take precedence over churches for interment, and "as soon as the epidemic had run its course the people reverted to their previous practice."[53]

The unpopularity of the burial reforms and the difficulty in implementing them across the span of Spanish America necessitated their repetition even as power shifted. In November 1813, the Cortes of Cadiz ordered that within the space of a month, all places lacking cemeteries begin making the necessary arrangements for construction of provisional cemeteries until such time as permanent ventilated cemeteries could be constructed.[54] The state promised to hold accountable anyone thwarting this initiative, regardless of class. Given the many issues facing the cortes, the fact that burial location became the subject of discussion demonstrates the degree to which funeral pageantry and mortuary customs historically had reinforced the social order. Establishing control over the dead provided a means of sacralizing and solidifying the new authorities' jurisdiction over the living.

After the monarchy's return, Fernando VII (1814–33) in 1819 issued still another cedula banning the practice of church burials.[55] It was this last cedula that finally elicited a response from New Mexico and resulted in real changes in New Mexican deathways. In December 1819,

Durango's bishop forwarded this most recent decree throughout the Archdiocese of Durango. Henceforth, corpses were to be removed in a public cart to the cemeteries that would be established away from towns. The dead would no longer be:

> interred six, eight, up to ten in a single plot, without separation of the sexes, burying secular and regular clergy with those who are not [clergy] in the same space and mixing up the cadavers and respectable remains of those anointed by God with others in the same space, which the sacred rites prohibit.[56]

Secular and regular clergy were to be buried along with the members of the confraternities of San Pedro, the poor, and outsiders in the vaults of the confraternities from this point forward. Significantly, those whose families had special vaults in parish churches, monasteries, or convents could maintain these places of distinction. Persons "of virtue or saintliness" were exempt from outdoor burial as well, provided that priests formally established proof of virtue or miracles.[57] The decree therefore reinstated the social privileges that the previous legislation had rescinded, no doubt reassuring elites and ecclesiastics throughout the Americas.

Referring to the documents of 1787 and 1804, the cedula reminded the parishes of the rules to observe in establishing the new cemeteries. Space should be adequate to accommodate burials anticipated in an average five-year period "with sufficient land for extraordinary circumstances."[58] In estimating the land needed, the king instructed that parishes calculate two bodies per burial plot; after three years these would have decayed sufficiently to allow for reuse of the grave. Like the discourse on public health, the approach here was rational and scientific, with demographics and the rate of decomposition considered in planning the new suburban cemeteries.

Instructions from Bishop Juan Francisco Márquez de Castañiza of Durango accompanied the king's decree and stressed the need for obedience out of respect for God, to safeguard public health, and "out of the loyalty owed to the sovereign."[59] Most interesting were the bishop's comments on theology. He wrote that if people had a true understanding of death, they would recognize the irrelevance of burial location, and he encouraged his flock to view the changes as a useful reminder of the body's nothingness. Less than two years before Mexican independence, Márquez de Castañiza contended that obedience to God's appointed on earth, the king of Spain, was far more critical to ensuring one's salvation than where one was interred.[60] Again, parish priests played the role of messengers and bore the responsibility of instructing the faithful, communicating to them:

> how indecorous it is that in the temple of our Lord, which should be adorned with the most exquisite of our decorations and perfumed with the most delicate incenses, one experiences the rather frequent indecencies of running into the bones of the dead in the churches, and one is unable to enter them [the churches] because of the terrible odor of decaying cadavers in the air, resulting in humors that are breathed in and constantly threaten the health of the towns.[61]

Echoing the discourse on hygiene, Márquez de Castañiza described how the darkness and poor ventilation that characterized most churches only exacerbated the dangers wrought by the dead's noxious emissions, preventing the gases' dissipation and allowing them to linger within the highly trafficked churches.

By now, the insalubrious nature of church burials had been communicated to priests and parishioners for decades; however, only after this most recent decree did resistance or obedience replace noncompliance in New Mexico. In several cases, however, issues aside from burial location were also at stake. For most parishes, for example, finances remained a sore point. Many churches had fallen into disrepair and lacked sufficient vestments, missals, and other essentials for performing the mass and administering the sacraments. Naturally, parishioners did not wish to pay more to the clergy than they already did. Many priests already thought themselves woefully undercompensated and could foresee a decrease in income with the new cemeteries, since burials there lacked the spiritual value or social cachet of burials near an altar or in a chapel. Like the actions of Santa Cruz and Taos rebels in 1837, New Mexicans' resistance to the reforms suggests the important role that individual parish priests might play, as well as the host of social issues that the reforms raised. This is nowhere more evident than in the Tewa pueblo of San Juan de los Caballeros, where the reforms underscored ethnic and class tensions suggestive of the fissures in vecino-pueblo relations visible elsewhere.

Located just north of Santa Cruz, about two hundred Indians called San Juan home in the early nineteenth century, and approximately seventeen hundred españoles lived nearby.[62] Dissatisfied with what they saw as their priest's selective application of the law, San Juan alcalde José Manuel Archuleta and two other community members in 1821 signed a petition addressed to the highest civil authority in the region, Comm. Gen. Alejo García Conde. The complainants alleged that Fray Mariano José Sánchez Vergara, who had served in New Mexico's different missions since 1794, only buried the community's poor outside while continuing to inter wealthy residents within the church. The authors poignantly asked, "Where does the idea come from, that he who is poor shall cease to love the temple?"[63] Further arguing that the cemetery had been frozen for six months and the ground was therefore impenetrable, they implored García Conde to remedy the situation in favor of religion and peace in the community. The commander general forwarded the complaints to the custos, who began judicial proceedings the following year, with three of San Juan's leaders coming forward to enumerate the community's problems with the friar.[64] They said that he refused to bury Indians inside the church, citing their failure to pay, and only allowed vecinos the privilege of church burial. They alleged, furthermore, that the friar deprived Indians of the tolling of bells, the high processional cross, and the cope—funerary extras that exacted additional expenditures, per the schedule of fees. San Juan Pueblo's concern with all the trappings of Roman Catholic ritual suggests that, far from being the heretics that Sánchez Vergara reportedly took them for, the Indians were indeed Christians. In fact, they had embraced baroque Roman Catholicism and its sensory trappings, which probably resonated with their own cultural and religious traditions. Their dissatisfaction with the friar stemmed from his refusal to grant them the trimmings required for an elaborate funeral and a burial within the church.

The unfolding testimony revealed that disposal of the dead represented just one of the community's concerns. In addition, the residents of San Juan charged the friar with physically abusing Indians on several occasions. Once, Sánchez Vergara allegedly had beaten an Indian whom the priest had ordered to dig a grave for a vecino's dead child. Afraid to be alone in the church at night, the Indian left the sanctuary, intending to return in the morning to do the job. When he found out, the friar allegedly pummeled the man. Others testified that Sánchez Vergara constantly harangued the Indians, accusing them of worshipping rocks and performing witchcraft. He would not let the Indians dance or participate in devotions to the saints, and—in front of the entire congregation, which one of the witnesses found most distressing—declared the Indians worthless and lazy. When giving his testimony, Sánchez Vergara freely admitted to the charges of corporal punishment, contending its occasional necessity. He also acknowledged preaching against the worship of rocks and feathers, claiming that the Indians venerated them as gods, not being true Christians at all. Though he did not contest most of the allegations, Sánchez Vergara did deny that he had buried anyone inside the church since the law banning the practice. Unfortunately, the friar, like his predecessors, was extremely vague in his burial book entries, and it is therefore impossible to determine where the truth lay in this case or establish long-term patterns of mortuary practices in San Juan.

The San Juan case highlights broader social changes taking place in New Mexico. Even before the formal abolition of their protected status shortly before independence, New Mexico's Pueblos found themselves increasingly at odds with the rapidly growing vecino population, which used legal and illegal means to gain access to pueblo lands.[65] In addition to their grievances against the friar, the petition that San Juan's leadership first addressed to Commander General García Conde expressed concern over threats to reduce pueblo landholdings and increase the first fruits they had to pay. Though the subsequent proceedings remain silent on these points, concentrating instead on the alleged abuse, land and economic issues likely underlay community tensions. Conflicts between vecinos and pueblos rose in the late eighteenth and early nineteenth centuries, and many of the legal proceedings after 1810 stemmed from pueblo-vecino land disputes.[66] Even the subtext of the clash with the friar appears economic and social in nature: the Indians contended that the vecinos received preferential treatment and the priest shamed the Indians before the vecino congregation.

Notwithstanding the apparent tensions between vecinos and pueblos, San Juan's leadership turned to two vecinos to assist the pueblo in its protest. When they decided the time had come to voice their concerns, the leadership solicited the assistance of a sympathetic vecino to travel to Durango and appeal to the bishop on the pueblo's behalf. Vecino Ignacio Madrid, selected in part because he knew the way to Durango, claimed familiarity with both the civil and ecclesiastical hierarchies and agreed to help the pueblo navigate the legal system. In Madrid, the pueblo hoped it had found a new advocate.

San Juan's leadership contended they had no other recourse, having been left "orphaned" since the death of the former *protector de indios*, the crown-appointed official who defended the interests of Indian communities in Spanish courts. Actually, this was only part of the story. The protector to whom the Indians referred had died a few years earlier, and his replacement probably did not sympathize with

San Juan's plight, for the new protector—Ignacio Sánchez Vergara—was none other than the despised friar's brother. Appointed to the post by the Audiencia of Guadalajara in 1817, he served as protector until a royal decree abolished the office shortly before independence, in 1821. According to San Juan's complaint, Sánchez Vergara the protector did not defend the pueblo's interests. Perhaps he did not even believe in the need for the post to which he had been named; he had once argued that the Indians of New Mexico no longer needed special status before the law, having already "emerged from their minority."[67]

Lacking a protector to represent their interests, and claiming only a limited knowledge of Spanish and the law, San Juan's leadership had no choice but to turn to Spanish vecinos to access the legal system. Once they had, their complaints were taken seriously and duly investigated. The following year, San Juan's leaders succeeded in ridding themselves of the friar. He moved on to a new post in Abiquiú, where in short order several citizens accused Sánchez Vergara of numerous "tyrannies," including leaving the dead unburied up to three days.[68] In addition to demonstrating vecino-pueblo tensions in this period, the San Juan case presages the more general social stratification increasingly evident in New Mexican mortuary practices, which would contribute to the 1837 Chimayó Rebellion.

Though decades passed before any New Mexican communities constructed true suburban cemeteries, priests in many settlements responded to the 1819 legislation with at least selective obedience. Priests increasingly were disinclined to bury the dead within either mission or parish churches. In Santa Fe, the parish priest hewed to the spirit of the law, while unhappy parishioners resisted the reforms as best they could. The family of don Mateo García, for example, insisted that his corpse be interred beneath the floors of the parish church dedicated to St. Francis. Though lacking embalming and refrigeration, the cadaver remained unburied for days that May of 1822, as the family pressured the priest to permit the traditional burial. Cura Juan Tomás Terrazas, however, eventually won out against the wishes of the family. He buried don Mateo in the campo santo next to the parish church, where he would continue to inter most of the parish dead.[69] Guadalupe church burials, however, were another matter. Santa Fe burial registers from 1816 to 1851 show numerous interments within the Guadalupe church.[70] The cost, however, increased considerably—to forty or fifty pesos—at the same time that the parish received only three pesos for a cemetery burial. While in 1816 don Pedro Pino paid to bury María Dolores, an Indian serving in

his household, within the Guadalupe chapel, thirty years later servants and the poor were unlikely to find rest beneath its floors.[71]
Archaeological evidence supports this finding, as the Guadalupe
burials were richer in burial goods and coffin embellishments than
those of their contemporaries interred in cemeteries in Alameda and
La Garita, Santa Fe.[72] Events in San Juan, therefore, differed little from
what began happening elsewhere in the region. While in San Juan—
which, recall, was surrounded and outnumbered by Spanish settlers
in neighboring communities—race allegedly determined who could
buy into the new burial hierarchy, in other communities wealth strat-
ified the dead, excluding most from the churches.

After decades of similar legislation that should have acted as a
warning if not actually an impetus for change, the 1819 decree signaled a jarring break from custom for the residents of Santa Cruz de
la Cañada as well. For more than one hundred years, Santa Cruz had
interred most of its dead within the parish church; in fact, only two
burials—notably, both of infants—had taken place in the campo
santo in the two years before Márquez de Castañiza's orders came.[73]
In the same month that the decree arrived, the once-meticulous Cura
Juan Tomás Terrazas became sloppy in recording burial location; suddenly, he was vague in his notations or did not note burial location at
all. This silence lasted for a short time even after Vicar Juan Manuel de
Jesús Rada replaced Terrazas the following month. Though perhaps
deliberately oblique in his citations, Terrazas in time reconciled himself—if not his parishioners—to the changes. With the charitable burial of a free mulatta, María Ramona—if not sooner—the parish in May
1821 began to bury its dead in the campo santo. Underscoring his personal commitment to the reforms, Vicar Rada even informed the
parish's mayordomo in writing that there were to be no exceptions to
cemetery burial, regardless of social status.[74] After just four years,
however, opposition replaced obedience.

In 1825, the ayuntamiento of Santa Cruz made a last-ditch effort
to end the practice of burying their dead in the cemetery. Four years
after Spain's rule had ended and one year after Mexico wrote its constitution, the ayuntamiento questioned the validity of the burial
reforms. Optimistic that independence or perhaps New Mexico's new
status as a territory of the Mexican nation had nullified the reforms,
the town's leadership said that "within all the residents of the parish a
general discontent and disconsolation have reigned" since the ban on
church burials.[75] The townspeople had not buried even a single
corpse in the church floor in four years and five months. Yet only with

"pain in our hearts" did the townsfolk obediently bury their dead in the cemetery; this anguish impelled the ayuntamiento to ask Vicar Rada for permission to revert to traditional burial practices.[76]

Notwithstanding the reference to the town's sorrow, the ayuntamiento firmly grounded its case in reason and hygiene, a language they hoped would resonate with the ecclesiastical hierarchy that comprised their real audience. Reassuring Rada that "few people die in New Mexico," and "little or no pestilence is seen here because of the natural health of the country," the ayuntamiento informed the parish priest of the adversity they had encountered in adhering to the reforms.[77] The layer of ice covering the ground during the six months of winter impeded outdoor burials, so only with the greatest trouble could the community dig graves. Forced to work outdoors in the harsh climate, the reforms actually jeopardized the health of the unfortunate gravediggers, whose tools sometimes even broke from the severe cold.[78] Finally, turning the very logic of the legislation against itself, the ayuntamiento maintained that because of these difficulties, corpses lay unburied for long periods of time; here resided the real public-health danger.

In addition to adopting the language of hygiene to achieve its own ends, the ayuntamiento clearly sought to capitalize on presumed ignorance of New Mexico. Had the king been aware of New Mexican circumstances, they implied, he never would have extended his ban on indoor burials to these distant lands, where the long, arduous winters made outdoor burials nearly impossible. Santa Cruz's claim of harsh winters echoed San Juan Pueblo's similar contention a few years earlier. While both communities may have exaggerated these pronouncements somewhat, their words also suggest that the Little Ice Age did indeed last until the mid-nineteenth century.[79] Whatever the case, the town asserted that its location distinguished it from the rest of Mexico and the king's decree had not taken into consideration the northern frontier's uniqueness. The ayuntamiento insisted, furthermore, that the region's climate made for little pestilence and few deaths, clearly hoping to undermine the environmental concerns so integral to contemporary theories of disease.

Although Santa Cruz boasted few literate citizens, the letter indicates that the town's leaders fully grasped the reasoning behind the reforms. Indeed, by cleverly manipulating the very enlightened logic that formed the basis for the legislation, the town sought to secure its exemption. Employing reasons that held greater sway than tradition and faith in an increasingly secular world, the letter described several public-health dangers facing Santa Cruz in light of the reforms. The ayuntamiento also professed concern at the impact on church revenues, which had waned with the inauguration of cheaper burials in the campo santo.

Though addressed to their parish priest, in reality the letter targeted a more distant audience. Vicar Rada would have been well aware of Santa Cruz's circumstances, since funerary and burial practices fell under his authority.[80] In any event, Rada was not new to the issue; just before his relocation to New Mexico he had served as parish priest in Canelas, Sonora. During his tenure there he had voiced some concerns with the reforms and told the bishop that it was simply impossible to comply with what he otherwise termed their "opportune, wise, and canonical disposition."[81] Financial hardship ranked foremost among his concerns for the parish, which could barely subsist on its existing income. The tremendous poverty of the people of Canelas made it impossible to secure either voluntary labor or materials from the community for the ventilated cemetery's construction. Like his predecessors, while in Canelas, Rada continued to inter the dead within the church or campo santo, according to their ability to pay.

The role Rada played in the petition sent by Santa Cruz's ayuntamiento remains unclear, but his concern with the parish coffers and the tone of his earlier correspondence suggest that, at the very least, he may have encouraged residents to articulate their displeasure in writing; certainly, the ayuntamiento's detailed description of the situation in Santa Cruz belies the fact that the letter was directed to him. Powerless to grant an exception to legislation that he perhaps found equally odious, Rada forwarded the community's concerns to his superiors in Durango. The pragmatic, legalistic response affirmed the validity of the new ways. Santa Cruz would in no way be exempt from the law, which had been adopted throughout Spanish America. The benefits of ventilated cemeteries outweighed any challenges the community faced.[82]

Shortly after Santa Cruz's failed appeal, Bishop Márquez de Castañiza sent the visitor general, Agustín Fernández de San Vicente, to New Mexico in 1826. After secularizing the parishes of Abiquiú, Belén, Taos, San Juan, and El Vado, Fernández de San Vicente disclosed that it was "foremost among my duties . . . to see to the establishment of ventilated cemeteries throughout this territory, which has been repeatedly ordered."[83] Fernández de San Vicente sent a circular instructing all the parishes of the changes. While referring only vaguely to "the ills" that the government sought to avoid with this legislation, by now it had to be crystal clear precisely what these words meant.[84] The key difference this time was that Fernández de

San Vicente was not content to settle for halting church burials and interring the dead in graveyards contiguous to churches, a tactic that some communities had used to sidestep the real issue. He actually expected parishes to construct ventilated cemeteries outside the town limits and cease burying any of the dead within settled areas.

The bishop's renewed interest in the reforms and Fernández de San Vicente's efforts ultimately resulted in changes across New Mexico, though some people continued trying to evade them. In some cases, they enjoyed short-term success, but the combination of legislation, more careful oversight from Durango, and time gradually wore away at resistant priests and their parishioners.[85] The variety of resistance and reasons proffered speaks to the diversity and creativity of New Mexicans. That the legislation chafed northern New Mexicans in particular becomes apparent not only in the formal protests of San Juan and Santa Cruz but also in parish correspondence.

Placed in the difficult position of implementing the unpopular and income-threatening legislation, many clergy—both secular and regular—undoubtedly found themselves torn as well. In general, however, it appears that despite their much smaller numbers, the secular clergy led the way in implementing the reforms in New Mexico. Though the crown had pushed for burial reform since the late eighteenth century, only with the introduction of the secular clergy—who took control in these key Spanish settlements—did New Mexican mortuary practices change in the 1820s and 1830s. Most of these men came from northern Mexico, including New Mexico. Trained at the seminary in Durango, they likely were exposed to the new piety as well as ideas of hygiene during their education. Considerably younger than the aging Franciscans who remained in New Mexico, these priests may have been less married to the traditional ways and perhaps felt some loyalty as well as obedience to the bishops—Bishop Márquez de Castañiza and later Bishop Zubiría—who ordained them in Durango and supported the reforms. The diocesan clergy arrived in New Mexico under the authority of the bishop of Durango, in contrast to the Spanish-born Franciscans, who historically had resisted Durango's control.

That the diocesan clergy served in many instances as the impetus for obedience to the twenty-year-old burial reforms is apparent in the case of Albuquerque, which illustrates the general trend. Fray Ambrosio Guerra had ministered to Albuquerque's parishioners for more than thirty years, with only a few interruptions. He consistently interred the dead within the church dedicated to San Felipe Neri, dutifully noting in the sacramental records where in the church floor they lay and whether or not they had received the last rites. He favored the transept for the burial of foundlings and other children, regardless of their ethnicity and their parents' ability to pay. He only occasionally buried people in the campo santo, though some charity cases wound up there over the years. Sometimes he identified these people as Utes or Comanches, but frequently he did not mention ethnicity, suggesting that they were in that increasingly generic category of castas who self-identified as españoles. Relocated to Sandia Pueblo at the end of 1817, his successor, Cura José Francisco Leyva y Rosas almost overnight began to use the campo santo for virtually all interments. When Guerra later took over for Leyva, he followed the secular priest's lead and relied almost exclusively on the campo santo.

Though the sudden break with tradition probably generated discontent in the parish, the documents do not provide any hint of dissent until a decade later, when the Fernández de San Vicente circular arrived in 1826. Leyva had returned again to San Felipe Neri by now, and he wrote for advice to Cura José Luis Rodríguez of Santa Fe. Though his letter to Rodríguez does not survive, we can surmise his concerns from the response he received. Rodríguez emphatically instructed Leyva to follow the official position on cemeteries expressed in the Fernández de San Vicente circular. He told Leyva to conform to the regulations as soon as possible and directed him to communicate to his parishioners the reforms' many benefits:

> It is necessary that you place yourself in accord with this illustrious constitutional government and that you rush to take the measures you see as prudent in order to expedite compliance with the circular promulgated by this government on May 10. If you encounter any difficulties, it is your duty as parish priest to smooth out these difficulties through your prudent exhortations to your parishioners, making them see the benefits that all will enjoy with the continuation of the campo santo in a ventilated site.[86]

As parish priest, he reminded Leyva, it was his responsibility to eliminate opposition and make sure that the reforms succeeded in their principal goal of "protecting the towns from corruption."[87] Just as under Spanish rule, priests represented the front line of promoting the transformation in burial geography after independence.

The Mexican government added to the considerable volume of legislation on the topic of subfloor burials by issuing yet another circular, which reached New Mexico by July 1833. Though the notice targeted a practice not even available locally—that of burying children inside religious communities—it reveals that despite the erosion of parish priests' authority in the late colonial period and the great anticlericalism of the liberals who in 1833 held power, the state still relied on clerical authority to promote its agenda. The government instructed priests to redouble their efforts so as to protect the public welfare and ensure the proper respect for places of worship. Liberal Vice Pres. Valentín Gómez Farías, himself a medical doctor, demanded that all ecclesiastical and civil authorities enforce existing religious and civil laws with greater zeal, or else risk cholera and the other epidemics plaguing Cuba.[88] Despite the cholera epidemic's arrival in Mexico that same year and the ongoing promulgation of decrees and circulars emphasizing the importance of the "new" regulations, not just New Mexicans but rural mestizo communities and Indian towns in Mexico continued to oppose burial reform.[89] Despite changing elite conceptions, popular pious practices remained as strong as ever.[90]

While available to only a few people, burial in a private chapel or in a chapel that had no resident priest allowed some to circumvent the mandates. Like the production of santos in the late eighteenth and early nineteenth centuries, private and public chapels proliferated in New Mexico in this period, spurred as much by economic growth as by population growth.[91] Sometimes family chapels offered a final resting place, but in most cases, community chapels served the purpose in areas lacking a permanent clerical presence. In some cases, priests who buried their parish dead obediently in the campo santo had no problem burying the dead in a chapel when going elsewhere in their jurisdiction. Thus in rural areas like Tomé and Alameda, near Albuquerque but far enough away to have their own chapels, the traditional burial ways endured even after 1819. Private chapels, which had not been specifically mentioned in any decree from either the crown or the Mexican government, finally came under attack, too. In 1841, burials in private chapels in Belén raised the ire of some church officials. Reminding Belén's residents that the church had "considerable moral force" at its disposable to ensure compliance with its precepts, Cura José de Jesús Luján of Santa Fe warned that burial inside chapels must immediately cease.[92]

Although he possessed several private chapels, one of Santa Fe's most generous church benefactors had given so much to the parish church that he felt entitled to burial within its chapel dedicated to San José.[93] In 1797, Bishop Olivares had granted merchant-rancher Antonio José Ortiz and his family members the right to burial within the chapel

Figure 3
Burial Locations Requested in Wills, 1700-1899

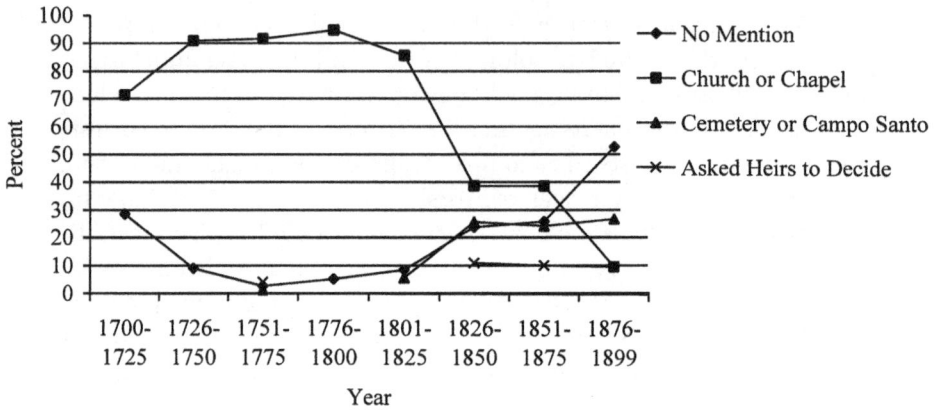

in gratitude for Ortiz's considerable philanthropy.[94] Ortiz had person-
ally assumed responsibility for the parroquia's rebuilding, renovation,
roof, bell towers, cemetery walls, a room for the chapel of the Third
Order, and a graveyard. As for the San José chapel, Ortiz had cleaned
and decorated it "exclusively with the objective that my body and that
of my spouse, my children, and all my family, be interred therein."[95]
Ortiz's complaint years later centered on the priest's insistence that
Ortiz pay for his and his family's interment, which violated Ortiz's
agreement with the bishop. Though it has been reported that his family buried Ortiz below the altar of the Rosario chapel in 1806 and his
wife, Rosa Bustamante, beneath the altar of the chapel dedicated to
the Virgin of Guadalupe adjoining their home on San Francisco Street,
the burial records are actually silent as to the location of either burial.[96] It is in fact likely that Ortiz prevailed and that in the end both he
and his bride of fifty-one years were interred in the San José chapel.
Though in his will—dated months before his correspondence with the
bishop—Ortiz requested burial in his home's private chapel, his wife
almost a decade later requested burial in the San Jose chapel, suggesting that this is where her husband's remains had found rest.

Though without question an exceptional case, even people of lesser
means and status preferred the traditional church burial well into the
mid-nineteenth century. While survivors were not always able to honor
their dying wishes, the baroque ideal of church burial endured through
the Mexican period regardless of gender, urban versus rural residency,
and season of the year. Of those who left wills, 93 percent specifically

Figure 4
Burial Locations Recorded in Albuquerque, Santa Fe, and Santa Cruz Burial
Registers, 1730-1850

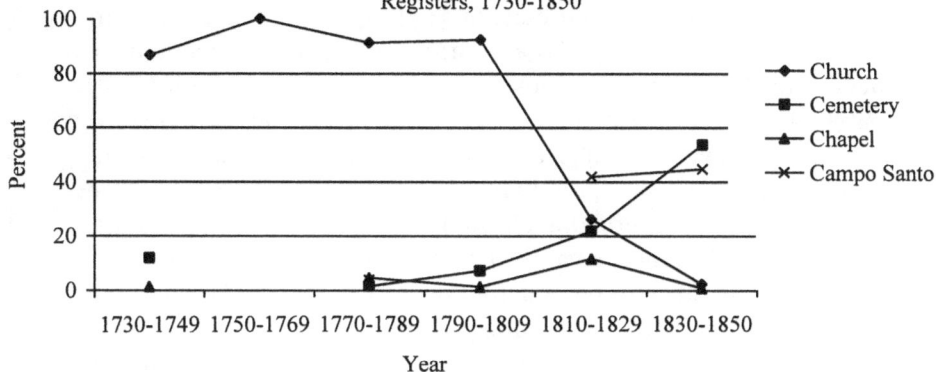

asked for a church burial from 1750 to 1821. After independence, this number fell radically, but even from 1822 through 1850 fully 42 percent of testators requested church burials, and only 18 percent requested a cemetery burial. The remainder left the decision up to their heirs (9 percent) or made no mention of burial location at all (21 percent), the latter being the most significant departure from the past. (The wills that the other 10 percent of testators left were vague or unclear as to intention.) Thus, notwithstanding the growing contact with outsiders with the opening of the Santa Fe Trail and the ongoing process of parish secularization, a significant proportion of people still sought burial as close as possible to the altar, in a favorite chapel or church. Although by the 1830s most of the population had to be well aware of the growing impossibility of fulfilling such requests, their wills testify to the enduring resonance of baroque ideals and corroborate studies finding that New Mexico in this period experienced a heightened religiosity, evidenced in santo production, church construction, and Penitente activities.[97] In communities where no resident priest resided, or where the priest was temporarily absent, parishioners resisted the reforms by burying the dead independently, within the church.[98]

Despite pockets of strong resistance, New Mexico did see changes. Though almost half of testators still elected interment within their parish church through at least the 1850s, at least among authorities the reforms had taken firm root, as evidenced by the burial registers, which show a radical shift away from church burial by 1821. Equally significant is the fact that people began removing themselves from the postmortem decision-making process entirely, evidence perhaps of a grudging concession to the new ways. Close to 40 percent of testators from 1822 through 1850 did not identify burial location at all, instead leaving the decision to their heirs or skipping this clause altogether.

Since the beginning of the reform movement, enforcement had been selective, contingent on local conditions, the inclination of the parish priest, and to a lesser degree, the identity of the deceased. Even as efforts to evade royal decrees against indoor burials wore thin, exceptions to the new paradigm emerged. Though wealth increasingly became the criteria that allowed one a church burial, no guarantees existed. Manuel Anaya, for example, left a generous bequest of silver coin to the church but found eternal rest in Albuquerque's campo santo in 1821.[99] That same year, the priest buried the unmarried María Toribia inside the parish church, beneath the choir, without explanation.[100] Despite his otherwise strict adherence to the burial reforms—he buried far more than 99 percent of parishioners in the cemetery—in 1829, Cura Antonio José Martínez buried his mother, María del Carmel, in the nave of the Taos church. He justified this act by noting that "the sepulcher belonged to her ancestors, her dead husband was in it, and she was the mother of the parish priest."[101] While the decrees prohibiting burial within churches made Martínez at least pause to justify his decision, whatever her qualities, it seems Martínez knew full well that the laws would not support a church burial in this case. His indignation with the actions of Taos rebels a few years later is somewhat ironic given that they only wanted their dead to receive the same treatment his mother had.

The tensions articulated by San Juan Pueblo in the 1820s appeared throughout New Mexico's parishes by the Territorial period. Now, only those with considerable influence or capital merited a privileged church burial. Bishop José Antonio Laureano de Zubiría y Escalante practically codified the shift in the once-querulous parish of Santa Cruz de la Cañada. During his 1850 visit, Zubiría granted the priest permission to bury people within the church if the mourners could pay eighteen to twenty-five pesos, reasoning that Mexican law no longer applied under U.S. authorities. A few years later, Bishop Jean-Baptiste Lamy confirmed the twenty-five peso cost for a church burial, which he observed did not include the fees for the parish priest.[102] By this time more than a generation had passed since the reforms' implementation, so of the few who could afford a church burial, even fewer elected one; a shift in thinking had taken effect in the space of a generation.[103] The same held true elsewhere in New Mexico. In Albuquerque, the only interment inside the church in 1848 was that of Isabel Luján, who died at age seventy-eight. Her burial cost twenty-five pesos, considerably more than the average cost of one to two pesos.[104] In 1852, the executors of the estate of Manuel Roybal and his wife María Manuela Trujillo paid twenty-five pesos for their burial in the church of Our Lady of Guadalupe in Pojoaque.[105] Thus, as a result of the reforms, New Mexicans in the end began to approximate the very hierarchical burials that had for so long characterized Spain and Mexico.

CEMETERY CONSTRUCTION

Even though compliance early on remained somewhat selective, by the 1820s some communities made at least half-hearted, plodding efforts to collect funds for cemetery construction. People may have been motivated in part by the realization that the small graveyards would not be able to keep up with their increased usage, especially as the population continued to grow. The walls of the campo santo around Santa Fe's parish church, for example, had to be extended, as Bruce Ellis writes. "By 1826, the tract [of the graveyard] had grown in stages from its 12-by-20 vara size [noted by Domínguez in 1776] to 26.25 by 61 varas east to west."[106] Added to the need for ventilated cemeteries in some communities was the requirement for separate cemeteries for the growing population of foreigners—non–Roman Catholics—who might die in the region.[107] In 1826, Santa Cruz's ayuntamiento ordered each head of household to contribute two hundred adobe bricks for the town's new ventilated cemetery.[108]

Of course, gathering adobes and collecting funds did not guarantee construction. Spurred on by citizens' complaints, Gov. José Antonio Chaves criticized the Santa Fe ayuntamiento in 1830 for its "inertia" on the matter of cemetery construction. Citing the fact that approximately fifteen hundred adobes had been gathered for the project, he concluded that only the council's apathy prevented the work's completion. After meeting in an extraordinary session, the outraged council notified Chaves that in a republic, the ayuntamiento could not force anyone to work on the cemetery and that up until that point they had been unable to contract any bricklayers to work on the job.[109] Three years later, the ayuntamiento remained in the discussion phase of cemetery construction. Though it had collected a considerable amount of money, no cemetery of any kind had been built, according to the cabildo records.[110] An impending ecclesiastical visit seems to have given the project the needed momentum, however, for when Bishop Zubiría visited Santa Fe in October 1833, he commented on the presence of a new campo santo.[111] Though burials had not commenced, the chapel had been built already, for the bishop used it as a point of reference in dictating how to divide the cemetery in sections reserved for children and adults.

By the 1840s, the parish priest routinely recorded burials "in the graveyard of this city of Santa Fe."[112] This was almost certainly the same cemetery that a construction crew in 2003 unwittingly unearthed in a residential neighborhood north of the city's central plaza, leading the Museum of New Mexico's Office of Archaeological Studies (OAS) to excavate over a two-year period the complete or partial remains of thirty-eight bodies. In his 1833 description of the cemetery, Bishop Zubiría wrote in part that "the cemetery shall be divided by a line from the door to the left-hand boundary of the chapel, leaving the northern section for burial of children and the other section for adults. Then, moving below the chapel to the door to the cemetery, it will be divided in six sections."[113] According to H. Wolcott Toll, this sketch matches what the OAS found at the site, which would have been north of the line Zubiría described and explains the overwhelming presence of children in the excavated section. The Archdiocese of Santa Fe stated at the time of the excavation that it possessed no record of the cemetery; the 1846 Gilmer map, however, indicates the presence of both the cemetery and a chapel, and the OAS found an 1885–86 map indicating the Roman Catholic Church's ownership of the land.[114] The archaeologists' preliminary findings indicated that the earliest burials uncovered dated to the 1830s to 1840s, suggesting that this was in fact the site of the city's first ventilated cemetery.[115]

No substantive change took place in Albuquerque for several decades, though the bishop likewise issued detailed instructions for a new cemetery during his visit in August 1833. The grounds were to be divided into sections, each of which would command a different price, from free charitable burials up to six pesos. Although Bishop Zubiría never dictated the actual location of the cemetery, he instructed the parish to identify someone who "being familiar with the cemetery is able to designate burial sites, in order to avoid the danger of opening some graves prematurely when the cadavers are still able to cause infection through their decomposition."[116] The caretaker's compensation would be 10 percent of all fees collected, the plot of his choice, and a complimentary burial for himself, his wife, and their children. More than fifteen years later, however, Albuquerque's leadership remained in the planning stages. Despite this impressive foot-dragging, it is significant that no one proffered arguments about the relative merits of establishing a ventilated cemetery. Agreed on the importance of the matter, the question only remained as to who would build the cemetery. Someone proposed that the community employ its most impoverished members—who would likely be buried free of charge in the new cemetery, anyway—to build the cemetery, thereby preventing them from becoming burdens on the parish church.[117] What came of this project ultimately remains unclear, for the city records are silent on the question of cemeteries. Thus it may be that the first true suburban cemetery in Albuquerque was that of Santa Bárbara, inaugurated with its first interment in 1870.[118]

At the nexus of public law and faith, in this most intimate and intensely personal of matters, it took considerable ecclesiastical and civil effort to change New Mexican customs. People resisted according to the local climate and the pressures from authorities in efforts to negotiate an acceptable solution. Priests sluggishly implemented burial reform because of their immediate financial concerns and the measure's unpopularity. Harder to document is the falsification or deliberate ambiguity of burial records.[119] Outright opposition through legal and extralegal means was popular in Santa Cruz and Taos. Individuals also resisted and negotiated. Already enjoying a relatively democratic burial system, New Mexicans could not be expected to embrace the reforms on the basis of egalitarianism as some in Mexico had done. The very selective implementation of the reforms might incite protest, as in the case of San Juan de los Caballeros.

As in other matters, the church hierarchy ultimately proved flexible and understanding of local conditions in its application of the model. The poverty of some parishes seems to have exempted them from establishing true suburban cemeteries. In Socorro, for example, Bishop Zubiría's chief concern was with the absence of windows in the church and the resultant filth from the many swallows that flew about. Windows and a baptismal font most occupied the notes of his visit there, and despite his obvious personal commitment to the "new" cemeteries, he made no mention of them in Socorro and other poor settlements. Bishop Zubiría likewise offered no criticism of the fact that the Santa Cruz church in 1833 used the churchyard for interments. Though this hardly followed the letter of the law, he undoubtedly recognized the impossibility of changing people overnight and seemed satisfied with the community's acceptance of outdoor burials—even if lacking a ventilated cemetery.

By the middle of the Mexican period, New Mexico had a two-tiered burial system in place.[120] Though still without true ventilated cemeteries, after the funeral mass people quickly exiled the dead from the church. The parish priest made exceptions for people who could pay, though, at least through the early Territorial period. Even in rural communities like Sapelló, near Las Vegas, though, burial inside the church was now reserved for those who could afford to pay inflated prices. Smaller communities like Sapelló might still allow subfloor burials, but the cost for burial in the nave of the church was twenty-five to fifty pesos, whereas for a mere six pesos, one could be buried in the church graveyard.[121] After half a century and three governments, concern for public health and hygiene had replaced salvation as the preeminent issue in burial. Some New Mexicans would request church burial as late as the 1890s, but for most of the population the baroque concern with burial in proximity to the saints had lost out to concern for safeguarding the living and pocketbook considerations. No longer integrated, the worlds of the living and the dead would continue to grow apart until cemeteries eventually came under civil authority by the end of the nineteenth century.

While the king and his ministers had sought through burial reform to apply a modern, enlightened approach to disease, power shaped the subtext of the debate over where to inter the dead. The state's efforts to control this most important of decisions formed a corollary to concomitant attempts—manifest in asylums, prisons, and streetlights—to maintain control of the living. As people increasingly questioned the social and political structures of the ancien régime, states across Europe extended their long-standing control of criminal and poor cadavers to all subjects. Legitimate official concern for public health entwined with the elusive need to control the body politic. Burial reform formed part of a larger process that proclaimed the ascendancy of doctors and affirmed changing notions of the constitution of authority and the individual's role in society. Shifting interment from churches to cemeteries, while potentially democratizing burial, also restricted the authority of parishes and localities as it undermined popular religious practices.

Furthermore, burial reform extended the reach of the state's jurisdiction over the individual beyond death. Just as families and individuals employed funerals to affirm their social authority, control over the body's disposal presented an opportunity for the state to assert its authority. While Thomas Laqueur contends that the funeral represents the "final pronouncement" on one's time on earth, in reality burial location serves as the ultimate, most enduring declaration of the individual in relation to the community.[122] By placing this most intimate of human activities under the aegis of the state, the enlightened Bourbon leadership and later the Mexican government, sought to usurp the traditional power of the parish church and the local community. In a time when death and its associated rites still fell within the cherished domain of families and communities, relinquishing control over burial location proved no small matter.

Realizing burial reform proved a process of ongoing negotiation that outlived the Spanish monarchy's control of the Americas. Each new decree underscored the inefficacy of earlier legislation. Whereas in central Mexico traditional elites headed the opposition when they felt their traditional privileges threatened, in New Mexico ordinary citizens, especially those in the Río Arriba, led the fight.[123] The viceroy in Mexico City, the bishop of Durango, Franciscan friars, secular clergy, and residents from New Mexico's villas and pueblos all engaged in a dialogue of power as they negotiated an acceptable space for the dead. While the 1837 rebels articulated the most aggressive position in these deliberations, the debate in a sense endured until the late nineteenth century, when the living finally relegated the dead to the new suburban cemeteries. Resistance to changes in burial location was grounded in popular piety but also had a firm basis in existing social, ethnic, and economic tensions. Far from isolated events, then, insurgents' extreme actions in 1837 formed part of a long-standing, emotional debate over where to inter the dead.

Transformations in the Second Half of the Nineteenth Century

I n 1857, long before early tourism promoters began extolling the virtues of New Mexico's healthy environment, encouraging those suffering from chronic ailments to visit its mineral springs and breathe its salubrious air, Massachusetts merchant John Kingsbury hoped that his wife Kate would benefit from Santa Fe's favorable environment. Though well aware of the risks of the long journey from Salem, he feared she would not survive another Massachusetts summer. In keeping with contemporary medical thought, a change of climate seemed to offer the only promise for her future, so the couple embarked for Santa Fe, where they had spent the first of their four years of marriage.

Crossing the plains in Kansas, however, young Kate succumbed to consumption and died. She arrived in Santa Fe eleven days later, encased in a metallic casket that her husband had hidden in the wagon train. Kingsbury buried his wife in the cemetery of the Independent Order of Odd Fellows, a secret fraternal organization of English origin established in Santa Fe in 1851.[1] Her obituary in the *Santa Fe Weekly Gazette* was suitably dramatic and melancholy, infused with the self-conscious sentimentality that characterized the

Northeast in this period. It contained all the necessary ingredients: the prior death of Kate Kingsbury's "darling little son," her own degenerating physical condition, and a detailed description of her beautiful death. This model of nineteenth-century sentimentality was complete with Kingsbury's decision to purchase the requisite paraphernalia for the cemetery. To properly honor her in the fashion of the time, he ordered an engraved white marble headstone, a footstone, and an iron fence to enclose the grave. These eventually came from the East, probably along the same route on which his wife had died.[2]

The events surrounding Kate Kingsbury's death are suggestive of the incipient changes in New Mexico in the second half of the nineteenth century. Kingsbury was part of a growing class of Anglo, Jewish, and other foreign merchants who would transform the New Mexican economy—and in turn, funerary practices—with goods provided by eastern manufacturers. His decision to bring a metal coffin from home on the journey to Santa Fe demonstrates not only his wife's frailty but also that Kingsbury coveted the latest in coffin technology. Though referred to as a coffin, the very fact that it was metallic indicates that it would have been classified as a "casket," a distinction that became increasingly important in the nineteenth century.[3] The word itself signaled a shift in values, ascribing as it did a new meaning to the corpse, which was encased like a jewel. A metal casket was an innovation even in the antebellum Northeast and would not have been available in New Mexico at this early date. Equally novel were the white marble grave markers and iron fencing that asserted individualism and demarcated one's property even in death. The cemetery where Kingsbury buried his beloved Kate also broke from New Mexican traditions. It was not part of any Roman Catholic church and had no religious affiliation at all but belonged to one of several fraternal orders that were "bastions of American culture" in Santa Fe facilitating political and economic alliances among non–Roman Catholics.[4]

The history of New Mexicans' evolving funerary customs in the second half of the nineteenth century is as much a history of business and economic enterprise as it is a social history. This is nowhere more evident than in Territorial newspapers, replete as they are with advertisements for coffins—often on the front page. As in much of the United States, the corpse itself began to become a commodity in this period. Practices that traditionally had been in the domestic sphere of women, such as cleaning and disposing of the corpse, eventually fell to a professional cadre of men. More often than not

19. Advertisement for "Professional Embalmer" appearing in *El Nuevo Mundo* (Albuquerque), July 9, 1898, image courtesy of New Mexico State University Library, Archives and Special Collections

they were transplants to New Mexico. Their names must have fallen clumsily off the tongues of Spanish speakers: Spiegelman, Derbyshire, Klattenhoff. Even the language of death changed, as New Mexicans added words like "undertaker," "embalmer," and "funeral director" to their growing English lexicon.

The attendant costs of burial reflected the changing notions of death. New Mexicans historically had counted on relatively inexpensive interments, unless their souls required an abundance of masses. A basic burial cost about four pesos in 1800, payable to the parish priest in some combination of wheat, corn, and chile. By the late nineteenth century, New Mexicans increasingly focused their resources on material goods rather than masses to help the soul. Instead of paying with grain or livestock for the manufactured coffins, printed funeral announcements, and fabric for mourning clothes, however, they now paid in cash. Without question, in rural communities little changed in this period, and even in urban areas not all could avail themselves of these new accouterments. For people who lived in areas with growing Anglo populations, though, even those who could not afford or who perhaps chose to reject these items could not fail to take notice of them.

New Mexico, then, was responding to conceptions of "domesticated death," which emerged in the northeastern United States in the first half of the nineteenth century. This romantic view of death and the attendant cult of memory manifested themselves in the rural cemeteries that mushroomed throughout the Northeast.[5] Like the suburban cemeteries that Carlos III had earlier promoted in Spain and the Americas, the movement toward rural cemeteries in the United States was born—at least initially—of public-health concerns. The new rural cemeteries also represented a very real shift taking place in the view of the dead, however. Religious optimism informed the elaborate mourning rituals, which focused on the reunion of the living and the dead in heaven. Elaborate and highly differentiated monuments to the dear departed replaced the uniform and simple grave markers of early churchyards. Printed booklets guided the cemeteries' many visitors through their gates to highlights on a tour of life-size statues of angels and gravestones modeled on utilitarian but emotionally charged objects like cradles. Andrew Jackson Downing in 1849 described the social significance accorded rural cemeteries, writing of Boston's Mount Auburn Cemetery. "Travelers made pilgrimages to the Athens of New England, solely to see the realization of their long cherished dream of a resting place for the dead, at once sacred from profanation, dear to the memory, and captivating to the imagination."[6]

His words suggest the concomitant changes in the view of the dead and ultimately in the treatment of the corpse itself. Proper mourning and keeping the dead "dear to the memory" increasingly required the use of special mourning clothes, lithographed memorial cards, beautiful containers for the dead, and eventually, embalming. Echoing the carefully crafted natural settings of the rural cemeteries, the new aesthetic manipulated nature by preserving and beautifying the corpse in a multitude of ways. "The dead person was reincarnated as a kind of hideous euphemism for a living one: it seems no accident that corpses were increasingly made to resemble dolls."[7]

Between 1850 and 1860, New Mexico's Anglo American population quadrupled, to sixty-three hundred. Though still a minority in the population of approximately ninety-three thousand, its economic power grew steadily and disproportionately to the population. Admittedly, these figures are somewhat misleading, as the 1850 census did not include El Paso, and both censuses included modern Arizona.[8] The migrants' impact on economic life, however, is undeniable. Likewise, in terms of mortuary practices, they brought northeastern deathways and the associated products with them to New Mexico, where they quickly spread in urban areas and gradually diffused among the rural populations as well.

Newspapers—themselves a relatively recent introduction to New Mexico—prominently displayed advertisements for undertakers and coffins on the front page, frequently emphasizing the eastern origins of their training and goods. Even a cursory review of these advertisements demonstrates that New Mexico kept apace of the rapidly evolving professional funeral industry, which began as a corollary to the furniture business. For many furniture dealers, coffins were initially a sideline. Most advertised a variety of coffins and caskets for sale but did not provide any related services. People could, at least as early as 1863, go to Simon Felger's Santa Fe Cabinet Shop for their coffin needs. In addition to manufacturing and selling all manner of bureaus, sofas, chairs, and tables "at reasonable prices . . . at the shortest notice, of the latest and most approved eastern styles," Felger announced the sale of coffins in bold letters in his Spanish-language advertising and in English ads proclaimed that he offered "undertaking" services.[9] The Albuquerque firm of Scott and Borchert offered "coffins and coffin trimmings" as well as furniture for sale at their Front Street store. Presumably, they felt that sales would be helped by graphics, and they employed an image of a casket, which featured prominently in their front-page ads.[10]

These early businesses did not offer one-stop shopping. People went to several different merchants to obtain what they needed to give their loved ones a burial that was decent by the new standards. The executors of Ana María Ortiz's estate went to at least a half-dozen different merchants to supply all the necessary accouterments for her funeral in 1881. While her forbears would have had little need or opportunity to purchase many of these items even a half-century before, by the time of her death, Ortiz's estate purchased a manufactured coffin and box—probably metallic or rosewood—from A. O. Robbins for fifty dollars. With stores in Las Vegas, Albuquerque, and Santa Fe, Robbins must have been one of the more successful dealers "in furniture, queensware, glassware, lamps, lamp fixtures, and undertaking goods."[11] From the Seligman Brothers general store, Ortiz's executors purchased a large quantity of crepe, lace, ribbon, and linen plus a pair of gloves. The gloves may have been for her corpse or for a family member's mourning costume, but the rest of the articles would have been used to display appropriate mourning at her home, in keeping with nineteenth-century standards of bereavement. Ilfield & Company, another dealer in general merchandise, sold the family candles. Felipe B. Delgado, who was, according to the bill, a "dealer in dry goods and family groceries, general merchandise, etc.," likewise sold four pounds of wax, presumably to provide light during the wake and funeral mass.[12] The New Mexico Printing and Publishing

Company printed 350 funeral notices to inform friends and acquaintances of Ortiz's passing and funeral arrangements. Spiegelberg Brothers, a general store established by Prussian brothers on the south side of the Santa Fe plaza in 1846, supplied flowers for the occasion.[13] Finally, her executors hired a nameless *retratista*, or portrait artist, to create a likeness of the dead woman.[14]

Postmortem portraits had been common among Mexico's wealthy in the colonial period and were increasingly common in the United States by the early nineteenth century. In colonial Mexico, painters took considerable poetic license in their creations. The favored subject matter was children, who sometimes appeared several years older in their portraits than their age in life. The artist might, for example, depict a child who had died in infancy as a toddler playing with a toy soldier. To the uninitiated onlooker, the painting would not obviously represent the dead, but might actually suggest a vivacious youngster. While only the very rich had been able to afford a painted likeness of their dead loved ones, tintypes, daguerreotypes, and the development of photography made such images more and more accessible to people in middle and eventually lower socioeconomic groups. The photograph, unlike the painting, however, did not allow the artist to transform the dead into a living image. Though children and adults alike might appear with eyes open in the photograph, the photographers did not generally attempt to disguise death. In time, conventions such as the presence of flowers clearly conveyed that the subject was dead. Rather than conceal death, the postmortem portrait memorialized it. Like embalming, the portrait temporarily stopped death, momentarily halting the inevitable process of decay by capturing the unchanging dead in portrait form.

Though the earliest New Mexican memorial portraits that survive in archives may only date to the 1880s (Illustration 11), the practice undoubtedly came to the region with the first daguerreotypists who migrated West.[15] Siegmund Seligman, a German immigrant who clerked for a time for the Spiegelberg Bros., opened what must have been New Mexico's first portrait studio in 1853.[16] Though it is uncertain how long the doors of this business remained open, among his early customers undoubtedly were those seeking the same type of memorial image popular in the antebellum United States. Even after Seligman went on to establish his own mercantile firm, itinerant photographers offered their services to the public. A father and son from St. Louis—Nicholas and William Henry Brown—in 1866 opened another photography studio in Santa Fe, where they marketed to both English- and Spanish-speaking customers. The pair traveled south to Chihuahua, their mobile studio making all manner of portraits along the way.[17]

Through the last quarter of the nineteenth century, throughout New Mexico—and particularly wherever Anglos and other foreigners were present—there is evidence of the steady development of a professional funeral industry, which provided not only coffins, but care of the corpse that would rival anything offered in the East. Remarkably, by 1848, embalming—a process that did not gain widespread popularity in the Northeast until the Civil War—was already available in Santa Fe. At this early date, embalming would have been, as in the East, primarily used in cases where a corpse required preservation for transportation over long distances. In this particular case, the obituary indicates that the body of one Mr. Alexander H. McKinstry had been embalmed for shipment "in the States."[18] Within a few decades, however, embalming became a central feature of funerary advertisements. *The Political Comet* in Las Vegas extolled the services of "K. Klattenhoff, dealer in Furniture, Queensware, Glassware, etc...Undertaking orders promptly attended to. Metallic Caskets, Imitation Caskets, etc."[19] H. W. Wyman, "Dealer in Coffins and Caskets, Embalming a Specialty" also offered his services to the Las Vegas public in the early 1880s.[20] Like Torrey, Anderson & Sloan in Albuquerque (formerly Robbins & Torrey), Wyman was prepared to respond even to telegraph orders. Rather than focus on the product itself, Wyman's ads feature an eye-catching stock image of stately white and black horses pulling a hearse. This graphic would have conveyed to readers the same elegance and regalness that a modern casket could provide. Deming advertised the undertaking services of C. H. Dane & Company, while Silver City supported Derbyshire Brothers Undertakers and Dealers in Furniture.[21]

By 1882, Albuquerque alone was home to at least five businesses supplying coffins and related goods and services to a population of less than ten thousand.[22] While initially many of these businesses clearly catered to newly settled easterners, the sheer number of businesses selling coffins and offering undertaking services in the last quarter of the nineteenth century indicates that Anglos were not the only clientele. Many Spanish-language newspapers featured these same ads in translation, demonstrating that the entrepreneurs targeted Spanish speakers directly. The new services and tastes were available to anyone who could afford them, regardless of ethnicity.

20. Advertisement for funerary goods appearing in *El Nuevo Mundo* (Albuquerque), June 26, 1897, image courtesy of New Mexico State University Library, Archives and Special Collections

When the railroads cut through New Mexico in the 1880s, they further nurtured the growth of these businesses, expanding the potential clientele and facilitating merchants' ability to supply the latest in caskets from the East. Technology accelerated the pace of change, as Clara Fergusson noted upon returning to Albuquerque after a two-year absence:

> When I left there was only the railway station about a mile from the houses in Old Town and a dusty lonely road stretching between. A man named Cromwell built a track between the two towns and a mule pulled the car. Later the line was electrified. When I returned from Germany the single street reaching toward Old Town was built up as far as Sixth Street. Another street ran along by the tracks....The new town was different from the old. Instead of quiet, low adobe houses shaded by cottonwoods, it was built of wood. There were stores, some of them with two story fronts, and nearly every other building was a saloon or a gambling house. The sidewalks were rickety boardwalks. There was a sense of excitement and feverishness and noise.[23]

Rather than have to rely on local manufactures, the railroad allowed merchants to purchase goods from as far away as New York, Milwaukee, and Minneapolis. E. Montfort of Albuquerque proudly declared in 1891 that his Gold Avenue office now featured "new undertaking rooms," indicating that his was a full-service establishment.[24] O. W. Strong, who entered the business early and would endure long after many had closed their doors or changed their names, in 1896 boasted that he carried "the largest lines of Undertaking Supplies consisting of cloth-covered and metallic caskets, robes, etc."[25] Strong provided a complete range of services, including the latest embalming techniques, and promised to care for corpses anywhere in New Mexico or Arizona. Like a few other undertakers, Strong eventually expanded his offerings to include the area's first ambulance service.

Archaeological sources confirm the story the newspapers tell: the almost complete transformation of deathways in urban areas during the latter half of the nineteenth century. The burials excavated in the Santuario de Guadalupe in Santa Fe exemplify this process. Though diverging from custom in their purchase of coffins, Santa Fe elites could, in time-honored tradition, continue to pay for burial within the chapel. New, imported traditions coexisted with old—if long-banned—customs. Some of the coffins were of machine-cut wood, with sectioned lids to allow for open casket funerals. Many of those found in the Santuario de Guadalupe included decorative detail: silver or copper braiding, bronze studs forming the shape of a Latin cross or the cross of Jerusalem on the lid and sides.[26] Here, silver handles affirmed the wealth of the dead, whereas the adult coffins uncovered in the former cemeteries at La Garita in Santa Fe and Alameda tended to be plain wooden boxes.[27] While only about 40 percent of nineteenth-century burials excavated at the old Alameda cemetery were coffined, a burial ground dating to the last quarter of the nineteenth century and found beneath a hospital parking lot in Albuquerque revealed that coffins were by this time the norm, even among middle-class Hispanics.[28]

Like the very fact of the burials' presence beneath the church, the Guadalupe burials show that this was a transitional period for New Mexican funerary customs. Fabric remnants and lace-collared hoods affirm what the wills suggest: only a few people continued to elect burial in the Franciscan habit. In rural areas, the traditional ways endured longer. The Federal Writers' Project interviewed one don Manuel Jesús Vasques in 1939, who obligingly related tales of his youthful days as a goatherd and carpenter in Peñasco. Born in 1856, he recalled making coffins in the 1870s, commenting that during the smallpox epidemic of 1875 he could not keep up with demand and "some of the dead were placed on poles and dragged to the cemetery by burros."[29] Though his business was brisk, elsewhere in New Mexico at the same time, excavated coffin materials reveal the reliance on coffins made of wood imported from the South and Gulf Coast of the U.S.[30]

Manufactured goods and professional services became dominant in urban areas, especially among middle-class Hispanic New Mexicans. By 1881, the priest's charge of forty pesos had become just one in a long list of items essential to a changing conception of death, a conception that in many ways mirrored that of the northeastern United States. Instead of calling upon local citizens to examine the bodies of those who had died under mysterious or violent circumstances, individual counties employed licensed medical doctors as coroners. Around the same time, Albuquerque and other towns created city cemeteries, secular burial grounds where anyone could be interred regardless of religion. Prudently located on the outskirts of population centers but without the necessary water, they were a far cry from the lush cemeteries of the Northeast.

Though the presence of immigrants and new trade goods wrought tremendous changes in New Mexican deathways in a very short time, the seed for the transformations seen in the late nineteenth century really had been planted by independence. The reduction in the will's spiritual clauses, falling pious bequests, and the decision to allow heirs to determine one's burial location all demonstrate the shift in consciousness taking place in New Mexico during the first half of the nineteenth century. The transition would not be without its opponents, and in many rural areas people continued to inter their dead according to traditional, homespun ways. The new sensibility toward death eventually triumphed, however, even in small outlying communities. Though not unquestioned, it did eventually become the standard of respectful, proper care for the deceased.

NOTES

INTRODUCTION

1. María Dolores Longina Chávez de Perea, Will, Bernalillo, Dec. 6, 1877, New Mexico State Records Center and Archives (hereafter cited as NMSRCA), Bernalillo County Probate Book C1/2, 58–62.

2. Russ Castronovo, *Necro Citizenship: Death, Eroticism, and the Public Sphere in the Nineteenth-Century United States* (Durham, NC: Duke University Press, 2001).

3. David J. Weber, *The Spanish Frontier in North America* (New Haven: Yale University Press, 1992), 5.

4. Gary Laderman, *The Sacred Remains: American Attitudes Toward Death, 1799–1883* (New Haven: Yale University Press, 1996), 37.

5. Oakah L. Jones Jr., *Los Paisanos: Spanish Settlers on the Northern Frontier of New Spain*, rev. ed. (1979; repr., Norman: University of Oklahoma Press, 1996), 165.

6. Pamela Voekel, *Alone Before God: The Religious Origins of Modernity in Mexico* (Durham, NC: Duke University Press, 2002), chap. 5–6.

7. Marc Simmons, *Spanish Government in New Mexico* (Albuquerque: University of New Mexico Press, 1968), 84–87.

8. Michael P. Carroll, *The Penitente Brotherhood: Patriarchy and Hispano-Catholicism in New Mexico* (Baltimore: The Johns Hopkins University Press, 2002), 39.

9. Historians and anthropologists alike have found this to be the case in many different times and places. See, for example, Mircea Eliade, "Mythologies of Death: An Introduction," in *Religious Encounters With Death*, ed. Frank E. Reynolds and Earle H. Waugh, 13–23 (University Park: Penn State University Press, 1977); and Philippe Ariès, *The Hour of Our Death*, trans. Helen Weaver (Oxford: Oxford University Press, 1991).

10. Carlos Eire, *From Madrid to Purgatory: The Art and Craft of Dying in Sixteenth-Century Spain* (Cambridge: Cambridge University Press, 1995), 215.

11. Archivo General de la Nación (hereafter cited as AGN), Inquisición, vol. 1468, exp. 3, fols. 78r–81v.

CHAPTER ONE

1. Vecino/a was used to designate a resident of a town who was a landowner. In New Mexico, the term generally also conveyed that someone was culturally Spanish. By the late colonial period, the term was also applied to Indians—Apache, *genízaro*, Pueblo—who were landowners. See, for example, Ambrosio Guerra to Real Consulado de Guadalajara, Albuquerque, June 12, 1801, Archivo Histórico del Arzobispado de Durango (hereafter cited as AHAD) 205:546–50; Andrés Reséndez, *Changing National Identities at the Frontier: Texas and New Mexico, 1800–1850* (Cambridge: Cambridge University Press, 2005), 53.

2. "Le respondió que no lo llamaba aunque se la llevara el diablo." Martín claimed to have married Ramírez to punish her father, who had returned to its rightful owner an ax that Martín had stolen. María Manuela Ramírez v. José Antonio Martín, San Juan Pueblo, May–June 1823, Mexican Archives of New Mexico (hereafter cited as MANM) 2: 1288–95.

3. Approximately five thousand individuals lived in El Paso. Fray Francisco Atanasio Domínguez, *The Missions of New Mexico, 1776*, ed. and trans. Eleanor B. Adams and Fray Angélico Chávez (Albuquerque: University of New Mexico Press, 1956), 217.

4. Alicia V. Tjarks, "Demographic, Ethnic and Occupational Structure of New Mexico, 1790," *The Americas* 35, no. 1 (1978): 45–88.

5. Antonio José Ríos-Bustamante, "New Mexico in the Eighteenth Century: Life, Labor and Trade in la Villa de San Felipe de Albuquerque, 1706–1790," *Aztlán* 7, no. 3 (1976): 380.

6. Magali M. Carrera, *Imagining Identity in New Spain: Race, Lineage, and the Colonial Body in Portraiture and Casta Paintings* (Austin: University of Texas Press, 2003), 5–6.

7. Ramón A. Gutiérrez, *When Jesus Came, The Corn Mothers Went Away: Marriage, Sexuality, and Power in New Mexico, 1500–1846* (Stanford: Stanford University Press, 1991), 174.

8. "Tengo a mi cargo, y administración 2952 almas, entre chico y grande… siendo sus clases los más genízaros (que es una mezcla de varias naciones) mulatos, coyotes y muy pocos españoles, aunque los más se tienen por estos últimos aunque no lo sean."

Ambrosio Guerra to Real Consulado de Guadalajara, Albuquerque, June 12, 1801, AHAD 205:546–50. Per Fray Angélico Chávez, I identify secular priests with the title *cura* and use fray or father only when referring to Franciscans. Fray Angélico Chávez, *The Archives of the Archdiocese of Santa Fe, 1678–1900* (Washington, DC: Academy of American Franciscan History, 1957), 5–6.

9. Robert E. Wright, OMI, "How Many Are 'A Few'? Catholic Clergy in Central and Northern New Mexico, 1780–1851," in *Four Hundred Years of Faith: Seeds of Struggle, Harvest of Faith: A History of the Catholic Church in New Mexico* (Santa Fe: Archdiocese of Santa Fe, 1998), 219–61.

10. Fray Juan Agustín de Morfí, *Account of Disorders in New Mexico, 1778*, ed. and trans. Marc Simmons (Isleta Pueblo: Historical Society of New Mexico, 1977), 12.

11. Ross Frank, *From Settler to Citizen: New Mexican Economic Development and the Creation of a Vecino Society, 1750–1820* (Berkeley: University of California Press, 2000), 139–51.

12. Andrés Reséndez, "Getting Cured and Getting Drunk: State Versus Market in Texas and New Mexico, 1800–1850," *Journal of the Early Republic* 22, no. 1 (Spring 2002): 77–103.

13. For more on the conflict among the Franciscans, Durango, and New Mexico's governors, see Jim Norris, *"After the Year Eighty": The Demise of Franciscan Power in Spanish New Mexico* (Albuquerque: University of New Mexico Press, 2000).

14. John L. Kessell, *The Missions of New Mexico Since 1776* (Albuquerque: University of New Mexico Press, 1980), 14.

15. David J. Weber, *The Mexican Frontier, 1821–1846: The American Southwest Under Mexico* (Albuquerque: University of New Mexico Press, 1982), 72.

16. Marta Weigle, *Brothers of Light, Brothers of Blood: The Penitentes of the Southwest* (Albuquerque: University of New Mexico Press, 1976), 22. Wright observes the same trend; Wright, "How Many Are 'A Few'?" 219–61.

17. Marc Simmons, "New Mexico's Spanish Exiles," *New Mexico Historical Review* (hereafter cited as *NMHR*) 59, no. 1 (1984): 67–79.

18. William B. Taylor, *Magistrates of the Sacred: Priests and Parishioners in Eighteenth-Century Mexico* (Stanford: Stanford University Press, 1996), 420–23.

19. Frank, *From Settler To Citizen*, chap. 2; Gutiérrez, *When Jesus Came*, chap. 10; Luis Navarro García, "The North of New Spain as a Political Problem in the Eighteenth Century," in *New Spain's Far Northern Frontier: Essays on Spain in the American West, 1540–1821*, ed. David J.

Weber, 201–15 (Albuquerque: University of New Mexico Press, 1979).

20. Memento mori refers to an object—e.g., a skull or a painting of a decomposing cadaver—used to remind the living of death. The phrase literally means "remember that thou must die."

21. Oswald and Mary Baca's study of the Río Abajo region found that children under age thirteen accounted for 54 percent of all deaths. See Oswald Baca, "Analysis of Deaths in New Mexico's Río Abajo During the Late Spanish Colonial and Mexican Periods, 1793–1846," *NMHR* 70, no. 3 (1995): 237–55. The definition of *párvulo* Baca uses, namely any child under age thirteen, is not necessarily consistent even within New Mexico. Numerous burial records in Albuquerque, for example, identify nine- and ten-year-olds as adults, and at least one burial record denotes a sixteen-year-old as a child.

22. On February 19, 1798, in San Felipe, a man died from an accidental gunshot while playing this game. It is unclear what the game entailed. As *tordo* is an adjective meaning "clumsy" or "stupid," perhaps the game was a test of some sort of skill. Chávez, *The Archives*, 235.

23. The Guadalupe excavation found numerous dental and vertebral pathologies suggestive of the sad state of public health in New Mexico's capital city. María Jorrín, "Summary Report: Santuario de Guadalupe Burials," University of New Mexico, Maxwell Museum of Anthropology, Oct. 24, 1990, in Edward E. Crocker Records from the Excavation and Restoration of the Santuario de Guadalupe (hereafter cited as Crocker Records), Center for Southwest Research (hereafter cited as CSWR), MSS 709 BC, box 1, fol. 9.

24. During the coldest months of the year the death toll rose notably, the result of airborne infections. Baca, "Analysis of Deaths," 246.

25. Marc Simmons, "Hygiene, Sanitation, and Public Health in Hispanic New Mexico," *NMHR* 67, no. 3 (1992): 209.

26. Amy Meschke, "Women's Lives Through Women's Wills in the Spanish and Mexican Borderlands, 1750–1846" (PhD diss., Southern Methodist University, 2004), 45.

27. Malcolm Ebright and Rick Hendricks, *The Witches of Abiquiu: The Governor, the Priest, the Genízaro Indians, and the Devil* (Albuquerque: University of New Mexico Press, 2006), chap. 6–10.

28. Robert D. Martínez, "Fray Juan José Toledo and the Devil in Spanish New Mexico: A Story of Witchcraft and Cultural Conflict in Eighteenth-Century Abiquiú" (master's thesis, University of New Mexico, 1997), 40.

29. Pedro Baptista Pino, *The Exposition on the Province of New Mexico, 1812*, ed. and trans. Adrian Bustamante and Marc Simmons (Santa Fe: Rancho de las Golondrinas; Albuquerque: University of New Mexico Press, 1995), 23.

30. Reséndez, "Getting Cured," 90–91.

31. Memoirs of Franz Huning, Huning-Ferguson Family Papers, CSWR, MSS 194BC, box 1.

32. Ariès argues for maternal indifference among the upper classes until the sixteenth or seventeenth century; Shorter agrees with Ariès but contends that among "ordinary people" indifference toward young children endured until at least the last quarter of the eighteenth century. See Philippe Ariès, *Centuries of Childhood: A Social History of Family Life* (New York: Knopf, 1962), 38–39; Edward Shorter, *The Making of the Modern Family* (New York: Basic Books, 1975), 169–75; see also Lawrence Stone, *The Family, Sex and Marriage in England, 1500–1800* (London: Weidenfeld and Nicholson, 1977). For opponents of this view, see Sylvia D. Hoffert, *Private Matters: American Attitudes Toward Childbearing and Infant Nurturing in the Urban North, 1800–1860* (Urbana: University of Illinois Press, 1999), 158–60; Alan MacFarlane, "Death and the Demographic Transition: A Note on English Evidence on Death, 1500–1750," in *Mortality and Immortality: The Anthropology and Archaeology of Death*, proceedings of a Meeting of the Research Seminar in Archaeology and Related Subjects held at the Institute of Archaeology, London University, June 1980, ed. S. C. Humphreys and Helen King, 249–59 (London: Academic Press, 1981); Mary Beth Norton, *Liberty's Daughters: The Revolutionary Experience of American Women, 1750–1800* (Boston: Little, Brown, 1980), 88–90; Nancy Schrom Dye, "Mother Love and Infant Death, 1750–1920," *The Journal of American History* 73, no. 2 (Sept. 1986), 329–53; Peter Slater, *Children in the New England Mind: In Death and in Life* (Hamden, CT: Archon, 1977), 18–19; Michel Vouvelle, *Ideologies and Mentalities*, trans. Eamon O'Flaherty (Chicago: University of Chicago Press, 1990). Dye suggests that some women's failure to name children or dwell on their activities in journals may have been the result of a different conception of personhood rather than lack of attachment to the child.

33. Murdo J. MacLeod, "Death in Western Colonial Mexico: Its Place in Village and Peasant Life," in *The Middle Period in Latin America: Values and Attitudes in the Seventeenth–Nineteenth Centuries*, ed. Mark D. Szuchman, 65 (Boulder: Lynne Rienner, 1989).

34. Le Goff writes that "these souls begin to acquire not only merit but also the power to transfer their merit to the living, to return service for service, to give assistance to men and women on earth. . . . The Communion of saints manifested itself to the full." Jacques Le Goff, *The Birth of Purgatory*, trans. Arthur Goldhammer (Chicago: University of Chicago Press, 1984), 356–57.

35. "No se trata de que estos hombres no experimentaran la angustia ante la amenaza de la nada; se trata de que su enorme fe terminaba por convertirse en un arma—o en un escudo—de eficacia contundente ante esa amenaza." Antonio García-Abásolo, *La vida y la muerte en Indias* (Córdoba: Publicaciones del Monte de Piedad y Caja de Ahorros, 1992), 21.

36. "El camino de esta vida no es como el de los peregrinos voluntario, sino necesario, como los condenados á la horca cuando salen desde la cárcel á la plaza. A la muerte estás condenado, y para ella caminas." Juan Eusebio Nieremberg, *De la diferencia entre lo terrenal y lo eterno* in *Tesoro de escritores místicos españoles: Obras escogidas de varios autores místicos españoles*, ed. Eugenio de Ochoa (Paris: Librería Europea, 1847), 426.

37. "Si temes lo que has ofendido a Dios, duélete de ello y consuélate, que no le ofenderás más si mueres… no pecarás más." Juan Eusebio Nieremberg, *Partida a la eternidad y preparación para la muerte* (Madrid: Imprenta Real, 1645), 10, quoted in Martín Eduardo Vargas Poo and Silvia Cogollos Amaya, "La teología de la muerte: Una visión española del fenómeno durante los siglos XVI al XVIII," in *Inquisición, muerte y sexualidad en el Nuevo Reino de Granada*, ed. Jaime Humberto Borja Gómez, 127 (Bogotá: Editorial Ariel-CEJA, 1996).

38. Antonio Arbiol, *Visita de enfermos y exercicio santo de ayudar a bien morir. Con las instrucciones más importantes para tan Sagrado Ministerio. Que ofrece al bien común Antonio Arbiol, religioso de la Regular Observancia de N. Seráfico P.S. Francisco de esta Santa Provincia de Aragón*, 2nd ed. (Zaragoza: Pascual Bueno, 1725), 29.

39. "¿Que importa, hermano, que seas grande en el mundo, si la muerte te ha de hacer igual con los pequeños? Llega un osario, que está lleno de huesos de difuntos, distingue entre ellos el rico del pobre, el sabio del necio, y el chico del grande; todos son huesos, todos calaveras, todos guardan una igual figura." Miguel de Mañara y Vicentelo de Leca, *Discurso de la verdad dedicado a la alta imperial magestad de Dios* (1725; repr., Seville: Imprenta San Antonio, 1961), 27. An ossuary is a repository for the bones of the dead. Many societies perform a secondary burial a few years after the original burial, when the flesh has completely been removed from the bones, and remove the clean bones to an ossuary.

40. Joaquín Hermenegildo Bolaños, *La portentosa vida de la muerte, empeatriz de los sepulcros, vengadora de los agravios del Altísimo y muy señora de la humana naturaleza*, ed. and with critical introduction by Blanca López de Mariscal (1792; repr. Mexico City: El Colegio de México, 1992), 221.

41. "La muerte se concibe como una irrupción salvaje e irracional

que pone en peligro la armonía social." Juan Pedro Viqueira, "El sentimiento de la muerte en el México ilustrado del siglo XVIII a través de dos textos de la época," *Relaciones* 2, no. 5 (1981), 45.

42. "Si Vuestra Merced le hubiera dicho a su alma: alégrate alma mía, porque ya tengo con qué pagarte muchas misas, con qué socorrer a los pobres necesitados, hacer muchas obras buenas, y en fin, tengo proporciones para ganarte el cielo, puede ser que entonces viviera Vuestra Merced mucho más de lo que pensaba, y no tuviera el susto que ahora tiene, y el dolor de ver su caudal en poder ajeno." Bolaños, *La portentosa vida de la muerte*, 258.

43. Domínguez, *Missions*, 220–33; Eleanor B. Adams, "Two Colonial New Mexico Libraries: 1704, 1776," *NMHR* 19, no. 2 (1944): 135–67; Eleanor B. Adams and Keith W. Algier, "A Frontier Book List—1800," *NMHR* 43, no. 1 (1968): 49–59. See also Eleanor B. Adams and France V. Scholes, "Books in New Mexico, 1598–1680," *NMHR* 17, no. 3 (1942): 226–70.

44. Joaquín del Pino, Will, Albuquerque, Dec. 7, 1768, NMSRCA, Miscellaneous Wills and Hijuelas, fol. 2.

45. Bernardo P. Gallegos, *Literacy, Education and Society in New Mexico, 1693–1821* (Albuquerque: University of New Mexico Press, 1992), 57–58.

46. Jones, *Los Paisanos*, 137.

47. Gallegos, *Literacy, Education and Society*, 53.

48. Scholes finds that about 37 percent of New Mexicans could sign their names in 1681 muster rolls but observes that more than 90 percent of those the Inquisition investigated could not sign. France V. Scholes, "Civil Government and Society in New Mexico in the Seventeenth Century," *NMHR* 10, no. 2 (1935), 71–111.

49. Norris, *"After the Year Eighty,"* 20–23.

50. Numerous examples from the Territorial period survive. Alvin O. Korte, "Despedidas as Reflections of Death in Hispanic New Mexico," *Omega* 32, no. 4 (1995–96): 245–67; and Rowena A. Rivera and Thomas J. Steele, SJ, "Territorial Documents and Memories: Singing Church History," *NMHR* 67, no. 4 (1992): 393–413.

51. Thomas J. Steele, SJ, *Santos and Saints: The Religious Folk Art of Hispanic New Mexico* (1974; repr., Santa Fe: Ancient City Press, 1994), 111. See also Paula Mues Orts, "Imágenes corporales: Arte virreinal de los siglos XVII y XVIII en Nueva España," in *El Cuerpo aludido: Anatomías y construcciones México, siglos XVI–XX*, 47–69 (Mexico City: Patronato del Museo Nacional de Arte, Conaculta—Instituto Nacional de Bellas Artes, 1998).

52. Clara García Ayluardo, "A World of Images: Cult, Ritual and Society in Colonial Mexico City," in *Rituals of Rule, Rituals of Resistance: Public*

Celebrations and Popular Culture in Mexico, ed. William H. Beezley, Cheryl English Martin, and William E. French, 77–93 (Wilmington, DE: Scholarly Resources, Inc., 1994); Voekel, *Alone Before God*, 18–24.

53. Memoirs of Franz Huning, Huning-Ferguson Family Papers, CSWR, MSS 194BC, boxes 1 and 2, fol. 6: Journal/Memoirs of Clara Huning Ferguson.

54. James William Abert, *Abert's New Mexico Report, 1846–47* (1848; repr. Albuquerque: Horn & Wallace, 1962), 57.

55. Domínguez, *Missions*, 75.

56. Frank, *A Land So Remote: Religious Art of New Mexico, 1780–1907* (Santa Fe: Red Crane Books, 2002), 1:15.

57. Steele, *Santos and Saints*, 66; Barbe Awalt and Paul Rhetts, *Our Saints Among Us: 400 Years of New Mexican Devotional Art* (Albuquerque: LPD Press, 1998), 173.

58. Thomas J. Steele, SJ, ed., *New Mexican Spanish Religious Oratory, 1800–1900* (Albuquerque: University of New Mexico Press, 1997), 93, citing Good Friday journal entry of Smith, dated April 9, 1852, in *Home Mission Record* 3, no. 8 (1852): 1.

59. Steele, *New Mexican Spanish Religious Oratory*, 23. The original is in the Archives of the Archdiocese of Santa Fe (hereafter cited as AASF), Loose Docs., Mission, 1825, n. 15.

60. Thomas J. Steele, SJ, and Rowena Rivera, *Penitente Self-Government: Brotherhoods and Councils, 1797–1947* (Santa Fe: Ancient City Press, 1985), 196–97.

61. Steele, *New Mexican Spanish Religious Oratory*, 37.

62. Weigle, *Brothers*, 170. See also E. Boyd Coll., NMSRCA, box 3, fol. F58; and William Wroth, *Images of Penance, Images of Mercy: Southwestern Santos in the Late Nineteenth Century* (Norman: University of Oklahoma Press, 1991), chap. 10.

63. Arbiol, *Visita de enfermos*, 105.

CHAPTER TWO

1. Juliana Fernández, Will, Santa Fe, May 21, 1785, Spanish Archives of New Mexico I (hereafter cited as SANM), 2:485–88.

2. The governor appointed the alcalde mayor to administer a district of several towns or a single community; he had both administrative and judicial functions. The teniente de justicia may have referred to an assistant to the alcalde mayor, who would have served in the alcalde mayor's absence. The alcalde de paz may be a synonym for the alcalde mayor. See Charles R. Cutter, *The Legal Culture of Northern New Spain, 1700–1810* (Albuquerque: University of New Mexico Press, 1995).

3. María de la Luz Pacheco, Will and receipts, Santa Fe, Apr. 1836, NMSRCA, Benjamin Read Coll., Series II, box 7, fol. F 11.

4. "Por lo que me parece que dicha Señora estaba ya sólo puesta en la carrera o agonía como dando cuenta ya a Nuestro Creador." Testimony of Domingo Fernández, Santa Fe, Sept. 16, 1814, NMSRCA, Ortiz Family Papers, box 1, fol. 5.

5. Ramón García, Will, Santa Fe, June 14, 1768, SANM I, 2:1016–20. "Hecho sin presencia de juez, y delante sólo de cinco testigos por haberme visto obligado a hacerlo en el punto del Cañon de Pecos, en el que no fué posible hacer uso de todos los requisitos legales en los términos siguientes." Juan Esteban Pino, Will, Cañon de Pecos, Dec. 5, 1838, NMSRCA, Benjamin Read Coll., Series I, box 5, fol. 245. Pino is identified as a thirty-eight-year-old "comerciante coronel y diputado" in the 1823 census of the Barrio de San Francisco in Santa Fe, MANM 3:231.

6. Domínguez, *Missions*, 244; Testimonio formal, y jurídico, del arancel mandado observar, en esta Provincia de Nuevo México por el Ilustrísimo Señor Don Benito Crespo, Dignísimo Obispo que fue de la capital, de Durango, Santa Fe, Jan. 30, 1807, AHAD 216:679–82.

7. Congregación de la Buena Muerte, *Dificultad imaginada y facilidad verdadera en la práctica de testamentos* (Mexico City, 1714). See also Susan Schroeder, "Jesuits, Nahuas, and the Good Death Society in Mexico City, 1710–1767," *Hispanic American Historical Review* 80, no. 1 (2000): 43–76.

8. *Luz a los vivos y escarmiento en los muertos* discussed in Vargas and Cogollos, "La teología de la muerte," passim.

9. "Memento Mori/Dispón tus cosas de suerte/Que te den vida en la muerte." Pedro Murillo Velarde, *Práctica de testamentos en la que se resuelven los casos más frecuentes que se ofrecen en la disposición de las últimas voluntades* (1755; repr., Santa Fe: Manderfield & Tucker, 1850), 5.

10. Eire, *From Madrid to Purgatory*, 23.

11. "Primeramente creo y confieso en el misterio inefable de la Santísima Trinidad Dios Padre, Dios hijo y Dios Espíritu Santo, tres personas distintas y ún solo Dios Verdadero. Creo que la segunda Persona que es Nuestro Señor Jesús Cristo encarnó en las purísimas entrañas de Nuestra Señora la Virgen María por obra del Espíritu Santo. Creo que nació de ella quedando Virgen antes del parto y después del parto y siempre Virgen y verdadera Madre de Dios. Creo que padeció muerte y pasión por redimirnos y salvarnos, creo que resucitó al tercer día. Creo que ha de venir a juzgar vivos y muertos, a premiar y castigar. Ultimamente creo y confieso todos

aquellos misterios que cree y confiesa Nuestra Santa Iglesia Católica Apostólica Romana y en esta fe y creencia quiero vivir y morir." Juliana Fernández, Will, Santa Fe, May 21, 1785, SANM I, 2:485–88.

12. "Yo Juan Esteban Pino confesando como confieso todos los misterios de nuestra santa fe." Juan Esteban Pino, Will, Cañon de Pecos, Dec. 5, 1838, NMSRCA, Benjamin Read Coll., Series I, box 5, fol. 245.

13. "En el nombre de Dios todopoderoso y de la siempre Virgen María concebida sin mancha de pecado original. Amén." María Antonia Andrea Martínez, Will, Santa Fe, May 22, 1834, NMSRCA, Donaciano Vigil Coll., box 7, fol. 316.

14. "Si Dios fuere servido de llamarme a juicio, ordeno mi testamento en la forma siguiente." Juliana Fernández, Will, Santa Fe, May 21, 1785, SANM I, 2:485–88.

15. "Para que nos defienda de nuestro común enemigo en la muerte." Joseph Baca, Will, Albuquerque, Aug. 29, 1766, SANM I, 6:774–97.

16. "Para en la hora de mi muerte destierren todo espíritu maligno, de cuya causa desde ahora y para siempre renuncio todas las pompas vanidades de este mundo." Gregorio Martín, Will [prob. Santo Tomás de] Abiquiú, Nov. 3, 1826, NMSRCA, María G. Durán Coll., exp. 1, fol. 6.

17. Juan Francisco Martín, Will, San Antonio del Embudo, Jan. 24, 1767, SANM I, 3:1362–67; quote from translated will in Donald Dreeson, ed., *WPA Translations of the Spanish Archives of New Mexico* (Albuquerque: Center for Southwest Research, University of New Mexico General Library, 1990), 13:146.

18. Reséndez, *Changing National Identities*, 233, 247. See also Andrés Reséndez, "National Identity on a Shifting Border: Texas and New Mexico in the Age of Transition, 1821–1848," *Journal of American History* 86, no. 2 (1999): 668–88.

19. "Hallándome en cama de la enfermedad que Dios Señor ha sido servido enviarme y temiéndome de la muerte como cosa natural y que no me coja desprevenido." Joaquín de Alderete, Will, Santa Fe, Apr. 9, 1767, SANM I, 1:320–23.

20. For Seville, see José Antonio Rivas Alvarez, *Miedo y piedad: testamentos sevillanos del siglo XVIII* (Seville: Deputación Provincial de Sevilla, 1986), 37. For Coahuila, see Alma Victoria Valdés, *Testamentos, muerte y exequias: Saltillo y San Esteban al despuntar el siglo XIX* (Saltillo, Mexico: Centro de Estudios Sociales y Humanísticos, 2000), 44. For Mexico's nobility, see Verónica Zárate Toscano, *Los nobles ante la muerte en México: Actitudes, ceremonias y memoria, 1750–1850* (Mexico City: El Colegio de México, Instituto

de Investigaciones Dr. José María Luis Mora, 2000), 43–44. In contrast to New Spain, only one New Mexican woman acknowledged that she was pregnant while making her will. Though she began her will by stating that she found herself in good health, Taos's Bárbara Montoya later mentioned that she was pregnant, suggesting that this was in fact a reason for her making the will. Bárbara Montoya, Will, Taos, Jan. 18, 1745, SANM I, 8:684–89.

21. Simón de Leyba, Will, Santa Fe, Oct. 15, 1783, SANM II, 11:664.

22. Nicolasa Vigil, Will, Chama, Oct. 2, 1765, SANM I, 5:1318–26.

23. "Y conociendo que soy mortal y que no sé cuando Dios Nuestro Señor sea servido de llamarme para sí y que ésta hora no me coja desprevenido." Gerónimo López, Will, Santa Fe, n.d. [1769], SANM I, 3:364–68.

24. "Conózcome por la mayor pecadora y que no tengo el dolor que debiera de haber ofendido a mi Dios, y Señor." Josefa Baca, Will, Albuquerque, June 10, 1746, SANM I, 1:700–34.

25. "Recelo que me saque de este miserable mundo." Donaciano Vigil, Will, Santa Fe, n.d. [1842], NMSRCA, Donaciano Vigil Coll., box 7, folder 319.

26. Popular thought frequently has accorded the words of the dying a unique sort of authority, holding such speech in a privileged position. As a result, an individual may say things on the deathbed otherwise prohibited by social norms. Erik Seeman, for example, discusses inversions of power (lay/clerical and male/female) on the deathbed in Erik R. Seeman, *Pious Persuasions: Laity and Clergy in Eighteenth-Century New England* (Baltimore: Johns Hopkins University Press, 1999), chap. 2.

27. "La muerte de el alma, no fue ordenada de Dios Nuestro Señor, sino es que los malos lo buscaron." Luis Jaramillo, Will, Santa Fe, Dec. 27, 1764, SANM I, 3:201–4.

28. "Ha de esperar el día de la resurrección para volver a formarse ya para nunca más morir." Gervacio Ortega, Will, San Buenaventura [Chimayó], Dec. 11, 1851, NMSRCA, Borrego-Ortega Papers, box 1, fol. 23.

29. María Chaves, Will, Nuestra Señora de la Soledad del Río Arriba, May 2, 1765, SANM I, 1:1389–92.

30. Nicolás Mares, Will, Santa Fe, Jan. 10, 1766, SANM I, 3:1140–43.

31. María Rosa Agustina Chacón, Will, Nuestra Señora del Carmen de la Cuchilla, Sept. 1, 1840, NMSRCA, Borrego-Ortega Papers, box 1, fol. 16.

32. "Estando para cerrar o dar fin a los días de mi vida, para morir como católico cristiano y con la disposición que se requiere para la mayor quietud y sosiego de mi alma y como que tengo hijos herederos forzosos de mis bienes." Romero's will was so deviant in

form that it was hotly contested after his death. Francisco Romero, Will, Las Trampas, Jan. 10, 1765, SANM I, 4:1180–82.

33. Pablo Manuel Trujillo. Will, San Gerónimo de Taos, Aug. 19, 1810, History Library, Mauro Montoya Coll., box 1, fol. 1 (Mexican Period).

34. In addition to leaving a sizable sum for the construction of the Chapel of Our Lady of Light (later known as "la Castrense") in his will, Juan Joseph Moreno and wife Juana Roybal gave generously to the chapel in Santa Fe's parish church dedicated to Our Lady of the Rosary, as noted in Domínguez's 1776 report. Moreno survived his illness in 1756 and lived more than a decade longer. Juan Joseph Moreno, Will, Santa Fe, Jan. 28, 1756, SANM I, 3:1042–56.

35. An hijo natural referred to a child born to unmarried parents but for whom no impediment to marriage existed. Joseph Baca, Will, Pueblo Quemado, Mar. 2, 1772, SANM I, 6:774–97. As late as 1887, a Santa Fe man uses this term to refer to the eight "natural" children he fathered.

36. "Declaro que como miserable frágil y pecadora tuve seis hijos." Josefa Baca, Will, Albuquerque, June 10, 1746, SANM I, 1:700–73.

37. According to the Sept. 9, 1814 certification of Fray Sebastián Alvarez, Bustamante had confessed her transgression to another priest at least two years before her death. Rosa Bustamante estate papers, Santa Fe, July 8, 1814, NMSRCA, Ortiz Family Papers, box 1, fols. 3, 5.

38. Suzanne Stamatov, "Family, Kin, and Community in Colonial New Mexico, 1694–1800" (PhD diss., University of New Mexico, 2003), 142.

39. Manuel Pudillo, Will, Santa Fe, Jan. 27, 1849, NMSRCA, Santa Fe County Records, Wills and Testaments, Book A, 16–20.

40. Petra Paula Padilla, Will, Santa Clara, July 20, 1816, NMSRCA, Mariano Chávez Family Papers, fol. 5.

41. "Bajo mi dominio sacrificando casi su existencia a beneficio mío: y reconocido de tan particulares favores quiero . . . mando y ordeno entre en iguales partes con mis citados hijos a gozar . . . lo que unidos han trabajado, pues no hallo otra cosa con que recompensarle sus fatigas." Juan Cristóbal Vigil, Will, Santa Fe, May 31, 1832, NMSRCA, Vigil Coll., box 7, fol. 314.

42. Joaquín Pino, Will, Albuquerque, Dec. 7, 1768, NMSRCA, Wills and Hijuelas Misc., fol. 2.

43. Inscription costs rarely appear in wills but are evident in the settlement of numerous estates. Joseph Ramo de Vera, Will, Santa Fe, March 11, 1754, SANM I, 5:1284–87.

44. María Pascuala de los Dolores Romero, Will, Santa Cruz de la Cañada, Feb. 23, 1846, NMSRCA, Borrego-Ortega Papers, box 1, fol. 18.

45. Juan Manuel Ortega, Will, Santa Fe, March 3, 1797, NMSRCA, Santa Fe County Probate Book E, 313–15.

46. Teodora Gertrudis Ortiz, Will, Santa Fe, July 9, 1800, SANM I, 1:889–92. Santa Fe's church dedicated to the Virgin of Guadalupe was built between 1795 and 1803. Kessell, *The Missions*, 44.

47. Gutiérrez, *When Jesus Came*, 171–72.

48. For a detailed discussion of the institution, its origins, and its impact in New Mexico, see James F. Brooks, *Captives and Cousins: Slavery, Kinship and Community in the Southwest Borderlands* (Chapel Hill: University of North Carolina Press, 2002).

49. Mónica Tomasa Martín, Will, San Gerónimo de Taos, April 11, 1770, SANM I, 3:1210–28.

50. Ramón Gutiérrez likens the institution to slavery, an assessment that wills often justify. Gutiérrez cites the sale of children born to criadas despite the mothers' formal opposition. Gutiérrez, *When Jesus Came*, 183.

51. "Debo a Ignacio Gonsales, vecino de San Buenaventura un indito de edad de siete años . . . debo a un hijo de Tomás Madrid, vecino de San Buenaventura una indita de seis años, que así mismo mando se pague de mis bienes." Andrés Montoya, Will, Santa Fe, June 17, 1740, SANM I, 3:841–44.

52. "Declaro tener cuentas con don Clemente Gutiérrez y no tengo presente la cantidad que me ha suplido pues lo que tengo presente es que le tengo entregadas dos indias a 50 pesos de plata por cada una." Domingo de Benavides, Will, Santa Fe, May 8, 1770, SANM I, 1:832–38.

53. "Cinco indias criadas, con ocho coyotitos." Francisco Romero, Will, Taos, Jan. 10, 1765, SANM I, 4:1180–82. Priests identified children as "coyotes" in baptismal registers, revealing mixed "Spanish"-Indian or casta-Indian parentage.

54. Gutiérrez, *When Jesus Came*, 199–200.

55. María de la Candelaria González, Will, Santa Fe, 1752, SANM I, 2:890–92.

56. Sandia Pueblo Burial Book, July 8, 1786, AASF 36:777.

57. Santa Fe Burial Book, Jan. 15, 1780, AASF 40:270.

58. May 1780, Santa Fe Burial Book, AASF 40:282–83.

59. Brooks, *Captives and Cousins*, 238.

60. David M. Brugge, *Navajos in the Catholic Church Records of New Mexico, 1694–1875* (1968; repr., Tsaile, AZ: Navajo Community College Press, 1985), 22–23; and Brooks, *Captives and Cousins*, 234, 250, and Appendix B.

61. Miguel Ortiz, Will, Santa Fe, May 27, 1814, Santa Fe County Probate Book E, NMSRCA, 213–20.

62. Diego Montoya, Will, Santa Fe, Nov. 9, 1818, NMSRCA, Hinojos Family Papers, box 1, fol. F 6.

63. Eduarda Rita Garduño, Will, Santa Fe, May 5, 1785, SANM I, 2:1068–70.

64. Francisco Martín, Will, San Antonio del Embudo, Nov. 14, 1764, NMSRCA, Benjamin M. Read Coll., Series II, box 7, fol. F 6, doc. 6.

65. "Que atiendan y miren por su madre y por sus demás hermanos como son obligados y que no hagan cosa ninguna sin parecer de su madre." Felipe Tafoya, Will, Santa Fe, Nov. 7, 1769, SANM I, 5:868–81.

66. "Que ningún hijo o hija vea para donde está un vicio, que todo vicio es contra Dios, y el honor del padre y madre." José Martínez, Will, San Acacio, May 25, 1854, NMSRCA, Taos County Probate Book B2, 73–76.

67. "Con igualdad desde lo primero hasta lo último encargándose sobre todo la paz y tranquilidad para que le gocen la bendición de Dios y la mía." María Micaela Baca, Will, Santa Fe, Apr. 22, 1830, NMSRCA, Twitchell Coll., fol. 134.

68. Bentura Mestas, Will, Santa Cruz, Dec. 14, 1835, NMSRCA, Renehan/Gilbert Papers, box 21, fol. 133.

69. "Es mi voluntad que después de mis días, de la mitad de los bienes que Dios me ha dado que me tocan se pague mi entierro, funeral y misas a la voluntad de mi mujer y mis hijos, que creo de ella y de ellos que no se olvidarán de mí, ella por compañera de tantos años y ellos por mis legítimos hijos." Gerónimo López, Will, Santa Fe, n.d. [1769?], SANM I, 3:364–68.

70. Juana Roybal, Will, Santa Fe, June 13, 1770, SANM I, 4:1236–40.

71. Teodora Gertrudis Ortiz, Will, Santa Fe, July 9, 1800, SANM I, 1:889–92.

72. María Rosa Agustina Chacón, Will, Nuestra Señora del Carmen de la Cuchilla, Sept. 1, 1840, NMSRCA, Borrego-Ortega Papers, box 1, fol. 16.

73. "Por si acaso algún día pudiere yo haber tomado alguna cosa que parezca poco y sea alguna cosa considerable, o por si en algún trato hubiere dado menos por lo que valía más para que Dios Nuestro Señor las distribuya según fuere su santa voluntad o que las deposite en el tesoro de su iglesia." Juan Antonio Ortiz, Will, Santa Fe, Aug. 23, 1795, NMSRCA, Ortiz Family Papers, box 1, fol. F 13, doc. 13.

74. Receipts included with José Viterbo Rivera will, Jan. 11, 1827, NMSRCA, Benjamin Read Coll., Series II, box 7, fol. F 11.

75. Receipts for masses and burial of don José Lázaro Trujillo, various dates, NMSRCA, Twitchell Coll., fol. 251.

76. Juan Montes Vigil, Will, Santa Fe, Apr. 30, 1762, SANM I, 5:1291–1313.

77. José Antonio Cruz, Will, Nuestra Señora del Carmen, Dec. 27, 1840, NMSRCA, Borrego-Ortega Papers, box 1, fol. 14.

78. Teresa Fernández de la Pedrera, Will, Santa Fe, May 11, 1785, NMSRCA, Hinojos Family Papers, box 1, fol. F 1.

79. Chávez notes that Bernardo de Sena was a foundling who came to New Mexico in 1693 at the age of nine. See Fray Angélico Chávez, *Origins of New Mexico Families: A Genealogy of the Spanish Colonial Period* rev. ed. (1954; repr., Santa Fe: Museum of New Mexico Press, 1992), 286. Bernardo de Sena, Will, Santa Fe, July 17, 1758, SANM I, 5:82–93.

80. Blas Griego to jefe político of New Mexico, Santa Fe, May 9, 1824, AHAD 253:99.

81. Gente de razón was used to describe Spaniards and non-Indians or Christians, including Christianized Indians, depending on the context. In this case, it appears to refer to Indians. Relación de Padre Menchero sobre el reino de Nuevo México, May 10, 1744, Biblioteca Nacional, Mexico—Archivo Franciscano (hereafter cited as BNM-AF), 19/407.1, fols. 1–44v.

82. In this respect, the situation of New Mexico's parish priests was not so different from other communities in New Spain. Elsewhere, priests exacted goods and even demanded labor as payment for services provided to their parishioners. Taylor, *Magistrates of the Sacred*, chap. 17.

83. A vara was about thirty-three inches in length. Hilario Archuleta, Will, Nambé, Oct. 24, 1781, NMSRCA, Twitchell Coll., fol. 141.

84. Ramón García, Will, Santa Fe, June 14, 1768, SANM I, 2:1016–21.

85. María Guadalupe Sánchez, Will, Santa Fe, n.d. [1833 or 1834], SANM I, 5:366–72.

86. Juana Roibal [Roybal], Will, Santa Fe, June 13, 1770, SANM I, 4:1236–40.

87. José Manuel Trujillo, Will, 1785, Puesto de San Joseph de Chama, SANM I, 5:900–905.

88. Juan Antonio Suaso, Will, San Antonio del Embudo, Apr. 26, 1818, NMSRCA, Suaso Family Coll., box 1, fol. 10.

89. Silvia Arrom, *Containing the Poor: The Mexico City Poor House, 1774–1871* (Durham, NC: Duke University Press, 2000).

90. "Mando se dé buenamente una corta limosna a doce mujeres las más pobres vergonzantes siendo mi deseo darles mucho más si pudiera." Rosa Bustamante, Will, Santa Fe, July 8, 1814, NMSRCA, Ortiz Family Papers, box 1, fol. 3.

91. Antonio José Ortiz, Will, Santa Fe, Jan. 31, 1805, NMSRCA, Ortiz Family Papers, box 1, fol. F 2.

92. Tomás Madrid, Will, Santa Fe, Jan. 27, 1830, MANM 11:416–19.

93. Josef Antonio Alarid, Will, Santa Fe, Mar. 12, 1822, SANM I, 1:447–59.

94. Juan Antonio Ortiz, Will, Santa Fe, Aug. 23, 1795, NMSRCA, Ortiz Family Papers, box 1, fol. F 3.

95. Curiously, Pescador states that the mandas forzosas originated in the decade between 1730 and 1740, and Voekel contends that they were in effect from approximately 1740 to 1806. Juan Javier Pescador, *De bautizados a fieles difuntos: Familia y mentalidades en una parroquia urbana: Santa Catarina de México, 1568–1820* (Mexico City: El Colegio de México, 1992), 290; Voekel, *Alone Before God*, 20.

96. Murillo, *Práctica de testamentos*, 28. See also Juan M. Rodríguez de San Miguel, *Pandectas Hispano-Megicanas ó sea Código General comprensivo de las leyes generales, útiles y vivas de las siete partidas*... (Mexico City: Librería de J. F. Rosa, 1852), 2:718. Pamela Voekel identifies a fourth: the redemption of Christian captives. Voekel, "Scent and Sensibility: Pungency and Piety in the Making of the *Gente Sensata*. Mexico 1604–1850" (PhD diss., University of Texas at Austin, 1997), 58.

97. Rosa Bustamante, Will, Santa Fe, July 8, 1814, NMSRCA, Ortiz Family Papers, box 1, fol. 3. E. Boyd translates this third clause in Bustamante's will as referring to the "benevolent orders," or local confraternities, and "the newest one" as meaning the church dedicated to the Virgin of Guadalupe. E. Boyd, *Popular Arts of Spanish New Mexico* (Santa Fe: Museum of New Mexico Press, 1974), 445.

98. "Digo yo Joseph Miguel de la Peña sindico de los lugares santos que recibí de Mariano Trujillo dos pares de medias que dejó el difunto su padre Lázaro Trujillo de mandas forzosas y para que conste dí este recibo hoy 20 de mayo de este presente año de 1778." Receipt, San Francisco de Nambé, May 20, 1778, NMSRCA, Twitchell Coll., fol. 251.

99. Francisco Romero, Will, Las Trampas, Jan. 10, 1765, SANM I, 4:1180–82.

100. Manuel de la Cruz Lucero, Will, Peña Blanca, May 1, 1878, NMSRCA, Bernalillo County Wills & Testaments Book C1/2, 206–8.

101. Voekel notes that most Veracruz and Mexico City testators omitted this clause. In Mexico City from 1750 to 1799, for example, fewer than 5 percent of testators chose a burial habit for themselves. Those who did specify burial attire preferred the habit of St. Francis over that of other religious. Voekel, "Scent and Sensibility," 46.

102. Bishop Francisco Gabriel Olivares y Benito describes the proper dress in a cordillera from Durango, July 16, 1799, AASF 52:521. See also Fray Angélico Chávez, "The Unique Tomb of Fathers Zárate and

de la Llana in Santa Fe," *NMHR* 40, no. 2 (1965): 101–15. See also Russ Gordon Montgomery, Watson Smith, and John Otis Brew, *Franciscan Awatovi: The Excavation and Conjectural Reconstruction of a Seventeenth-Century Spanish Mission Establishment at a Hopi Indian Town in Northeastern Arizona* (Cambridge, MA: Peabody Museum, Harvard University, 1949), 202–3.

103. Fernando Martínez Gil, *Muerte y sociedad en la España de los Austrias* (Madrid: Siglo Veintiuno, 1993), 384; Voekel, *Alone Before God*, 33.

104. Eire, *From Madrid to Purgatory*, 110.

105. "Sucede muchas veces, que los enfermos, sabiendo el gran tesoro de indulgencias que hay en la Tercera Orden de Nuestro Seráfico Padre San Francisco, piden el hábito, y la profesión, para morir con ese gran consuelo espiritual, y socorro de sus almas." Arbiol, *Visita de enfermos*, 31.

106. Rivas Álvarez, *Miedo y piedad*, 128.

107. Zárate Toscano, *Los nobles ante la muerte*, 231–36. In Spain, some testators wore the habits of more than one religious order to reap additional benefits. Based on the correlation of occupation and burial costume preference, Rivas Álvarez suggests that the custom was imported from outside of Spain. Rivas Álvarez, *Miedo y piedad*, 128. This tradition's popularity in Spain varied slightly geographically but endured well into the twentieth century, according to Eire.

108. Eire, *From Madrid to Purgatory*, 107. In contrast to Spain, there is no suggestion in New Mexico that testators ever wore more than one habit for burial.

109. "Con la vestidura y bendición del hábito de Nuestro Seráfico Padre San Francisco." Bárbara Baca, Will, Santa Fe, Dec. 30, 1838, NMSRCA, Twitchell Coll., fol. 166.

110. Fray Cayetano de Otero received thirty pesos from the estate of Capt. don Pedro Cháves for a *mortaja*, or burial garment. Receipt in the estate settlement of Pedro de Cháves, 1736, SANM I, 8:436–39. See also Receipt signed by Juan Bermejo, Santa Fe, Oct. 5, 1785, SANM I, 8:1234.

111. Patente by Fray Silvestre Vélez de Escalante, San Francisco de Nambé, July 5, 1779, AASF, Loose Docs., Mission, 1769, n. 2, AASF 52:375–79.

112. Estate of Manuel Gallegos, receipt signed by Antonio Ortega, n.p., Oct. 22, 1764, SANM I, 2:1001.

113. Receipt signed by Juan Bermejo, Santa Fe, Oct. 5, 1785, SANM I, 8:1234.

114. Frank, *From Settler to Citizen*, 92.

115. Burials 8, 11, 12, and 21 include these features. Crocker Records, CSWR, MSS 709 BC, box 1.

116. Mary D. Taylor, "The Jerusalem Cross: The Sub-floor Burials in the Santuario de Guadalupe, Santa Fe, New Mexico: Their Relationship to the Tercer Orden de San Francisco and the Cofradía de Nuestro Padre Jesús Sometimes Known as 'Penitentes,'" n.p., 1989. This paper uses the presence of these fabrics to bolster the case that the Guadalupe Chapel became the site of Penitente burials in the nineteenth century. Crocker Records, CSWR, MSS 709 BC, box 1, fol. 19.

117. Catalina Durán estate, May 23, 1752, Santa Fe, SANM I, 2:277–79.

118. For an overview, see Philippe Ariès, "The Reversal of Death: Changes in Attitudes Toward Death in Western Societies," in *Death in America*, ed. David Stannard, 134–58 (Pittsburgh: University of Pennsylvania Press, 1975).

119. Antonio José Martínez, *Manualito de párrocos, para los autos del ministerio más precisos, y auxiliar a los enfermos*. Tomado del de el P. Juan Francisco López. (Taos: Imprenta del Presbitero Antonio José Martínez a cargo de J. M. Baca, 1839), 52. NMSRCA, Benjamin Read Coll., Series II, fol. 48. This and all subsequent translations of the Latin from this source courtesy of Fray Thomas J. Steele, SJ.

120. José Manuel Martínez, Will, Plaza de San José de Abiquiú, Feb. 25, 1842, NMSRCA, Miscellaneous Colonial Docs. 19B, box serial no. 15792, item 45.

121. For a general discussion of economic and population changes, see Frank, *From Settler to Citizen*, chap. 5.

122. Ríos-Bustamante, "New Mexico in the Eighteenth Century," 375.

123. Reséndez, *Changing National Identities*, 233, 247.

CHAPTER THREE

1. "Digo yo, don Luis Montoya Cabeza de Vaca, teniente de caballería de la urbana milicia de Santa Fe y demás de la provincia que certifico bajo mi palabra de honor, que el día cinco de Marzo de este año de mil ochocientos, se me ofreció mandar llamar a el padre caballero que le pusiera a mi difunta hija los santos oleos. No quiso venir. Volvieron el día seis a llamarlo no quiso volver. El día siete no quiso venir. Fui yo personalmente y habiéndole tocado la puerta me mandó entrar, y con palabras muy indecorosas y ofensivas, me dijo que mi hija estaba tan mala como él y que los oleos no le eran de ningún sufragio a ningún cristiano." Though Montoya's phrasing is vague, his daughter most certainly was alive at the time that he called for the priest, for the sacraments could not be administered postmortem. Certification of Luis Montoya Cabeza de Vaca, Santa Fe (?), Nov. 10, 1800, AHAD 203:301–3.

2. Martínez, *Manualito de párrocos*, 12.

3. "Imponderable es el peligro que corremos a la hora de la muerte, punto de que depende la eternidad, y momento crítico de la eterna dicha ó condenación de nuestras almas; y por eso decisivo trance, en que el infernal dragón, cuyo poder es incomparable, como dicen las Escrituras Sagradas (Job 41, y 24) hace los mayores esfuerzos, y asesta todas sus baterías contra los moribundos, como que sabe le resta poco tiempo." *Exôrcismo para favorecer a los moribundos en su más afligido trance, el que pueden practicar todos los fieles en todo tiempo y ocasión.* (Puebla: Reimpreso en la Oficina del Real Seminario Palafoxiano, 1787), NMSRCA, Prince Collection Historical Documents, box 5, fol. 4, no. 6.

4. Martínez, "Fray Juan José Toledo," 71–72.

5. "Efecto desde ahora y para la hora de mi muerte, quiero invocar por mi protectora y abogada y defensora a la santísima Virgen, santo de mi nombre, y angel de mi guarda, que todos quiero sean en la presencia de Dios Nuestro Señor mis intercesores y me defiendan hasta ponerme salvo en la presencia de su divina majestad." Miguel Lucero, Will, Albuquerque, Jan. 20, 1766, SANM I, 3:327–34.

6. Antonio Sais, Will, Albuquerque, Nov. 2, 1770, SANM I, 5:224–27.

7. Martínez, *Manualito de párrocos*, 7.

8. Domínguez, *Missions*, 95.

9. Rodríguez, *Pandectas*, 53.

10. One record of interest is the Jan. 1, 1790, burial book entry for one Juana María, daughter of Mariano Romero and Juana María Tenorio. The infant received the "agua de necesidad" from one Olalla Segura, presumably the midwife. This may be the same Olalla [spelled here Olaya] identified ten years earlier as a *coyota*, widow of the deceased Manuel de Coza. Comanches had killed Coza in Cieneguilla, where he had gone to plant. See Santa Fe Burial Book, AASF 40:374 and 40:225.

11. José Esquivel Artecian for Juan Francisco Márquez de Castañiza to priests and ecclesiastics of the bishopric of Durango, Durango, Oct. 15, 1816, AASF, Patentes 48:006.

12. Martínez, *Muerte y sociedad*, 385.

13. Fanny Calderón de la Barca, *Life in Mexico: The Letters of Fanny Calderón de la Barca*, ed. by Howard T. Fisher and Marion Hall Fisher (New York: Anchor Books, 1966), 117.

14. Rosa Bustamante, Will, Santa Fe, July 8, 1814, NMSRCA, Ortiz Family Papers, box 1, fol. 3.

15. Fernández de San Vicente Visitation, Santa Fe, Sept. 8, 1826, AASF 45:531–32.

16. "Le serán unas luces y adornos mucho más aceptables que todas las riquezas, velas y antorchas de los altares más suntuosos, brillantes, adornados y llenos de ardientes achas, aunque no alcanzará a contarlas el guarísmo." Fortino Hipólito Vera, *Notas del Compendio histórico del Concilio III Mexicano* (Amacameca, Mexico: Imp. del Colegio Católico a cargo de G. Olvera, 1879), 62.

17. Domínguez, *Missions*, 80.

18. Joseph Martos, *Doors to the Sacred: A Historical Introduction to Sacraments in the Catholic Church* (Garden City, NY: Doubleday & Co., 1981), 382.

19. "De esta manera se les dará a los miserables enfermos este socorro importantísimo, no se dejará su administración, para aquel estado en que sería un milagro, que el Sacramento causáre su efecto propio de dar salud al cuerpo." Bishop [Juan Francisco Márquez de Castañiza] to priests, Durango, Dec. 21, 1819, AASF, Patentes, no. 45, 48:74.

20. Lansing B. Bloom, "The Death of Jacques D'Eglise," *NMHR* 2, no. 4 (1927), 373.

21. "En esta misión de Nuestra Señora de los Dolores de Sandia en siete de marzo, de mil setecientos ochenta y ocho años, yo Fray José Mariano Rosete, Ministro de dicha misión, di sepultura eclesiástica al cuerpo difunto de Manuela, Moquina, casada que fue con Cristóbal, Tigua. Murió como a los veinte y cinco años de edad; recibió el sacramento de la Penitencia y por su mala costumbre de estos indios, no me llamaron para darle la extrema unción." March 7, 1788, Sandia Burial Book, AASF 36:707.

22. Martos, *Doors to the Sacred*, 387.

23. According to Chávez, Carache did not confess because his throat was so badly cut. This, however, is not the version of the story that González tells. Ramón González to Esteban Aumatell, San Juan Pueblo, Jan. 3, 1799, AASF, Loose Docs., Mission, 1799, n. 1, 53:268–69.

24. March 9, 1798, Santa Cruz Burial Book, AASF 39:515.

25. "Dar este espiritual consuelo y socorro importantísimo a su alma, para que así confortado se prepare con mayores veras para una buena muerte." Decree signed by Bishop Pedro [Tamarón y Romeral] of Durango, May 21, 1760, Albuquerque Burial Book, AASF 34:188–92.

26. No January entry in either the Santa Fe parish or Castrense Chapel burial records appears to match this woman. "Últimamente, Señor, el 11 de enero del presente año falleció en casa del soldado distinguido don Bernal una india que de orden del Señor Gobernador se le había puesto iba ya para dos meses, y después de haberla yo

administrado, vístome dicho Bernal para sepultarla, y ya abierto el sepulcro (el que aún permanece clamando por su cuerpo) pasó el Señor Cura Interino de esta villa de Santa Fe don José María Bivián de Ortega a dicha casa a una hora tan incómoda como a la una de la tarde, extrajó el cuerpo, lo depositó en la iglesia, e inmediatamente le dió sepultura en el cementerio, y así vea V.S. Ilustrísima hasta donde hemos llegado, por lo que esto y todo lo acaecido lo dejo a la alta y prudente consideración de V.S. para que ponga el remedio correspondiente." Francisco de Hozio to Francisco Gabriel de Olivares y Benito, Santa Fe, Feb. 26, 1800, AHAD 203:272–73.

27. José María Bivián de Ortega to Olivares y Benito, Santa Fe, Aug. 6, 1800, AHAD 203:294–300, and Sobre Sacristías Mayores, 1800 AHAD 203:312–30.

28. Certificate of Antonio José Ortiz, Santa Fe, Nov. 18, 1800, AHAD 203:284.

29. Certificate of Juan José Silva, Santa Fe, Nov. 18, 1800, AHAD 203:262. Other correspondence from Santa Fe residents defending the priest before the bishop of Durango is in AHAD 203:262–73, 203:277–78, and 203:282–84.

30. José Ignacio Sánchez to Mariano Sánchez, Isleta, Apr. 25, 1815, AASF, Loose Docs., Mission, 1815, n. 13, 53:839–41. After decades of being a *visita* of Isleta, Albuquerque, or Belén, in 1821 Tomé got its own priest.

31. José de la Prada to bishop of Durango, Nuestra Señora de Guadalupe de Pojoaque, Nov. 20, 1786, AHAD 159:248.

32. José Francisco Leyva to Vicente Simón González de Cossío, Albuquerque, June 16, 1820, AHAD 243:713–14.

33. "Que la iglesia del Paso del Norte, que podemos llamar la más atendida en toda la provincia está peor que una bodega de pulquería de las de México." Juan Bautista Ladrón del Niño de Guevara to Juan Francisco Márquez de Castañiza, Durango, Oct. 23, 1820, AASF, Accounts Book LXII 45:285–302.

34. "En la Misión de Picurís es pecado mortal celebrar con aquellos ornamentos." Ladrón del Niño de Guevara to Márquez de Castañiza, Durango, Oct. 23, 1820, AASF, Accounts Book LXII 45:285–302.

35. "Sólo en la capital se hallaban dos cantores que debían servir aquella parroquia; más de ellos uno tan perverso, que fue necesario que el Gobernador le desterrase de la villa, de lo que es fácil inferir la ninguna pompa, o solemnidad con que se celebran las funciones, oficios divinos e entierros y demás sufragios en aquella provincia." Ladrón del Niño de Guevara to Márquez de Castañiza, Durango, Oct. 23, 1820, AASF, Accounts Book LXII 45:285–302.

36. The numbers of those receiving some or all of the sacraments in Albuquerque and Santa Cruz declined from 97 percent in both communities in the period from 1790 to 1809 to 68 percent in Albuquerque and 73 percent in Santa Cruz from 1830 through 1850. This shift could, of course, reflect many causes, including a more dispersed or mobile population and greater accuracy in record keeping.

37. Testimonies against don Gregorio Oliden, AGN, Inquisición, vol. 1193, S/E, fols. 309r–16r. See also Richard E. Greenleaf, "The Inquisition in Eighteenth-Century New Mexico," *NMHR* 60, no. 1 (1985): 29–60.

38. Taylor, *Magistrates of the Sacred*, 107. See also David J. Weber, *Bárbaros: Spaniards and Their Savages in the Age of Enlightenment* (New Haven: Yale University Press, 2005), 117–18.

39. Rick Hendricks, "The Exile and Return of Fray Isidro Cadelo, 1793–1810," *NMHR* 70, no. 2 (1995): 129–57; Gutiérrez, *When Jesus Came*, 312–13.

40. "De suerte Señores Gobernadores de la Mitra, que solamente hemos sufrido todo ésto primeramente por sujetarnos a la voluntad de Dios, que quizás así lo dispone, o a nuestra mala suerte y peca- dos que de este modo se nos castigan, o tal vez al desen- tendimiento del prelado local de esta custodia que le es constante y notoria la reprehensible conducta y falta gravísima de adminis- tración espiritual de los sacramentos, y no ha dado todavía el menor paso a proporcionarnos el socorro que tanto deseamos y cuya falta no podemos sufrir ya pues, en contra de nuestras con- ciencias." José Francisco de Herrera et. al. to bishopric, San Gerónimo de Taos, June 15, 1823, AHAD 250:475–77.

41. Steele and Rivera, *Penitente Self-Government*, 80, 198–200.

42. Weigle, *Brothers*, 175–76.

43. Arbiol, *Visita de enfermos*, 93.

44. Jan. 4, 1825, Galisteo Burial Book, AASF 35:740.

45. Declaration of Fray Miguel de Menchero, Santa Barbara, May 10, 1744, in Charles Wilson Hackett, trans. and ed., *Historical Documents Relating to New Mexico, Nueva Vizcaya and Approaches Thereto, to 1773*, collected by Adolph F. A. Bandelier and Fanny R. Bandelier (Washington, DC: Carnegie Institution of Washington, 1937), 3:408. Menchero was the *calificador* of the Holy Office of the Inquisition, responsible for examining texts.

46. May 7, 1777, Picurís Pueblo Burial Book, AASF 36:1044.

47. June 14, 1819, Albuquerque Burial Book, AASF 34:440.

48. July 28, 1819, Albuquerque Burial Book, AASF 34:441.

49. "Así pagamos el bien los del mundo." José Antonio Casados to Eulogio Valdéz, San Miguel del Vado, July 4, 1850, AASF, Loose Docs., Mission, 1850, n. 2, 55:801–2.

50. "Entregó el alma a su criador." Josef Mariano de la Peña to Mariano Josef Sánchez, Pajarito, n.d. (1820), AASF, Loose Docs., Mission, 1820, n. 36, 54:291.

51. "Bien, le considero, consternadísimo, por la separación de su esposa, más, al mismo tiempo Dios le ha proporcionado un conocimiento de que es una deuda, indispensable, a todo mortal y sin saber el cuando de su exigencia." Mariano [José Sánchez Vergara?] to the lord governor, Jémez, Aug. 18, 1807, AASF, Loose Docs., Mission, 1807, n. 14, 53:650.

52. "Dios ha sido servido de llamar a juicio a la Luz mi esposa." Toribio González to Francisco Montoya, Jémez (?), Dec. 4, 1807, AASF, Loose Docs., Mission, 1807, n. 16, 53:653.

53. Simmons, *Spanish Government in New Mexico*, 115. Each friar received an annual stipend of 330 pesos.

54. Frank, *From Settler to Citizen*, 148–49.

55. "Añado, que para obviar fraudes, en grave perjuicio de las Almas, conduce mucho para bien espiritual y temporal de los habitantes de toda esta provincia, que corra moneda acuñada, y se olviden los pesos de la tierra, que ni los que los inventaron los entendieron, y menos los que existen los entienden. A dichos pesos, les llamo yo, pesos imaginarios. Pues veo, que hay pesos, que a razón de plata unos importan la 4a parte de un real, otros medio real, otros un real, otros dos reales españoles. Y por esto no hay quien los entienda; de lo cual resultan fraudes, usuras, y engaños en perjuicio de las conciencias, y perdición eternal de las almas." José Mariano Rosete to Real Consulado of City of Guadalajara, Santa Cruz, June 9, 1801, AHAD 205:543–45.

56. "Soy un hombre anciano pobre cargado de familia." Blas Griego complaint to jefe político, Albuquerque, May 9, 1824, AHAD 253:99–101.

57. Bishop Benito Crespo y Monroy, Durango, Oct. 23, 1731, AASF, Loose Docs., Mission, 1731, n. 3, 51:1158–60.

58. Juana Galvana, Funeral receipts, Zia, May 9, 1753, SANM I, 1:1365–66.

59. Manuel Olguín, Estate settlement, Santa Fe, Jan. 14, 1778, SANM I, 4:296–314.

60. Pedro Bautista Pino to José Bivián de Ortega, Santa Fe, n.d., and Bivián de Ortega to Pino, Mar. 4, 1801, n.p., AASF, Loose Docs., Mission, 1801, n. 6, 53:343–44.

61. The italics are part of the translation provided in Domínguez, *Missions*, 30.

62. Fray Diego Muñoz Jurado, Defamation case, Santa Cruz de la
    Cañada, 1781, AASF, Loose Docs., Mission, 1781, n. 7, 52:581–625.

63. "Es opinión común en el país que cuanto adquieren y trabajan los
    individuos de él, lo absorben los religiosos por los bautismos,
    casamientos y entierros que hacen, cuyo arancel que rige de más de
    cincuenta años a esta parte es sumamente alto y arreglado a plata o
    su equivalente." De la Concha also noted that some people went
    into servitude to pay for the church's fee for marriage. Fernando de
    la Concha, Informe, to the comandante general of the Provincias
    Internas, don Jacobo Ugarte y Loyola, Santa Fe, Nov. 1, 1790, AGN,
    Provincias Internas, vol. 161, exp. 5, 89r–93r.

64. Frank, *From Settler to Citizen*, 199. See also the detailed discussion
    in José Mariano Rosete to Santiago Fernández de Sierra, Sandia,
    Feb. 8, 1789, AASF, Loose Docs., Mission, 1789, n. 1, 52:851–53.

65. W. W. H. Davis, *El Gringo; or New Mexico and Her People* (1857; repr.,
    Lincoln: University of Nebraska Press, 1982), 229.

66. "Porque se entierran los vecinos de la misma manera que los
    Indios." José María Bivián de Ortega to Francisco Gabriel de
    Olivares y Benito, Santa Fe, June 19, 1800, AHAD 203:798–99.

67. "Ni en las partidas de entierros ni en las de casamientos se encuen-
    tra distinción de castas como es corriente en los aranceles para los
    respectivos derechos que deban exigirse." José Francisco Leyva to
    Juan Francisco Márquez de Castañiza, Albuquerque, July 15, 1821;
    copy of document courtesy of Fray Thomas J. Steele, SJ; original is
    in the AHAD.

68. Adult burials could cost more, of course, depending on the services,
    and the parish directory lists a range of thirty-six to fifty pesos for
    adult funerals. Directorio Parroquial con arreglo y costumbre,
    1814–17, Archivo de la Iglesia de Nuestra Señora de Guadalupe del
    Paso del Río del Norte, Catholic Archives of Texas (hereafter cited as
    CAT), Various Spanish and Mexican Photostats, 102.2.

69. Domínguez, *Missions*, 76.

70. Manuel Rada to bishop of Durango, Santa Cruz de la Cañada,
    Apr. 30, 1821, AHAD 246:235–41.

71. Notwithstanding this trend, regardless of the year, as people aged,
    they tended to spend more on their burials, based on the burial reg-
    isters for these same communities.

72. Gutiérrez, *When Jesus Came*, 312.

73. "Es verdad lo que dice el bendito Padre, que dice misa todos los
    días, pero la dice para sí, por que no hace señal con las campanas
    como está dicho, porque el no espera a nadie." Juan Armijo's
    response to Manuel Bellido, Cochití, Dec. 30, 1821, MANM 1:293–95.

74. Juan José Ornelas to bishop of Durango, Santa Cruz de la Cañada, n.d., AHAD 231:761–63. According to Chávez, Lombide served in Santa Cruz from Jan. 1802 to Nov. 1803.

75. Fernández San Vicente Visitation, May 1826, AASF, Accounts 45:544–45.

76. The first example refers to Cura Rada's complaint against Fray Diego Marines de Arellano, in Manuel Rada to [señor gobernador de la sagrada mitra], don Pedro Millan Rodrigues, Santa Cruz, May 16, 1824, AHAD 252:1055–58. The second case refers to accusations made against Fray Esteban Aumatell in José María Bivián de Ortega to bishop of Durango [Francisco Gabriel de Olivares y Benito], Santa Fe, Aug. 6, 1800, AHAD 203:294–300. There had been tension between the secular priests and the Franciscans since the first secular clergy arrived in the province in 1798. See Norris, "*After The Year Eighty*," 136–39, 150–53. Rada also railed against Fray Manuel Bellido for marrying foreign men to New Mexican women; see Reséndez, *Changing National Identities*, 134–35.

77. Jerome J. Martínez y Alire, "The Influence of the Roman Catholic Church in New Mexico under Mexican Administration: 1821–1848," in *Four Hundred Years of Faith: Seeds of Struggle, Harvest of Faith: A History of the Catholic Church in New Mexico*, ed. Thomas J. Steele, SJ, Paul Fisher Rhetts, and Barbe Awalt, 329–44 (Santa Fe: Archdiocese of Santa Fe, 1998).

78. It should be noted that the secular clergy did not confine themselves to criticizing the Franciscans and on occasion pointed out the weaknesses of other priests as well. See, for example, José Francisco Leyva's critique of Father Madariaga. José Francisco Leyva to vicar general [don Juan Rafael Rascón], San Miguel del Vado, Feb. 18, 1831, AHAD 515:732–34.

79. Arancel, Albuquerque, Aug. 9, 1833, AASF, Accounts 45:690–94.

80. These costs represented a significant reduction in cost over Durango's 1751 arancel, which dictated that the burial of a Spaniard with a high cross, cope, and sung mass cost twenty-four pesos, four reales and the burial of a non-Spaniard cost twelve pesos with a high cross and eight pesos with a low cross and no cope. It is unclear whether this schedule of fees was ever in effect in New Mexico, for the Crespo arancel predated it and was repeatedly copied, well into the nineteenth century. Arancel promulgated by Antonio José Melo and Pedro Anselmo Sánchez de Tagle, Durango, July 10, 1751, AHAD 59:98–100.

81. Receipt signed by Juan Bermejo, Santa Fe, Oct. 5, 1785, SANM I, 8:1234.

82. Cuaderno en que se manifiesta el repartimiento de los herederos del difunto don Antonio José Ortiz, Santa Fe, Aug. 14, 1806, NMSRCA, Ortiz Family Papers, box 1, fol. F2, docs. 9–13.

83. Pescador, *De bautizados*, chap. 5.

84. This figure is based on analysis of the burial records from Albuquerque, Santa Fe, and Santa Cruz. For those years that the records provide the necessary details, the colonial burial registers for the pueblos of Picurís, San Juan, Santa Clara, Nambé, and Cochití all corroborate these findings for the Spanish villas, demonstrating that upwards of 90 percent of burials in these communities also took place within the churches. Burial registers are located in AASF reels 34–43.

85. Santa Clara Burial Book, AASF 38:548–71.

86. Voekel, *Alone Before God*, 107.

87. Alicia Tjarks argues, for example, that Texas represented a place of opportunity for eighteenth-century Mexicans, who enjoyed a greater degree of social mobility there than elsewhere in the viceroyalty. Using a very different approach, Ana María Alonso finds that warfare, wealth, and living in a "civilized" manner all served as sources of honor and status in the north. Alicia V. Tjarks, "Evolución urbana de Texas durante el siglo XVIII," *Revista de Indias* 33–34 (Jan. 1973–Dec. 1974): 605–36. See also Alicia V. Tjarks, "Comparative Demographic Analysis of Texas, 1777–1793," *Southwestern Historical Quarterly* 77 (Jan. 1974): 291–338, and Tjarks, "Demographic," 45–88; Ana María Alonso, *Thread of Blood: Colonialism, Revolution, and Gender on Mexico's Northern Frontier* (Tucson: University of Arizona Press, 1995), 54–55.

88. Santa Fe Burial Book, May 26, 1789, AASF 40:282.

89. Albuquerque Burial Book, Dec. 9, 1819, AASF 34:445.

90. Antonio Severino Martínez, Will, Taos, June 8, 1827, NMSRCA, Minge-Martínez Papers, box 1, fol. 1.

91. Few people requested anniversary masses in their wills. Lázaro Atencio, Will, Abiquiú, Aug. 1, 1777, SANM I, 1:388–94.

92. Rosa Bustamante, Will, Santa Fe, July 8, 1814, NMSRCA, Ortiz Family Papers, box 1, fol. 3.

93. Domínguez, *Missions*, 20.

94. Fray Andrés Varo had in 1749 identified confraternities dedicated to the Blessed Sacrament (*el santísimo*) and Our Lady of the Rosary (Nuestra Señora la Conquistadora) in Santa Fe, another to the Blessed Sacrament and one to Our Lady of Carmel in Santa Cruz, and one to the Poor Souls in Purgatory in Albuquerque. Informe de Fray Andrés Varo al ministro provincial, Fray Bernardo de Arratia,

sobre las misiones de la Custodia de Nuevo México, Hospicio de
Santa Bárbara de México, Jan. 23, 1749, BNM-AF, 19/407.1, fols. 1–44v.

95. Report by Fray Buenaventura Merino, Santa Fe, Oct. 14, 1794, AASF,
Loose Docs., Mission, 1794, n. 15, AASF 53:123–26. The confraternity
for the Poor Souls had been transferred from Bernalillo when its
chapel there was abandoned at an unknown date. José Bivián de
Ortega to Francisco Gabriel de Olivares y Benito, Santa Fe, Aug. 4,
1800, AHAD 203:285–87.

96. José Bivián de Ortega to Francisco Gabriel de Olivares y Benito,
Santa Fe, Nov. 7, 1799, AHAD 192:667–71.

97. Frank, *From Settler to Citizen*, 60–61.

98. AASF, Loose Docs., Mission, 1807, n. 6, 53:636–37.

99. For a provocative discussion of the Day of the Dead and its origins,
see Stanley Brandes, "Sugar, Colonialism, and Death: On the Origins
of Mexico's Day of the Dead," *Comparative Studies in Society and
History* 39, no. 2 (1997): 270–99, and Stanley Brandes, "Iconography
in Mexico's Day of the Dead: Origins and Meaning," *Ethnohistory* 45,
no. 2 (1998): 181–218.

100. Directorio parroquial con arreglo y costumbre, 1814–17, Archivo de la
Iglesia de Nuestra Señora de Guadalupe del Paso del Río del Norte,
CAT, Various Spanish and Mexican Photostats, 102.2.

101. Charlie Carrillo, conversation with the author, July 12, 2006.
According to Carrillo, who supervised the excavation for the community of Abiquiú, fire destroyed the field notes.

102. Charlie Carrillo, conversation with the author, July 12, 2006; Betsy
Petrick, "Abiquiu Rebuilds Its Heritage," *Suntrails USA* 1, no. 1 (1978):
18–47. New Mexicans used *talco*—pulverized mica—to decorate
altars, crosses, and other sacred objects. E. Boyd, *Popular Arts*, 310.

103. The Santa Fe cemetery at La Garita included numerous crowned
infants, some with shiny fabric or the noted iron crowns and/or
daggers, the latter believed to have been placed in imitation of the
Virgin of Sorrows. H. Wolcott Toll et al., "La Garita Camposanto:
Work at a Forgotten Cemetery Under Kearny Road, Santa Fe, New
Mexico, 2003 and 2005," Archaeology Note 358 (Santa Fe, NM:
Office of Archaeological Studies, Department of Cultural Affairs,
forthcoming), 29–32. For the Alameda excavation, no report is yet
available. Richard C. Chapman, e-mail messages to the author,
July 27–Aug. 1, 2006.

104. Gutierre Aceves, "Images of an Eternal Innocence," *Artes de México*
15 (1992): 84–89. A similar artistic tradition in Protestant North
America grew in popularity from 1830 to 1860; Laderman, *The
Sacred Remains*, 77.

105. Josiah Gregg, *Commerce of the Prairies*, ed. Max L. Moorhead (1844; repr., Norman: University of Oklahoma Press, 1954), 185. The Huning-Ferguson papers also include several apt descriptions; Memoirs of Franz Huning, Huning-Ferguson Family Papers, CSWR, MSS 194BC, boxes 1 and 2, fol. 6: Journal/Memoirs of Clara Huning Ferguson.
106. Abert, *Abert's New Mexico Report*, 45.
107. Interview with Mrs. Clara Fergusson, Library of Congress, Manuscript Division, Works Progress Administration Federal Writers' Project Coll., Sept. 14, 1936, http://memory.loc.gov/ammem/wpaintro/wpahome.html.
108. Domínguez, *Missions*, 311.
109. Lorenzo de Córdova, *Echoes of the Flute* (Santa Fe: Ancient City Press, 1972), 49. A more recent oral history affirms the importance of song in traditional northern New Mexican funerals, noting that during the "Entriega de los Difuntos, (Commendation of the Dead) sung at the place of the funeral or the camposanto . . . the musician assumes the voice of the deceased person saying good-bye to the ones left behind. Other verses relate to scriptural passages and the beliefs about what transpires with the soul or spirit following death of the body. The culmination is the community's handing over to God the soul of the dead person." Cipriano Vigil, *Entriegas of Northern New Mexico and Southern Colorado* (Santa Fe: History Library, Museum of New Mexico, 1987), 3.
110. A document of unknown New Mexican provenance indicates the use of a small carpenter's horse (a "burrito") as a bier. Noticia de lo que se necesita en esta Parroquia, n.p., AASF, Loose Docs., Mission, 1800, n. 14, 53:326–27.
111. "En fin: si me hubieran llamado, según correspondía, hubiera ido, pues en tal caso ningún Padre Ministro ignora lo que deba hacer." José Mariano Rosete to Vice-Custos Santiago Fernández de Sierra, Sandia, Feb. 8, 1789, AASF, Loose Docs., Mission, 1789, n. 1, 52:851–53.
112. "Vino (el Señor Lindón) con gran frescura, riéndose, como si hubiera muerto, no su padre sino algún perro: vino, digo, no a ajustar el funeral, sino a mentir, haciéndose del más infeliz pobre, y desgraciado, que no tenía más que pagar, que un caballo grande en edad, pero de servicio. Admití el caballo de servicio. Díjome, quería el entierro con misa cantada. Respondíle que si la misa era cantada, me había de dar dos sarapes más . . . En eso quedamos, y él admitió." José Mariano Rosete to Vice-Custos Santiago Fernández de Sierra, Sandia, Feb. 8, 1789, AASF, Loose Docs., Mission, 1789, n. 1, 52:851–53.
113. "Trajeron el difunto cuerpo al cementerio de esta iglesia: no el *Lindón*, quizá se le hizo afrenta traer en hombros a su difunto padre;

pusiéronle al cuerpo difunto algunas candelas, las que no daban luz, por defecto del aire, entráronlas a la iglesia, pusiéronlas sobre el altar, donde se ponen los paramentos, para bautizar. Y tuvo (nuestro consabido) el atrevimiento de entrarse al templo, a hacer un cigarro, encenderlo, en las propias candelas del difunto, y comenzar a humar; y hubiera seguido en tal desacato, si un indio sacristán indignado por tal acción, no lo hubiera echado a empujones de la iglesia. Medrados estamos. Que ya los indios respetan más (aunque sea en esta ocasión) la casa de Dios, que no los hijos de Cristianos viejos. A cuyas indignas acciones me he estado, como si fuése de mármol; pues según toco las cosas me conviene parecer estatua." José Mariano Rosete to Vice-Custos Santiago Fernández de Sierra, Sandia, Feb. 8, 1789, AASF, Loose Docs., Mission, 1789, n. 1, 52:851–53.

CHAPTER FOUR

1. Proceedings against Manuel Gallego for the murder of María Espíritu Santo Roybal, San Antonio del Rancho, Feb. 3–Apr. 22, 1834, Sender Coll., doc. 124, 1:724–51.

2. Irma Barriga Calle, "La experiencia de la muerte en Lima, siglo XVII," *Apuntes* 31 (Segundo Semestre 1992), 86.

3. "La división y separación del cuerpo y alma en el compuesto humano." *Diccionario de Autoridades*, facs. ed., 3 vols. (1726–37; Madrid: Editorial Gredos, 1990), 2:625.

4. Eliade, "Mythologies of Death," 15.

5. Eliade, "Mythologies of Death," 15; Ariès, *The Hour*, chap. 8; Viqueira, "El sentimiento," 32.

6. "Ya estaba su alma en la eternidad." Dec. 15, 1798, Sandia Burial Book, AASF 36: 781.

7. Eire, *From Madrid to Purgatory*, 431. Carolyn Bynum Walker points out the paradox in medieval society, where people regarded fragmentation and dissection with both favor and horror. Carolyn Bynum Walker, *Fragmentation and Redemption: Essays on Gender and the Human Body in Medieval Religion* (New York: Zone Books, 1991), chap. 7.

8. Miruna Achim, "Fractured Visions: Theaters of Science in Seventeenth-Century Mexico" (PhD diss., Yale University, 1999), 25–28.

9. "Que en una cortada que le dieron al afeitarlo, le salió sangre tan fresca como si estuviese vivo y le corrió hasta la punta de la barba." Jan. 4, 1825, Galisteo Burial Book, AASF 35:740.

10. Fray Angélico Chávez, "The Mystery of Father Padilla," *El Palacio* 54, no. 11 (1947): 251–68.

11. "Se ha ido elevando desde el punto de profundidad en que fue sepultado hasta llegar a la superficie del pavimento lado del Evangelio del presbiterio." Examination of the remains of Fray Juan José de Padilla, Isleta Pueblo, July 7, 1819, AASF, Loose Docs., Mission, 1819, n. 20, 54:155–57.

12. Chávez, "The Mystery," 259.

13. Chávez, "The Mystery," 260.

14. "Hasta las mujeres y niños le ven, y admiran sin terror y a todos mostrando reverencia." Examination of the remains of Fray Juan José de Padilla, Isleta Pueblo, July 7, 1819, AASF, Loose Docs., Mission, 1819, n. 20, 54:155–57.

15. NMSRCA, Fray Angélico Chávez Coll., box 1, fol. 14, and Fray Angélico Chávez History Library, Mauro Montoya Coll., box 4, fol. 9.

16. Bando de policía y buen gobierno que presentó al muy Ylltre. Ayuntamiento de Santa Fe el Lic. don Antonio Barreyro, asesor general del territorio de Nuevo México, Santa Fe, Jan. 2, 1833, MANM 16:584–95.

17. Walker, *Fragmentation*, chap. 6.

18. Agustín de Vetancourt, *Teatro mexicano: descripción breve de los sucesos ejemplares, históricos y religiosos del Nuevo Mundo de las Indias*, 4 vols., Colección Chimalistac (1698; repr., Madrid: Editorial Porrúa, 1960), 4:198, 327.

19. Vetancourt cited in Chávez, "The Unique Tomb," 101–15.

20. João José Reis, *Death is a Festival: Funeral Rites and Rebellion in Nineteenth-Century Brazil*, trans. H. Sabrina Gledhill (Chapel Hill: University of North Carolina Press, 2003), 153.

21. Vargas and Cogollos, "La teología de la muerte," 117–42.

22. Domínguez, *Missions*, 146.

23. Juan Pedro Viqueira Albán, *Propriety and Permissiveness in Bourbon Mexico*, trans. Sonya Lipsett-Rivera and Sergio Rivera Ayala (Wilmington, DE: Scholarly Resources, 1999), 31.

24. Recently arrived in Santa Fe, Fray Diego Muñoz Jurado complained to the bishop about the matter, without clear resolution. During his tenure in office, Bishop Benito Crespo y Monroy (1723–36) had apparently ordered the destruction of an offending home in the same area. Diego Muñoz Jurado to bishop [José Joaquín Granados], Santa Clara, Sept. 16, 1794, AHAD 187:320–21.

25. On prohibited activities, see AGN, Reales Cédulas Originales, vol. 195, exp. 40, fols. 77–80. Even the festivities around the Day of the Dead came under attack in Mexico City; see Viqueira, *Propriety*, 117–19.

26. José Ignacio Suárez to Francisco Gabriel de Olivares y Benito, El Paso, May 1, 1800, AHAD 203:304–6.

27. According to Martínez, the competition for burial near an altar was instrumental in the proliferation of chapels, the growth of confraternities—each of which had its own altar—and the multiplication of private chapels in Asturias. Martínez, *Muerte y sociedad*, 439. Pascua Sánchez traces this same tradition to the tremendous popularity of Marian devotions in the eighteenth century. María José de la Pascua Sánchez, "La solidaridad como elemento del 'buen morir.' La preparación de la muerte en el siglo XVIII (El caso de Cádiz)," in *Muerte, religiosidad y cultura popular siglos XIII–XVIII*, ed. Eliseo Serrano Martín, 343–64 (Zaragoza: Institución Fernando el Católico, 1994), 361.

28. Antonio Urban Montaño, Will, Los Palacios (juris. of Santa Fe), Oct. 28, 1772, SANM I, 5:1138–41.

29. Francisco Ortiz Niño Ladrón de Guevara, Will, Santa Fe, Feb. 25, 1749, SANM I, 4:255–59. Wills as late as the last quarter of the nineteenth century echoed this request.

30. Joseph Baca, Will, Albuquerque, Aug. 29, 1766, SANM I, 6:774–97.

31. Voekel, *Alone Before God*, 107.

32. Informe que hizo el Reverendo Padre Fray Carlos Delgado a Nuestro Reverendo Padre Ximeno sobre los execrables hostilidades y tiranías de los gobernadores y alcaldes mayores contra los indios, en consternación a la custodia, 1750, AGN, Historia, v. 25, S/E. The incident with the Sumas took place in El Paso.

33. See, for example, Reis, *Death is a Festival*, 148–52. Michel Foucault, *Discipline and Punish: The Birth of the Prison*, trans. Alan Sheridan (1977; repr., New York: Vintage Books, 1995), 55.

34. Robert J. Torrez, "Crime and Punishment in Spanish Colonial New Mexico," Research Paper 34 (Albuquerque: Center for Land Grant Studies, 1994), 187.

35. Torrez, "Crime," 186.

36. Jan. 26, 1779, Santa Fe Burial Book, AASF 40:264.

37. "Respecto a que esta Señora con la enfermedad que Dios ha sido servido enviarle, me parece no debe ser oída en ningún tribunal de justicia, en virtud de faltarle el entendimiento natural que Dios le dió, y por cuyo motivo se debe contar que su hijo Mariano la sobrevivió a ella, y no ella a su hijo." Because Márquez does not appear elsewhere in the historical record, it is impossible to determine the nature of her illness. Statement of Juan Rafael Ortiz, Santa Fe, Apr. 23, 1811, SANM I, 3:1476–78.

38. Statement of María Márquez de Ayala, Pojoaque, May 10, 1811, *WPA Translations*, 19:83.

39. "Pero vuelvo a decir que está muerta y sin sentidos de poder hacer

defensa sobre este [illegible] porque hace veinte cinco años que no se la administran los santos sacramentos con lo que prueba que está muerta y la sobrevivió." Statement of José García de la Mora, Santa Fe, June 3, 1811, SANM I, 3:1481–83.

40. "Sólo por un género de caridad y recompensa por haberle faltado su hijo ya difunto y contemplarla, ya al morir como de cuenta de don Juan Ortiz enterarla y darle mortaja con un entierro de arancel corriente." Statement of Manuel García, Santa Cruz de la Cañada, Aug. 3, 1811, SANM I, 3:1489–91.

41. Eliade, "Mythologies of Death," 15.

42. Archaeologists noted a powdery substance that may have been lime in the excavations at the Guadalupe church in Santa Fe. Seventeenth- and eighteenth-century burials in St. Augustine also exhibited traces of lime and were rarely coffined. See Joan K. Koch, "Mortuary Behavior Patterning and Physical Anthropology in Colonial St. Augustine," in *Spanish St. Augustine: The Archaeology of a Colonial Creole Community*, ed. Kathleen Deagan, 187–227 (New York: Academic Press, 1983).

43. Visitor Juan Bautista Ladrón del Niño de Guevara noted, for example, the presence of "andas para los difuntos," or a litter to carry the dead, in the parish church at San Juan. Acts of the Guevara Visitation, San Juan de los Caballeros, 1817–20, AASF, Accounts 45:158–76.

44. Bárbara Baca, Will, Santa Fe, Dec. 30, 1838, NMSRCA, Twitchell Coll., fol. 166.

45. Rosa Bustamante, Will, Santa Fe, July 8, 1814, NMSRCA, Ortiz Family Papers, box 1, fol. F 3.

46. Voekel, *Alone Before God*, 91.

47. Edward Crocker, personal communication with the author, Apr. 1999.

48. William T. Brown, e-mail message to the author, Aug. 11, 2006.

49. Richard C. Chapman, e-mail messages to the author, July 27– Aug. 1, 2006.

50. María Dolores Morales, "Cambios en las prácticas funerarias. Los lugares de sepultura en la ciudad de México, 1784–1857," *Historias* 27 (Oct. 1991–Mar. 1992), 100.

51. Notes on Burial, n.d., NMSRCA, Woodward Penitente Coll., box 8, fol. 149. It should be noted, however, that more recent excavations in nineteenth-century burial grounds in Santa Fe and Alameda found numerous burials oriented with their heads to the west and south, respectively. Toll et al., "La Garita Camposanto," 33; William T. Brown, e-mail message to the author, Aug. 11, 2006.

52. Koch describes similar findings at St. Augustine. Koch, "Mortuary," 221.

53. Noticia de lo que se necesita en esta Parroquia, AASF, Loose Docs., Mission, 1800, n. 14, 53:326–27.

54. In the cemeteries, wooden grave markers might be used, but given their constant exposure to the elements, these were no more permanent than the grave itself. It was not until the end of the nineteenth century that New Mexicans used carved stone markers to demarcate graves; see Roland Dickey, *New Mexico Village Arts* (Albuquerque: University of New Mexico Press), 1949; Nancy Hunter Warren, "New Mexico Village Camposantos," *Markers* 4 (1987), 115–29. See also John R. Stilgoe, "Folklore and Graveyard Design," *Landscape* 22, no. 3 (1978), 22–28. According to Ariès, it was not until the end of the eighteenth century that common people began marking their graves with visible tombs and inscriptions. Ariès, *The Hour*, 272.

55. Gregg, *Commerce*, 185.

56. Crocker Records, CSWR, MS 709BC, box 1, fol. 6.

57. Some of the disturbances relate to water conduits and gas pipelines placed at the site, but many resulted from the imposition of new burials over existing ones. Richard C. Chapman, e-mail messages to the author, July 27–Aug. 1, 2006; William T. Brown, e-mail message to the author, Aug. 11, 2006.

58. Gregg, *Commerce*, 185.

59. John L. Stephens, *Incidents of Travel in Central America, Chiapas, and Yucatán*, 2 vols. (1841; repr., New York: Dover, 1969), 2:371–72.

60. Domínguez, *Missions*, 257.

61. Voekel, "Scent and Sensibility," 94.

62. Martínez, "Fray Juan José Toledo," 32.

63. Voekel, "Scent and Sensibility," 94.

64. Morales, "Cambios," 100.

65. Case of Pedro de Chávez, San Agustín de Isleta, 1729, AGN, Inquisición, v. 871, exp. 13, 333r–63v.

66. "Templos vivos de Dios." Agustín Fernández de San Vicente Visitation, Santa Fe, Sept. 8, 1826, AASF, Accounts 45:526.

67. Weigle, *Brothers*, 24–25.

68. Acts of the Ladrón del Niño de Guevara Visitation, Santa Fe, 1817–20, AASF, Accounts 45:35–37.

69. Abert, *Abert's New Mexico Report*, 45.

70. Real Cédula para que los vice-patronos y prelados de Indias y Filipinas procedan de común acuerdo al arreglo de cementerios, y reforma de los abusos que se noten, conforme a las Reales disposiciones que se expresan, Palacio, Apr. 16, 1819 (Durango, Dec. 6, 1819), AASF, Patentes 47:609–10, and AGN, Reales Cédulas Originales, vol. 220, exp. 154, fol. 2.

71. Burial entry for three girls, each named Juana María, Apr. 11, 1798, Sandia Burial Book, AASF 36:791. In the priest's absence, the community interred two of the girls together in March; the third was buried adjacent to their grave.

72. "Se le dió sepultura eclesiástica en esta parroquia, al cadáver de Cristóbal Segura, español y vecino de ésta, viudo de Juana Brito no testó por que no tuvo qué, ni recibió ningún sacramento por su muerte repentina. En el mismo día y en el propio sepulcro se le dió sepultura a José Floretino, párvulo, hijo de padres no conocidos." Apr. 9, 1818, Santa Fe Burial Book, AASF 40:864.

73. May 26, 1777, Albuquerque Burial Book, AASF 34:258–60.

74. Bruce Ellis, *Bishop Lamy's Santa Fe Cathedral* (Albuquerque: University of New Mexico Press, 1985), 161. A 1957 excavation found several mass graves in the northern half of Santa Fe's parish church, probably evidence of the nineteenth-century need to accommodate more of the community's dead. Ellis notes only that these burials were "of late date," adding, "Only seven were more or less fully exposed. Of the seven, two were mass reburials, uncoffined, of disarticulated bones laid in adjoining pits about three feet long and two feet wide, dug six feet below top floor level ... About a foot above each pit was a coffined burial, the full-sized coffins of planed pine boards fastened with wide-headed badly corroded wrought-iron nails. Both coffins were painted black, one bearing a simple wide-lined geometric design in white on its exposed edge. Next to these, toward the central axis of the nave, were three coffined burials stacked vertically." Ellis, *Bishop Lamy's*, 166.

75. Ariès, *The Hour*, passim.

76. José G. Rigau-Pérez, "Surgery at the Service of Theology: Postmortem Cesarean Sections in Puerto Rico and the Royal Cedula of 1804," *Hispanic American Historical Review* 75, no. 3 (1995): 377–404.

77. This law complicates previous scholarship on the history of abortion in the United States, which asserts that until "quickening," the fetus was not considered alive.

78. As king of the Two Sicilies, under the title Carlos VII, Carlos III had promulgated similar legislation in 1749, emphasizing the spiritual importance of the postmortem cesarean section and warning that disobedience was equivalent to homicide. Rosemary Keupper Valle, "The Cesarean Operation in Alta California During the Franciscan Mission Period (1769–1833)," *Bulletin of the History of Medicine* 48, no. 2 (1974): 265–75. Carlos III had sent a similar decree to Spain's bishops in 1761. Rigau-Pérez, "Surgery," 385.

79. "Circular para la pronta práctica de la operación cesárea" in Rodríguez, *Pandectas*, 349.

80. Valle, "The Cesarean," 272.

81. A reprint of Rodríguez's text, with notes, appears in "'Con la sangre de todo un dios': *La caridad del sacerdote para con los niños encerrados en el vientre de sus madres difuntas.* Y notas sobre la operación cesárea *post mortem* en el periodo novohispano tardío," ed. Juan Carlos Ruiz Guadalajara, *Relaciones* 94 (2003): 201–48.

82. "Circular para la pronto práctica de la operación cesárea" in Rodríguez, *Pandectas*, 349.

83. Adam Warren, "Piety and Danger: Popular Ritual, Epidemics, and Medical Reforms in Lima, Peru, 1750–1860" (PhD diss., University of California, San Diego, 2004), chap. 3.

84. Though Moll and others cite a 1779 operation in Santa Clara, California, as the first postmortem cesarean section in Latin America, Valle finds no corroborating evidence in the documentary record for California. She cites a 1799 Santa Clara operation as the first. Aristides A. Moll, *Aesculapius in Latin America* (Philadelphia: WB Saunders Co., 1944), 163; Valle, "The Cesarean," 267–68.

85. Rigau-Pérez translates the Spanish term "criatura" as "creature," though "fetus" is more accurate. Rigau-Pérez, "Surgery," 381. The cedula and accompanying instructions are in AHAD 211:21–26.

86. Valle, "The Cesarean," 267.

87. Cedula on obligations of civil officers, surgeons, and ecclesiastics, Aranjuez, Apr. 13, 1804, SANM II, 15:241–44.

88. Abert, *Abert's New Mexico Report*, 129.

89. This is the cedula's language; translation from Rigau-Pérez, "Surgery," 380.

90. "Ni, las tentaciones aparentes, nos eximimos de tan rigurosa obligación." Isidoro Barcenilla to New Mexican missions and parishes, Apr. 18, 1815, Zia, AASF, Loose Docs., Mission, 1815, n. 12, 53:834–37.

91. "De los niños, no extraídos, del vientre, de sus difuntas madres." Isidoro Barcenilla to New Mexican missions and parishes, Apr. 18, 1815, Zia, AASF, Loose Docs., Mission, 1815, n. 12, 53:834–37.

92. See also Proceedings against Andrés Márquez for the murder of Juan Valdez, Santa Fe, June 4, 1826, MANM 5:1016–22.

CHAPTER FIVE

1. In both communities, at least one burial appears to have taken place under these conditions, though the burial registers are silent

or vague for these months in Taos and Santa Cruz. Fernando Ortiz to José Antonio Laureano de Zubiría y Escalante, Santa Cruz, Oct. 8, 1837, AGN, Justicia, t. 138, leg. 48, 162–63, copy in University of California at Berkeley, Bancroft Library; Antonio José Martínez to José Antonio Laureano de Zubiría y Escalante, Taos, Sept. 25, 1837, AGN, Justicia, t. 138, leg. 48, 166–68, copy in University of California at Berkeley, Bancroft Library, full translation in Janet Lecompte, *Rebellion in Río Arriba, 1837* (Albuquerque: University of New Mexico Press, 1985), 123–34.

2.   Antonio José Martínez to José Antonio Laureano de Zubiría y Escalante, Taos, Sept. 25, 1837, AGN, Justicia, t. 138, leg. 48, 166–68, full translation in Lecompte, *Rebellion*, 123–34.

3.   For Guatemala, see Douglass Sullivan-González, *Piety, Power and Politics: Religion and Nation Formation in Guatemala, 1821–1871* (Pittsburgh: University of Pittsburgh Press, 1998), chap. 3, and Greg Grandin, *The Blood of Guatemala: A History of Race and Nation* (Durham, NC: Duke University Press, 2000), chap. 3. For Brazil, see Reis, *Death is a Festival.*

4.   Reséndez, *Changing National Identities*, 183.

5.   In the year before the rebellion, the governor sent four punitive expeditions against the Navajos; the last of these, in December 1836, was especially brutal because of the harsh winter weather. See Reséndez, *Changing National Identities*, chap. 6.

6.   Reséndez, *Changing National Identities*, 180.

7.   Reséndez, *Changing National Identities*, 188. On the social and ethnic composition of the rebels, see also Fray Angélico Chávez, *But Time and Chance: The Story of Padre Martínez of Taos, 1793–1867* (Santa Fe: Sunstone Press, 1981), 51–55. Most Pueblos in both the Río Arriba and the Río Abajo supported the rebellion, as did many Plains Indians. See also Brooks, *Captives and Cousins*, 273–80.

8.   Taylor, *Magistrates of the Sacred*, 14. This is not to say that the church did not at times cooperate with or benefit from reforms; the church hierarchy and individual clerics were in fact at times supporters of different reforms. See also Weber, *Bárbaros*, 109.

9.   Guenter B. Risse, "Medicine in the Age of Enlightenment," in *Medicine in Society: Historical Essays*, ed. Andrew Wear, 149–95 (New York: Cambridge University Press, 1992).

10. On the importance of clerical fees—and, in non-Indian parishes, funeral fees especially—to clergy, see Taylor, *Magistrates of the Sacred*, 134–38.

11. Voekel, *Alone Before God*, 122.

12. Voekel, *Alone Before God*, 145.

13. "Pues aunque podrían servir para recordar nuestra mortalidad,
acaso no evitarían el perjuicio de la infección que se va a precaver."
Baltasar Melchor Gaspar María de Jovellanos, "Informe sobre la disciplina eclesiástica antigua y moderna relativa al lugar de las sepulturas," *Obras Históricas*, ed. Elviro Martínez (1786; repr., Mexico
City: Editorial Porrúa, 1984), 182.

14. "Don Juan Durán, que era un hombre lleno de humores, despedía
un hedor insufrible." In fairness to don Juan Durán, it should be
noted that the burial had been disturbed several times, allowing for
the release of the stench. Jovellanos, "Informe," 182. Similar stories
warning of the deadly fumes were widespread elsewhere in Europe
and in the Americas at this same time. For a discussion of these
currents of thought in New York and New Haven, for example, see
David Charles Sloane, *The Last Great Necessity: Cemeteries in
American History* (Baltimore: The Johns Hopkins University Press,
1991), 37–40.

15. Voekel, *Alone Before God*, chap. 7. Michael Sappol discusses this
idea in the eighteenth-century United States. Michael Sappol, *A
Traffic of Dead Bodies: Anatomy and Embodied Social Identity in
Nineteenth-Century America* (Princeton: Princeton University Press,
2002), chap. 2.

16. Sappol, *A Traffic of Dead Bodies*, 49.

17. See Carlo M. Cipolla, *Miasmas and Disease: Public Health and the
Environment in the Pre-Industrial Age*, trans. Elizabeth Potter (New
Haven: Yale University Press, 1992); María Jesús Merinero Martín,
Percepción social de la enfermedad en tiempos de la ilustración
(Cáceres: Universidad de Extremadura, 1995).

18. The perceived connection between odor and disease grew after
1760. See Alain Corbin, *The Foul and the Fragrant: Odor and the
French Social Imagination* (1982; repr., Cambridge, MA: Harvard
University Press, 1986).

19. Cipolla, *Miasmas and Disease*, 5.

20. Cipolla, *Miasmas and Disease*, 7. One Italian anatomist even
devised a contraption—the eudiometer—that purported to measure the air's corruption. Voekel, *Alone Before God*, 185.

21. Jean-Pierre Clement, "El nacimiento de la higiene urbana en la
América Española del siglo XVIII," *Revista de Indias* 43, no. 171
(1983): 77–95. Heavily influenced by French medical thought,
Spanish authorities were not alone in promoting these ideas. The
French and British cases parallel these developments in Spain.
Cipolla, *Miasmas and Disease*, passim.

22. Clement, "El nacimiento," 82.

23. Donald Cooper, *Epidemic Disease in Mexico City, 1761–1813: An Administrative, Social, and Medical Study* (Austin: University of Texas Press, 1965), 34.

24. Corbin notes a similar dissonance in elite concerns and the popular classes' perceptions of daily life, observing that "the great majority of the population had no exposure to the new discipline except through hospitals, prisons, or barracks. The dissemination of the codes of hygiene scarcely entered the educational realm before the 1860s." Corbin, *The Foul*, 211. Knaut contends that people—especially the new merchant elite—in Veracruz were more receptive to reform measures than Mexico City's residents, because of Veracruz's greater susceptibility to yellow fever, tremendous economic growth, and population makeup in the late eighteenth century. Andrew L. Knaut, "Yellow Fever and the Late Colonial Public Health Response in the Port of Veracruz," *Hispanic American Historical Review* 77, no. 4 (1997): 619–44.

25. Cooper, *Epidemic Disease*, 59. Similar methods had a long history in Europe. See Corbin, *The Foul*, 97, 103.

26. Voekel, *Alone Before God*, 140.

27. Correspondence among the Conde de Floridablanca, the Conde de Revillagigedo, and the king of Spain, 1791–93, Archivo General de Indias (hereafter cited as AGI), Estado 20, n. 94, Estado 21, n. 24, and Estado 21, n. 75. See Marcela Dávalos, *Basura e Ilustración: La limpieza de la Ciudad de México a fines del siglo XVIII* (Mexico City: Instituto Nacional de Antropología e Historia, 1997), and Cooper, *Epidemic Disease*, for discussions of urban waste management and public-health policies attempted in New Spain's capital city.

28. Cabildo records, Santa Fe, Apr. 12, 1832, CSWR, MSS 76 BC, box 1, fol. 1.

29. Bando de policia y buen gobierno que presentó al muy Ylltre. Ayuntamiento de Santa Fe el Licenciado d. Antonio Barreyro, asesor general del territorio de Nuevo México, Santa Fe, Jan. 2, 1833, MANM 16:584–95; Cabildo records, Santa Fe, Jan. 6, 1833, CSWR, MSS 76 BC, box 1, fol. 1.

30. This emphasis on personal responsibility echoes findings on central Mexico. Voekel, *Alone Before God*, 191–93.

31. "Consta por la experiencia que la generación de la peste nace de la corrupción de los cadáveres, o putrefacción intensa fetidíssima de algunos estanques que quanto por el efecto de ventilación se elevan vapores venenosos, corruptivos y quitan del medio al viviente." Silvia Cogollos Amaya and Martín Eduardo Vargas Poo, "Las discusiones en torno a la construcción y utilidad de los 'dormitorios' para los muertos (Santafé, finales del siglo XVIII)," in *Inquisición, muerte y sexualidad en el Nuevo Reino de Granada*, ed. Jaime Humberto

Borja Gómez (Bogotá: Editorial Ariel-CEJA, 1996), 150.

32. Cogollos and Vargas, "Las discusiones," 156.

33. Dr. Mauricio de Echandi quoted in Voekel, *Alone Before God*, 185.

34. Real Cédula para el restablecimiento de la disciplina de la Iglesia en el uso y construcción de cementerios, según el Ritual Romano, Apr. 3, 1787, in *Novísima Recopilación de las leyes de España dividida en XII libros, mandada formar por el Señor Don Carlos IV*, t. I, Libs. I y II (Madrid, 1805), 18–19.

35. "Viva la providencia saludable/que a Dios da culto y a los hombres vida,/huya la corrupción abominable de su sagrada casa esclarecida./Respírese en el templo el agradable/aromático olor que a orar convida,/triúnfen ya los/inciensos primitivos/y no maten los muertos a los vivos." Cited in José Manuel López Gómez, *Salud pública y medicina en Mérida, 1700–1833* (Extremadura: Asamblea de Extremadura, 1990), 214.

36. Real cédula que pide informe con justificación y brevedad posible sobre su establecimiento, fuera de poblado de cementerios, Madrid, Mar. 27, 1789, AHAD 168:75–77, and AGN, Reales Cédulas Originales, vol. 142, exp. 165, fol. 2.

37. "En ciertas estaciones del año eran tantos los que se enterraban, que en algunas iglesias apenas podía pisarse sin tocar sepulturas blandas y hediondas." Real cédula que pide informe con justificación y brevedad, Madrid, Mar. 27, 1789, AHAD 168:75–77, and AGN, Reales Cédulas Originales, vol. 142, exp. 165, fol. 2.

38. Joseph Powell, conversation with the author, Feb. 11, 1999.

39. Although not on record as having been received in New Mexico, the tremendous loss of colonial New Mexican documents may explain the order's absence from the archives. Furthermore, record keeping was highly inconsistent in New Mexico's parishes, a shortcoming that many visiting officials criticized. The absence of the decree in surviving documents in no way undermines the likelihood that the decree was received. In fact, an 1821 report from Santa Cruz informed the bishop that the parish had no record of decrees issued by his predecessors. Manuel Rada to bishop, Santa Cruz de la Cañada, Apr. 30, 1821, AHAD 246:235–41.

40. Having received few responses to the decree, Madrid complained to New Spain's viceroy a decade later. Francisco Cerda to viceroy of New Spain [Miguel José de Azanza], Madrid, June 20, 1798, AGN, Reales Cédulas Originales, vol. 170, exp. 51, fol. 1.

41. Francisco Gabriel de Olivares y Benito to parishes of New Mexico, Durango, July 12, 1799, AASF, Patentes, 1745–1810, Albuquerque 40:1124–25.

42. José María Bivián de Ortega to Francisco Gabriel de Olivares y Benito, Santa Fe, June 18, 1800, AHAD 203:786–88.

43. "Y aunque fuera excesiva, creo de nada sirviera: por cuanto está su pavimento, tan cubierto de osamenta, que ya no hay lugar, que se rompa, que deje de salir gran fetor [hedor] abominable." José Mariano Rosete to Francisco Gabriel de Olivares y Benito, Santa Cruz de la Cañada, Apr. 26, 1800, AHAD 203:791–92.

44. Ambrosio Guerra to Francisco Gabriel de Olivares y Benito, Albuquerque, June 28, 1800, AHAD 192:652–53. While other parishes' responses may have been lost in the ensuing years, it is likely that these three parishes were indeed the only ones to respond to the bishop's directive. As Ortega noted, although he had sent the bishop's circular to all towns and missions of the province, only Rosete had responded. José Bivián de Ortega to Francisco Gabriel de Olivares y Benito, Santa Fe, June 18, 1800, AHAD 203:786–88.

45. Real Cédula sobre establecimiento de cementerios ventilados en los dominios de Indias, Aranjuez, May 15, 1804, and Circular del Consejo dando reglas para la construcción de cementerios, June 28, 1804, AGN, Reales Cédulas Originales, vol. 192, exp. 55, fol. 2.

46. "Haciendo entender a los curas el mérito, que contraerán en contribuir a tan loable fin, no siendo otro el mío, que el mayor decoro, y decencia de los templos, y de la salud pública, que tanto me interesa." Real Cédula sobre establecimiento de cementerios ventilados, Aranjuez, May 15, 1804, AGN, Reales Cédulas Originales, vol. 192, exp. 55, fol. 2.

47. Circular del Consejo dando reglas para la construcción de cementerios, June 28, 1804, Archivo Histórico Nacional (hereafter cited as AHN), Cons. Lib. 1502, no. 56.

48. The vara was a standard unit of measurement, with one vara equal to approximately thirty-three inches.

49. "Dando el buen ejemplo con dicha determinación de concluir la carrera de esta miserable vida con una disposición tan laudable a favor de la humanidad, y por la salud y conservación de sus semejantes." Francisco Gabriel de Olivares y Benito to the dean and cabildo of the cathedral chapter, all prelates of the city of Durango et. al., Durango, Sept. 15, 1806, AHAD 476:220–22.

50. "Igual número de días de indulgencia por cada Pater Noster, y Ave María del Santísimo Rosario y demás oraciones de que usa la Santa Iglesia, a todas las personas de ambos sexos, que acudan a orar por las ánimas de los fieles difuntos en la iglesia de Santa Ana donde se harán los funerales, conforme al reglamento separado, y en la capilla del cementerio, e igualmente a todos los que concurrieron a

contemplar en los sagrados misterios de la pasión de Nuestro Señor Jesucristo, por cada una de las estaciones del Vía Crucis que se colocará alrededor de dicha portalería, y también a los que pasando por la inmediación de dichos cementerios levantaren el corazón a Dios, pidiendo a Su Majestad Santísima conceda su bendición y paz a las ánimas de los difuntos; y últimamente concedemos igual gracia a todas las personas que en los parajes expresados trajesen a la memoria aunque sea por un corto rato, la certidumbre de la muerte, a cuyo recuerdo se debe el menosprecio de los momentos presentes, y la atención a la eternidad de futuro." Francisco Gabriel de Olivares y Benito to the dean and cabildo of the cathedral chapter, all prelates of the city of Durango et. al., Durango, Sept. 15, 1806, AHAD 476:220–22.

51. In addition to Voekel, *Alone Before God*, chaps. 2, 3, see Brian Larkin, "The Splendor of Worship: Baroque Catholicism, Religious Reform, and Last Wills and Testaments in Eighteenth-Century Mexico City," *Colonial Latin American Historical Review* 8, no. 4 (1999): 405–42 and Taylor, *Magistrates of the Sacred*, 265–70; and Mario Góngora, *Studies in the Colonial History of Spanish America* (Cambridge: Cambridge University Press, 1975), 177–205. For Spain, a good starting point is William J. Callahan, "Two Spains and Two Churches, 1760–1835," *Historical Reflections* 2 (1975): 157–81.

52. Morales, "Cambios," 100–101.

53. Cooper, *Epidemic Disease*, 27.

54. Cortes to viceroy of New Spain [Félix María Calleja del Rey], Isla de León, Nov. 11, 1813, AGN, Reales Cédulas Originales, vol. 209, exp. 197, fol. 276.

55. Real Cédula para que los vice-patronos y prelados de Indias y Filipinas procedan de común acuerdo al arreglo de cementerios, y reforma de los abusos que se noten, conforme a las Reales disposiciones que se expresan, Palacio, Apr. 16, 1819 (Durango, Dec. 6, 1819), AASF, Patentes 47:609–10, and AGN, Reales Cédulas Originales, vol. 220, exp. 154, fol. 2.

56. "Sepultando en una sola zanja seis, ocho y hasta diez sin división de sexos, enterrándose los sacerdotes seculares y regulares con los que no lo son en un mismo lugar y recinto, y confundiendo los cadáveres y respetables cenizas de los ungidos del Señor con los demás, contra lo que está mandado y previenen los sagrados ritos." Real Cédula, Palacio, Apr. 16, 1819, AGN, Reales Cédulas Originales, vol. 220, exp. 154, fol. 2.

57. "Con la prevención de que las personas de virtud o santidad cuyos cadáveres podrían enterrarse en las iglesias, según la misma ley,

hubiesen de ser aquellas por cuya muerte debían los ordinarios eclesiásticos formar procesos de virtudes o milagros, o depositar sus cadáveres conforme a las decisiones eclesiásticas." Real Cédula, Palacio, Apr. 16, 1819, AGN, Reales Cédulas Originales, vol. 220, exp. 154, fol. 2.

58. "Además quede algún terreno sobrante para ocurrencias extraordinarias." Real Cédula, Palacio, Apr. 16, 1819, AGN, Reales Cédulas Originales, vol. 220, exp. 154, fol. 2.

59. "Y la fidelidad que debemos a nuestro soberano." Bishop of Durango to New Mexico parishes, Dec. 6, 1819, AASF, Patentes 47:611–12.

60. "Quiere también que Vosotros les haga entender el justo aprecio que deben merecerles los cementerios sagrados, los sufragios que en ellos mismos se aplican por los difuntos, cuyas cenizas descansan en ellos y que si todos formáremos una idea verdadera de la muerte y de la nada de Nuestro cuerpo, nos sería indiferente que se sepultase en tal o tal lugar siendo sagrado y nuestras almas se hallarían delante de Dios con el mérito de haber obedecido lo que nos manda el rey que el mismo Señor nos ha dado para que nos gobierne." Bishop of Durango to New Mexico parishes, Dec. 6, 1819, AASF, Patentes 47:611–12.

61. "Cuan indecoroso es que en el templo del Señor que deberíamos adornar con las más exquisitas de nuestras alhajas y perfumar con los más finos inciensos, se advierte las indecencias bastantemente frecuentes por desgracia de tropezar con los huesos de los difuntos en las iglesias y no poderse asistir a ellas, por el hedor de los cadáveres corrompidos a que es consiguiente la de los aires que respiran y exponen constantemente la salud de los Pueblos." Bishop of Durango to New Mexico parishes, Dec. 6, 1819, AASF, Patentes 47:611–12.

62. Kessell, *The Missions*, 91.

63. "De donde previene desamorarse del templo el que es pobre." José Manuel Archuleta et. al. to Alejo García Conde, San Juan de los Caballeros, Oct. 11, 1821, SANM I, 6:1712–13. See also *WPA Translations*, vol. 21, 123–24.

64. Complaint of Indians of San Juan Against Fray Manuel Sánchez Vergara; Request for Outside Protector, Jan. 1–Mar. 18, 1822, MANM 1:1184–98.

65. Frank, *From Settler to Citizen*, 201–5.

66. Frank, *From Settler to Citizen*, 203.

67. This opinion is referenced in a document from the Junta Provincial dated Feb. 21, 1821. Charles R. Cutter, *The Protector de Indios in*

Colonial New Mexico, 1659–1821 (Albuquerque: University of New Mexico Press, 1986), 100.

68. Rafael Trujillo and Miguel García to governor [Facundo Melgares], Abiquiú, Sept. 1822 MANM 1:1110–11.

69. May 23, 1822, Santa Fe Burial Book, AASF 40:918.

70. Archaeological evidence indicates that burials in the Santuario de Guadalupe continued well into the late nineteenth century.

71. Oct. 3, 1816, Santa Fe Burial Book, AASF 40:812.

72. Toll et al, "La Garita Camposanto," 32; William T. Brown, e-mail message to the author, Aug. 11, 2006.

73. The letter from Santa Cruz, dated Aug. 1825, notes that the decree had arrived four years and five months earlier, or March 1821, though the same circulars had arrived in Albuquerque by early April 1820. Ayuntamiento of Santa Cruz de la Cañada to Juan Manuel de Jesús Rada, Santa Cruz de la Cañada, Aug. 28, 1825, AASF, Loose Docs., Mission, 1825, no. 10, 54:692–94. Santa Cruz de la Cañada Burial Book, AASF, reel 34.

74. Ramón Frega (?) to Juan Manuel de Jesús Rada, Santa Cruz, June 10, 1821, AASF, Santa Cruz Patentes, 50:15–16.

75. "En todos los habitantes de esa feligresía reina un general descontento, y desconsuelo." Ayuntamiento of Santa Cruz de la Cañada to Juan Manuel de Jesús Rada, Santa Cruz de la Cañada, Aug. 28, 1825, AASF, Loose Docs., Mission, 1825, n. 10, 54:692–94.

76. "Se ha obedecido por todo ese vecindario, aunque si, viendo con dolor de su corazón enterrar sus cadáveres en el cementerio." Ayuntamiento of Santa Cruz de la Cañada to Juan Manuel de Jesús Rada, Santa Cruz de la Cañada, Aug. 28, 1825, AASF, Loose Docs., Mission, 1825, n. 10, 54:692–94.

77. "Pues muy pocos son los que mueren, pocas o ningunas pestes se advierten por lo naturalmente sano del país." Ayuntamiento of Santa Cruz de la Cañada to Juan Manuel de Jesús Rada, Santa Cruz de la Cañada, Aug. 28, 1825, AASF, Loose Docs., Mission, 1825, n. 10, 54:692–94.

78. "A estos infelices les resulta graves daños por estar tanto tiempo dentro del hielo trabajando." Ayuntamiento of Santa Cruz de la Cañada to Juan Manuel de Jesús Rada, Santa Cruz de la Cañada, Aug. 28, 1825, AASF, Loose Docs., Mission, 1825, n. 10, 54:692–94.

79. Weber, *Spanish Frontier*, 10. An 1801 report from Santa Cruz also affirms that the region suffered with six months of winter. José Mariano Rosete to Real Consulado of City of Guadalajara, Santa Cruz, June 9, 1801, AHAD 205:543–45.

80. Curiously, at the end of his first month in Santa Cruz four years earlier, he had written a detailed report to the bishop commenting on the sorry state of the parish, which he said did not even have a campo santo. Whether he did not recognize the space outside the church as a burial ground or was actually referring to the lack of a ventilated cemetery is unclear. Juan Manuel de Jesús Rada to bishop, Santa Cruz de la Cañada, Apr. 30, 1821, AHAD 246:235–41.

81. "Pero a esta tan oportuna, sabia y canónica disposición para poner la actualmente en ejecución se oponen los siguientes obstáculos." Rada also noted that his predecessors never had established an outdoor cemetery. Juan Manuel de Jesús Rada to Juan Francisco Márquez de Castañiza, Canelas, July 30, 1820, AHAD 243:711–12.

82. Agustín Fernández de San Vicente to ayuntamiento of Santa Cruz de la Cañada, Santa Fe, July 1, 1826, AASF, Loose Docs., Mission, 1825, n. 10, 54:692–97.

83. "Siendo una de mis primeras obligaciones... procurar en todo este territorio la erección de cementerios ventilados que con tanta repetición se ha mandado, ya por Reales Cédulas del gobierno español, que aun están vigentes." Agustín Fernández de San Vicente to priests and ministers of New Mexico, Santa Fe, May 10, 1826, AASF, Patentes 48:144, and AASF, Loose Docs., Mission, 1826, n. 25, 54:783.

84. "Para evitar de este modo los males que ha tenido presentes el gobierno al tiempo de expedir sus citadas resoluciones." Agustín Fernández de San Vicente to priests and ministers of New Mexico, Santa Fe, May 10, 1826, AASF, Patentes 48:144.

85. After the death of Bishop Márquez de Castañiza in 1825, no bishop served Durango for six years. Vacancies became common throughout Mexico, resulting from a conflict between the Vatican and the Mexican government, and by 1829 Mexico had no bishops whatsoever. José Ignacio Gallegos, *Historia de la iglesia en Durango* (Mexico City: Editorial Jus, 1969), 257; Weber, *Mexican Frontier*, 70.

86. "Es necesario que Vesa se ponga de acuerdo con ese ilustre ayuntamiento constitucional, y que apure por su parte cuantos arbitrios le dicte su prudencia, a fin de que tenga puntual cumplimiento la circular expedida por este gobierno en 10 del último mayo. Que si se pulsaron algunas dificultades, á V. como párroco pertenece el allanarlas por medio de exhortaciones prudentes hacia sus feligreses, haciéndoles ver el beneficio que a todos resultará de la construcción del campo santo en un sitio ventilado." José Luis Rodríguez to José Francisco Leyva, Santa Fe, June 10, 1826, AASF, Loose Docs., Mission, 1826, n. 11, 54:753–54.

87. "Su objeto principal, que es preservar a los pueblos de la corrupción." José Luis Rodríguez to José Francisco Leyva, Santa Fe, June 10,
1826, AASF, Loose Docs., Mission, 1826, n. 11, 54:753–54. See also José
Luis Rodríguez to José Francisco Leyva, Santa Fe, June 10, 1826,
AASF, Accounts 45:603–4.

88. Vice president [Valentín Gómez Farías] to José Antonio Laureano de
Zubiría y Escalante to the parishes of New Mexico, Mexico City,
Apr. 23, 1833, AASF, Patentes 49:255–56.

89. Voekel, "Scent and Sensibility," 386.

90. Taylor, *Magistrates of the Sacred*, 299, 450.

91. The 1826 Fernández de San Vicente visitation is replete with author-
izations for the construction of private and public chapels and ora-
tories. Likewise, Frank counted more than thirty licenses for new
churches and chapels in the 1833 visitation of Bishop don José
Antonio Laureano de Zubiría y Escalante. Frank, *From Settler to
Citizen*, 182.

92. "La Santa Iglesia también tiene medios de fuerza moral para com-
peler a sus hijos al cumplimiento de sus preceptos y disposiciones."
Rafael Ortiz to José de Jesús Luján, Santa Fe, June 22, 1841, AASF,
Accounts 46:871–72.

93. Felipe Mirabal has identified three chapels belonging to Ortiz: Our
Lady of Guadalupe in Ortiz's rancho of San Antonio in Pojoaque,
Our Lady of Guadalupe at his home in Santa Fe, and Our Lady of
the Rosary chapel in northern Santa Fe. Felipe R. Mirabal, e-mail
message to the author, Aug. 8, 2006.

94. Ellis, *Bishop Lamy's*, 61.

95. "Sólo con el fín de que en ella sean sepultados mi cuerpo, el de mi
esposa, hijos y los de toda mi familia." Antonio José Ortiz to
Francisco Gabriel de Olivares y Benito, Santa Fe, Nov. 16, 1805,
AHAD 212:415–16. See also Kessell, *The Missions*, 37.

96. Nancy Ligon de Ita, *The Ortiz Family of New Mexico* (San Mateo, CA:
Nancy Ligon de Ita, 1998), 15; Aug. 13, 1806, Santa Fe Burial Book,
AASF 40:504, and Aug. 16, 1814, Santa Fe Burial Book, AASF 40:572.

97. Weigle, *Brothers*, 37.

98. See, for example, Apr. 22, 1830, Picurís Burial Book, AASF 36:1225.

99. Oct. 12, 1821, Albuquerque Burial Book, AASF 34:463.

100. May 26, 1821, Albuquerque Burial Book, AASF 34:458.

101. "Y fue sepultada en el cuerpo de la iglesia, a mérito de ser el sepulcro de sus mayores, y su difunto esposo en ella, y madre del cura
mismo que soy el párroco." Her husband, Severino Martínez, had
been buried two years earlier in the church because he was a
church benefactor. Apr. 25, 1829, Taos Burial Book, AASF 42:95.

102. Jean-Baptiste Lamy to José de Jesús Luján, Santa Fe, July 4, 1855, AASF, Loose Docs., Diocesan 56:402–3.
103. Zubiría made it clear that these funds from subfloor burials were to be kept separate and used for repairs of the church and its decorations. Only one person was interred in the church in the period from 1850 to 1853. José Antonio Laureano de Zubiría y Escalante, Sept. 17, 1850, Santa Cruz de la Cañada Burial Book, AASF 39:1127–28.
104. Jan. 17, 1848, Albuquerque Burial Book, AASF 34:901.
105. Manuel Roybal and María Manuela Trujillo estate settlement, Jacona area, Dec. 2, 1852, NMSRCA, Frank Romero Papers, box 1, fol. 2.
106. Ellis, *Bishop Lamy's*, 80.
107. Ministerio de Relaciones Interiores y Exteriores, July 7, 1824, AGN, Ayuntamientos, vol. 3, exp. 1.
108. Proceedings of the Ayuntamiento of Santa Cruz de la Cañada, Santa Cruz, May 28, 1826, NMSRCA, Sender Coll., 1:523, and Communication from Gov. Antonio Narbona to alcalde constitucional of Santa Cruz de la Cañada, July 3, 1826, NMSRCA, Sender Coll. 1:535–37.
109. Gov. José Antonio Chaves to Santa Fe Ayuntamiento, Santa Fe, June 18, 1830, MANM 10:930–33, and Ayuntamiento of Santa Fe to Gov. José Antonio Chaves, Santa Fe, June 18, 1830, MANM 10:656–58.
110. Cabildo records, Santa Fe, Mar. 30, 1833, CSWR, MSS 76 BC, box 1, fol. 1.
111. Visitation of Bishop José Antonio Laureano de Zubiría y Escalante, Santa Fe, Oct. 18, 1833, NMSCRA, Microfilm of Zubiría Visitation (1 reel), 47r–48v.
112. "En el campo santo de esta ciudad de Santa Fe." Santa Fe Burial Book, AASF 41:1–187. Burials continued to take place in the individual churches' graveyards as well during this time.
113. "Primeramente el campo santo se dividirá por una línea que desde la puerta vaya a dar a la orilla izquierda de la capilla, quedando destinada toda la parte del norte para entierros de párvulos y la otra para los de adultos. Después bajando de la capilla de la puerta del campo santo se dividirá este en seis tramos." Visitation of Bishop José Antonio Laureano de Zubiría y Escalante, Santa Fe, Oct. 18, 1833, NMSCRA, Microfilm of Zubiría Visitation (1 reel), 47r–48v.
114. Julie Ann Grimm, "Emergency Money Will Be Used to Pay For Excavation," *The Santa Fe New Mexican*, Oct. 17, 2003; John Arnold, "City Funds Cemetery Research," *Albuquerque Journal*, Oct. 17, 2003. A survey conducted in 1936 still shows the cemetery's presence. Toll et al., "La Garita Camposanto," 3, 29.

115. Natasha Williamson, "Historical Artifacts From LA 120430" (unpublished preliminary report, Museum of New Mexico, Office of Archaeological Studies, Dec. 12, 2003).

116. "Es preciso que haya uno, que teniendo conocimiento del campo santo pueda designar los lugares de sepultura, para evitar el peligro de que se abran algunos sepulcros fuera de tiempo y cuando los cadáveres se hallen todavía en estado de causar infección con su corrupción." José Antonio Laureano de Zubiría y Escalante, Arancel, San Felipe de Neri de Albuquerque, Aug. 9, 1833, AASF, Accounts 45:690–94. See also Visitation of Bishop José Antonio Laureano de Zubiría y Escalante, Albuquerque, Aug. 9, 1833, NMSCRA, Microfilm of Zubiría Visitation (1 reel), 22v–24v.

117. Manuel Gallegos et. al., Oct. 15, 1849, Albuquerque, AASF, Accounts 45:798–800. The commander general of the Provincias Internas, Pedro de Nava, had suggested to the king that criminal labor be used for cemetery construction as early as 1796. King of Spain [Carlos IV] to Bishop of Durango [Francisco Gabriel de Olivares y Benito], San Lorenzo, Dec. 1, 1798, AHAD II, 110:179–83.

118. The first recorded burial in Santa Barbara Cemetery was that of Rafael Apodaca on Mar. 8, 1870. Book C, "Libro de defunciones de la Parroquia de Albuquerque desde Octubre 1859 a Diciembre 1891," AASF, reel 96A, no frame number. Thanks to Brian Graney for this citation.

119. This hypothesis is supported by the limited archaeological record, which dates numerous burials (from 1816 to 1852) in Santa Fe's Santuario de Guadalupe, for example. Crocker Records, CSWR, MS 709BC, box 1. Las Trampas folklore suggests that subfloor burials took place in secret as late as 1905. E. Boyd, *Popular Arts*, 446.

120. According to Jordan, subfloor burials continued in Texas for these same reasons of wealth and status. Terry G. Jordan, *Texas Graveyards: A Cultural Legacy* (Austin: University of Texas Press, 1982), 66.

121. Libro de Fábrica, 1860–71, Sapelló, AASF, Loose Docs., Diocesan, 1860, n. 29, 57:148–65. The richer burial goods and coffins found in the Santuario de Guadalupe versus the Alameda and La Garita cemeteries confirm this conclusion.

122. Thomas Laqueur, "Bodies, Death, and Pauper Funerals," *Representations* I, no. 1 (1983): 109–31.

123. For a succinct overview of the elite position see Pamela Voekel, "Piety and Public Space: The Cemetery Campaign in Veracruz, 1789–1810," in *Latin American Popular Culture: An Introduction*, eds. William H. Beezley and Linda A. Curcio-Nagy, 1–25 (Wilmington, DE: Scholarly Resources, 2000). In Guatemala, resistance was especially strong within indigenous communities. Sullivan-González, *Piety*, 38–45.

EPILOGUE

1. The cemetery was located on the site where today the Masonic Temple is; its burials were moved around the turn of the century to Fairview Cemetery and National Cemetery. John M. Kingsbury, *Trading in Santa Fe: John M. Kingsbury's Correspondence with James Josiah Webb, 1853–1861*, eds. Jane Lenz Elder and David J. Weber (Dallas: Southern Methodist University Press, 1996), 34n74.

2. The obituary is reproduced in Kingsbury, *Trading*, 51, 57–60, 82–83.

3. Laderman, *The Sacred Remains*, 46.

4. Chris Wilson, *The Myth of Santa Fe: Creating a Modern Regional Tradition* (Albuquerque: University of New Mexico Press, 1997), 185.

5. Many texts address these changes in greater detail. See Ann Douglass, *The Feminization of American Culture* (1977; repr., New York: The Noonday Press, 1998); James J. Farrell, *Inventing the American Way of Death, 1830–1920* (Philadelphia: Temple University Press, 1980); Karen Halttunen, *Confidence Men and Painted Women: A Study of Middle-Class Culture in America, 1830–1870* (New Haven: Yale University Press, 1982); and Laderman, *The Sacred Remains*.

6. Andrew Jackson Downing, "Public Cemeteries and Public Gardens," *The Horticulturist and Journal of Rural Art and Rural Taste* 4, no. 1 (1849): 1–12.

7. Douglass, *Feminization*, 209.

8. Kingsbury, *Trading*, xx.

9. *El Nuevo Mejicano* (Santa Fe) Apr. 25, 1863, t. 1, n. 17.

10. *Albuquerque Evening Democrat*, July 20, 1882, 1.

11. Ana Maria Ortiz funeral expenses, Santa Fe, Nov.–Dec., 1881, AASF, Loose Docs., Diocesan, 1881, n. 7, 58:14–21.

12. Felipe likely was related to the very successful merchant Simón Delgado, to whom Bishop Lamy sold the Castrense Chapel in 1859. The wills of José Manuel Fernando Delgado and Felipe Delgado are in the NMSRCA, Santa Fe County Probate Books D and E, respectively.

13. Solomon Jacob Spiegelberg arrived in 1844, and four brothers followed him to Santa Fe. Wilson, *The Myth of Santa Fe*, 68.

14. Ana Maria Ortiz funeral expenses, Santa Fe, Nov.–Dec., 1881, AASF, Loose Docs., Diocesan, 1881, n. 7, 58:14–21.

15. The Museum of New Mexico Photo Archives house several such images. Many studies and collections for this phenomenon exist, including Jay Ruby, *Secure the Shadow: Death and Photography in America* (Cambridge: MIT Press, 1995), and Stanley B. Burns, *Sleeping Beauty: Memorial Photography in America* (Altadena, CA: Twelvetree, 1991).

16. The first known photograph taken in New Mexico is the famous daguerreotype of Padre Antonio José Martínez of Taos. Van Deren Coke, *Photography in New Mexico* (Albuquerque: University of New Mexico Press, 1979), 2.

17. Wilson incorrectly states that the Browns opened Santa Fe's first studio. Wilson, *The Myth*, 82.

18. *Santa Fe Republican*, Sept. 12, 1848.

19. *The Political Comet* (Las Vegas, NM), Nov. 4, 1882.

20. *Las Vegas Daily Optic*, Mar. 8, 1884, vol. V, n. 104.

21. *The Kingston Clipper* (Kingston, NM), Mar. 8, 1884, vol. 1, n. 6.

22. The 1880 census did not include a figure for Albuquerque alone because the town had fewer than 10,000 residents. Bernalillo County had 17,225 people. *New Mexico Blue Book* (Albuquerque: Secretary of State, 1882).

23. Interview with Mrs. Clara Fergusson, Library of Congress, Manuscript Division, Works Progress Administration Federal Writers' Project Collection, Sept. 14, 1936, http://memory.loc.gov/ammem/wpaintro/wpahome.html.

24. *Adobeland* (Albuquerque), June 13, 1891, vol. 2, no 2.

25. *Albuquerque City Directory*, 1896.

26. Exterior fabric remnants suggest additional decoration in the form of fabric crosses and possible draping. These cloth embellishments are consistent with those reported in rural northern New Mexico in the early twentieth century. Here, it was local women who decorated the coffin interior with black fabric and the exterior with white crosses. Randy Thompson to Archaeological Review Committee, Santa Fe, Oct. 25, 1993, in Crocker Records, CSWR, MS 709BC, box 1; Córdova, *Echoes of the Flute*, 15.

27. Crocker Records, CSWR, MS 709BC, box 1; Toll et al., "La Garita Camposanto," 13; William T. Brown, e-mail message to the author, Aug. 11, 2006.

28. St. Joseph Hospital Excavation, LA 49791, Maxwell Museum of Anthropology, University of New Mexico, Laboratory of Human Osteology. According to then-State Historian Stanley M. Hordes, the patients at St. Joseph's Hospital were at the time 92 percent Anglo and only 8 percent Hispanic. If the cemetery was one for patients who had died, it suggests the ethnic segregation of burials, common in the United States. Correspondence between Stanley M. Hordes and Stan Rhine, Feb. 19, 1985–Feb. 28, 1985, University of New Mexico, Laboratory of Human Osteology; William T. Brown, e-mail message to the author, Aug. 11, 2006.

29. Interview with Simeon Tejada, Library of Congress, Manuscript

Division, Works Progress Administration Federal Writers' Project Collection, Apr. 17, 1939, http://memory.loc.gov/ammem/wpaintro/wpahome.html.

30. According to Richard G. Holloway's evaluation of coffin materials from the Seven Rivers Cemetery in Artesia, 67 percent of excavated coffins were made of Southern Pine, not available in New Mexico. Bobbie Ferguson, "'And They Laid Them to Rest in the Little Plot Beside the Pecos': Final Report on the Relocation of Old Seven Rivers Cemetery Eddy County, New Mexico" (Denver: Denver Office, Bureau of Reclamation, 1993), 2:E1.

BIBLIOGRAPHY

ARCHIVAL SOURCES

Archives of the Archdiocese of Santa Fe (AASF), Santa Fe, NM

Archivo Franciscano, Biblioteca Nacional de México (AF-BNM),
    Mexico City

Archivo General de Indias (AGI), Seville

Archivo General de la Nación, (AGN), Mexico City, Mexico City Ramos:
    Ayuntamientos, Historia, Inquisición, Justicia, Provincias Internas,
    Reales Cédulas Originales

Archivo Histórico del Arzobispado de Durango (AHAD), New Mexico State
    Library, Southwest Collection, Las Cruces, NM

Archivo Histórico Nacional, Madrid (AHN)

Center for Southwest Research (CSWR), University of New Mexico,
    Albuquerque, NM

City of Albuquerque, Clerk's Office

Fray Angélico Chávez History Library, Museum of New Mexico,
    Santa Fe, NM

Mexican Archives of New Mexico (MANM)

New Mexico State Records Center and Archives (NMSRCA), Santa Fe, NM

Rio Grande Historical Collections, New Mexico State Library,
    Las Cruces, NM

Spanish Archives of New Mexico (SANM), Series I and Series II

Territorial Archives of New Mexico (TANM)

PUBLISHED PRIMARY SOURCES

Abert, James William. *Abert's New Mexico Report, 1846–47.* 1848. Reprint,
    Albuquerque: Horn & Wallace, 1962.

Arbiol, Antonio. *Visita de enfermos y exercicio santo de ayudar a bien
    morir. Con las instrucciones más importantes para tan Sagrado*

Ministerio. Que ofrece al bien común Antonio Arbiol, religioso de la Regular Observancia de N. Seráfico P. S. Francisco de esta Santa Provincia de Aragón. 2nd ed. Zaragoza: Pascual Vueno, 1725.

Baxter, Sylvester. "Along the Rio Grande." *Harper's* 70, no. 419 (1885): 687–701.

Bolaños, Fray Joaquín Hermenegildo. *La portentosa vida de la muerte, emperatriz de los sepulcros, vengadora de los agravios del Altísimo y muy señora de la humana naturaleza.* 1792. Reprint, Mexico City: El Colegio de México, 1992.

Calderón de la Barca, Fanny. *Life in Mexico: The Letters of Fanny Calderón de la Barca,* edited by Howard T. Fisher and Marion Hall Fisher. New York: Anchor Books, 1966.

Congregación de la Buena Muerte. *Dificultad imaginada y facilidad verdadera en la práctica de testamentos.* Mexico City, 1714.

Davis, W. W. H. *El Gringo; or New Mexico and Her People.* 1857. Reprint, Lincoln: University of Nebraska Press, 1982.

Documentos para servir a la historia del Nuevo México, 1538–1778. Colección "Chimalistac" de libros y documentos acerca de la Nueva España 13. Madrid: Ediciones J. J. Porrúa-Turanzas, 1962.

Domínguez, Fray Francisco Atanasio. *The Missions of New Mexico, 1776.* Edited and translated by Eleanor B. Adams and Fray Angélico Chávez. Albuquerque: University of New Mexico Press, 1956.

Downing, Andrew Jackson. "Public Cemeteries and Public Gardens." *The Horticulturist and Journal of Rural Art and Rural Taste* 4, no. 1 (1849): 1–12.

Dreeson, Donald, ed. *WPA Translations of the Spanish Archives of New Mexico.* Albuquerque: Center for Southwest Research, University of New Mexico General Library, 1990.

Emory, W. H., with J. W. Albert, P. St. George Cooke, and A. R. Johnston. *Notes of a Military Reconnaissance, From Ft. Leavenworth, in Missouri, to San Diego, in California.* Washington, DC: Wendell and Van Benthuysen, Printers, 1848.

Exôrcismo para favorecer a los moribundos en su más afligido trance, el que pueden practicar todos los fieles en todo tiempo y ocasión. Puebla: Reimpreso en la Oficina del Real Seminario Palafoxiano, 1787.

Gregg, Josiah. *Commerce of the Prairies.* Edited by Max L. Moorhead. 1844. Reprint, Norman: University of Oklahoma Press, 1954.

Hackett, Charles Wilson, trans. and ed. *Historical Documents Relating to New Mexico, Nueva Vizcaya and Approaches Thereto, to 1773.* Collected by Adolph F. A. Bandelier and Fanny R. Bandelier. 3 vols. Washington, DC: Carnegie Institution of Washington, 1923–37.

Jovellanos, Gaspar Melchor de. "Informe sobre la disciplina eclesiástica antigua y moderna relativa al lugar de las sepulturas." In *Obras Históricas*. Edited by Elviro Martínez. 1786. Reprint, Mexico City: Editorial Porrúa, 1984.

Kingsbury, John M. *Trading in Santa Fe: John M. Kingsbury's Correspondence With James Josiah Webb, 1853–1861*. Edited by Jane Lenz Elder and David J. Weber. Dallas: Southern Methodist University Press, 1996.

Magoffin, Susan Shelby. *Down the Santa Fe Trail and Into Mexico: The Diary of Susan Shelby Magoffin, 1846–1847*. Edited by Stella M. Drumm. 1926. Reprint, Lincoln: University of Nebraska Press, 1982.

Mañara y Vicentelo de Leca, Miguel de. *Discurso de la verdad dedicado a la alta imperial magestad de Dios*. 1725. Reprint, Seville: Imprenta San Antonio, 1961.

Martínez, Antonio José. *Manualito de párrocos, para los autos del ministerio más precisos, y auxiliar a los enfermos*. Tomado del de el P. Juan Francisco López. Taos: Imprenta del Presbitero Antonio José Martínez a cargo de J. M. Baca, 1839.

Morfí, Fray Juan Agustín de. *Account of Disorders in New Mexico, 1778*. Edited and translated by Marc Simmons. Isleta Pueblo: Historical Society of New Mexico, 1977.

Murillo Velarde, Pedro. *Práctica de testamentos en la que se resuelven los casos más frecuentes que se ofrecen en la disposición de las últimas voluntades*. 1755. Reprint, Santa Fe: Manderfield & Tucker, 1850.

Nieremberg, Juan Eusebio. *De la diferencia entre lo terrenal y lo eterno. In Tesoro de escritores místicos españoles: Obras escogidas de varios autores místicos españoles*, edited by Eugenio de Ochoa, 359–493. Paris: Librería Europea, 1847.

Novísima Recopilación de las leyes de España dividida en XII libros, mandada formar por el Señor Don Carlos IV. t. I, Libs. I y II. Madrid, 1805.

Pino, Pedro Baptista. *The Exposition on the Province of New Mexico, 1812*. Edited and translated by Adrian Bustamante and Marc Simmons. Santa Fe: Rancho de las Golondrinas; Albuquerque: University of New Mexico Press, 1995.

Rodríguez, Fray José Manuel. "'Con la sangre de todo un dios': *La caridad del sacerdote para con los niños encerrados en el vientre de sus madres difuntas*. Y notas sobre la operación cesárea *post mortem* en el periodo novohispano tardío," edited by Juan Carlos Ruiz Guadalajara. *Relaciones* 94 (2003): 201–248.

Rodríguez de San Miguel, Juan M. *Pandectas Hispano-Megicanas ó sea Código General comprensivo de las leyes generales, útiles y vivas de las siete partidas recopilación novísima, la de Indias, autos y providencias conocidas por de Montemayor y Beleña, y cédulas posteriores hasta el año de 1820, con exclusión de las totalmente inútiles de las repetidas, y de las expresamente derogadas.* Vol. 2. Mexico City: Librería de J. F. Rosa, 1852.

Sánchez, Pedro. *Memorias sobre la vida del Presbiterio Don Antonio José Martínez.* Santa Fe: Impresora del Nuevo Mexicano, 1903. In *Northern Mexico on the Eve of the U.S. Invasion.* Edited by David J. Weber. New York: Arno Press, 1976.

Sibley, George Champlain. *The Road to Santa Fe: The Journal and Diaries of George Champlain Sibley.* Edited by Kate L. Gregg. Albuquerque: University of New Mexico Press, 1952.

Stephens, John L. *Incidents of Travel in Central America, Chiapas, and Yucatán.* 1841. 2 vols. Reprint, New York: Dover, 1969.

Tamarón y Romeral, Pedro. *Bishop Tamarón's Visitation of New Mexico, 1760.* Edited and translated by Eleanor B. Adams. Albuquerque: Historical Society of New Mexico, 1954.

Vera, Fortino Hipólito. *Notas del Compendio histórico del Concilio III Mexicano.* Amacameca, Mexico: Imp. del Colegio Católico a cargo de G. Olvera, 1879.

Vetancourt, Agustín de. *Teatro mexicano: descripción breve de los sucesos ejemplares, históricos y religiosos del Nuevo Mundo de las Indias.* 1698. Reprint, Madrid: Editorial Porrúa, 1960.

THESES, DISSERTATIONS, MANUSCRIPTS, AND PUBLISHED SECONDARY SOURCES

Aberle, S. D., J. H. Watkins, and E. H. Pitney. "The Vital History of San Juan Pueblo." *Human Biology* 12, no. 2 (1940): 141–87.

Aceves, Gutierre. "Images of An Eternal Innocence." *Artes de México* 15 (1992): 84–89.

Achim, Miruna. "Fractured Visions: Theaters of Science in Seventeenth-Century Mexico." PhD diss., Yale University, 1999.

Adams, Eleanor B. "The Chapel and Cofradía of Our Lady of Light in Santa Fe." *New Mexico Historical Review* 22, no. 4 (1947): 327–41.

———. "Two Colonial New Mexico Libraries, 1704, 1776." *New Mexico Historical Review* 19, no. 2 (1944): 135–67.

Adams, Eleanor B., and Keith W. Algier. "A Frontier Book List—1800." *New Mexico Historical Review* 43, no. 1 (1968): 49–59.

Adams, Eleanor B., and France V. Scholes. "Books in New Mexico, 1598–1680." *New Mexico Historical Review* 17, no. 3 (1942): 226–70.

Agueda Méndez, María. "La muerte burlada en textos populares mexicanos (siglo XVIII)." *CMHLB [Cahiers du Monde Hispanique et*

Luso-Brésilien] Caravelle 65 (1995): 11–22.

Ahlborn, Richard Eighme. "The Will of a New Mexico Woman in 1762." *New Mexico Historical Review* 65, no. 3 (1990): 319–55.

Alonso, Ana María. *Thread of Blood: Colonialism, Revolution, and Gender on Mexico's Northern Frontier.* Tucson: University of Arizona Press, 1995.

Álvarez Santaló, Carlos, María Jesús Buxó I Rey, and Salvador Rodríguez Becerra, eds. *Vida y muerte: La imaginación religiosa.* Barcelona: Editorial Anthropos, 1989.

Arellano, E. "Descansos." *New Mexico Magazine* 64, no. 2 (1986): 42–45.

Ariès, Philippe. *Centuries of Childhood: A Social History of Family Life.* New York: Knopf, 1962.

———. *The Hour of Our Death.* Translated by Helen Weaver. Oxford: Oxford University Press, 1991.

———. *Images of Man and Death.* Cambridge: Harvard University Press, 1985.

———. "The Reversal of Death: Changes in Attitudes Toward Death in Western Societies." In *Death in America*, edited by David Stannard, 134–58. Pittsburgh: University of Pennsylvania Press, 1975.

Arrom, Silvia. *Containing the Poor: The Mexico City Poor House, 1774–1871.* Durham, NC: Duke University Press, 2000.

Awalt, Barbe, and Paul Rhetts. *Our Saints Among Us: 400 Years of New Mexican Devotional Art.* Albuquerque: LPD Press, 1998.

Ayluardo, Clara García. "A World of Images: Cult, Ritual and Society in Colonial Mexico City." In *Rituals of Rule, Rituals of Resistance: Public Celebrations and Popular Culture in Mexico*, edited by William H. Beezley, Cheryl English Martin, and William E. French, 77–93. Wilmington, DE: Scholarly Resources, Inc., 1994.

Baca, Oswald G. "Analysis of Deaths in New Mexico's Río Abajo During the Late Spanish Colonial and Mexican Periods, 1793–1846." *New Mexico Historical Review* 70, no. 3 (1995): 237–55.

Baca, Oswald G., and Mary Ann Baca. *A Compilation of Burial Records of the Central New Mexico Villages of Tomé, San Fernando, Los Enlames, Valencia, Peralta, Casa Colorada, and Manzano, 1793–1795 and 1809–1845.* Albuquerque: Center for Regional Studies and Southwest Hispanic Research Institute, University of New Mexico, 1993.

Baroja, Julio Caro. *Las formas complejas de la vida religiosa (Religión, sociedad y carácter en la España de los siglos XVI y XVIII).* Madrid: SARPE, 1985.

Barreiro Mallón, Baudilio. "La nobleza asturiana ante la muerte y la vida." In *Actas del II Coloquio de Metodología Histórica Aplicada.*

La documentación notarial y la historia, 2:27–60. Santiago de Campostela: Junta de Decanos de los Colegios Notariales de España, Secretariado de Publicaciones de la Universidad de Santiago, 1984.

Barriga Calle, Irma. "La experiencia de la muerte en Lima, siglo XVII." *Apuntes* 31 (Segundo Semestre 1992): 81–102.

———. "Sobre el discurso jesuita en torno a la muerte presente en la Lima del siglo XVII." *Histórica* 19, no. 2 (1995): 165–95.

Bender, Thomas. "The 'Rural' Cemetery Movement: Urban Travail and the Appeal of Nature." *New England Quarterly* 47 (June 1974): 196–211.

Benrimo, Dorothy. *Camposantos: A Photographic Essay*. Fort Worth: Amon Carter Museum, 1966.

Bloom, Lansing B. "The Death of Jacques D'Eglise." *New Mexico Historical Review* 2, no. 4 (1927): 369–75.

Borja Gómez, Jaime Humberto, ed. *Inquisición, muerte y sexualidad en el Nuevo Reino de Granada*. Bogota: Editorial Ariel-CEJA, 1996.

Boyd, E. *Popular Arts of Spanish New Mexico*. Santa Fe: Museum of New Mexico Press, 1974.

Brading, David. "Tridentine Catholicism and Enlightened Despotism in Bourbon Mexico." *Journal of Latin American Studies* 15 (May 1983): 1–22.

Brandes, Stanley. "Iconography in Mexico's Day of the Dead: Origins and Meaning." *Ethnohistory* 45, no. 2 (1998): 181–218.

———. "Sugar, Colonialism, and Death: On the Origins of Mexico's Day of the Dead." *Comparative Studies in Society and History* 39, no. 2 (1997): 270–99.

Brooks, James F. *Captives and Cousins: Slavery, Kinship and Community in the Southwest Borderlands*. Chapel Hill: University of North Carolina Press, 2002.

Brugge, David M. *Navajos in the Catholic Church Records of New Mexico, 1694–1875*. 1968. Reprint, Tsaile, AZ: Navajo Community College Press, 1985.

Burns, Stanley B. *Sleeping Beauty: Memorial Photography in America*. Altadena, CA: Twelvetree, 1991.

Callahan, William J. "Two Spains and Two Churches, 1760–1835." *Historical Reflections* 2 (1975): 157–81.

Cannon, Aubrey. "The Historical Dimension in Mortuary Expressions of Status and Sentiment." *Current Anthropology* 10, no. 4 (1989): 437–58.

Carr, Christopher. "Mortuary Practices: Their Social, Philosophical-Religious, Circumstantial, and Physical Determinants." *Journal of Archaeological Method and Theory* 2, no. 2 (1995): 105–95.

Carrera, Magali M. *Imagining Identity in New Spain: Race, Lineage, and the Colonial Body in Portraiture and Casta Paintings*. Austin: University of Texas Press, 2003.

Carroll, Michael P. *The Penitente Brotherhood: Patriarchy and Hispano-Catholicism in New Mexico*. Baltimore: The Johns Hopkins University Press, 2002.

Castronovo, Russ. *Necro Citizenship: Death, Eroticism, and the Public Sphere in the Nineteenth-Century United States*. Durham, NC: Duke University Press, 2001.

Chávez, Fray Angélico. *Archives of the Archdiocese of Santa Fe, 1678–1900*. Washington, DC: Academy of American Franciscan History, 1957.

———. *But Time and Chance: The Story of Padre Martínez of Taos, 1793–1867*. Santa Fe: Sunstone Press, 1981.

———. "Doña Tules, Her Fame and Her Funeral." *El Palacio* 57, no. 8 (1950): 227–34.

———. "The Mystery of Father Padilla." *El Palacio* 54, no. 11 (1947): 251–68.

———. *Origins of New Mexico Families: A Genealogy of the Spanish Colonial Period*. Santa Fe: Historical Society of New Mexico, 1954. Reprint. Revised edition, with a new forward by Thomas E. Chávez. Santa Fe: Museum of New Mexico Press, 1992.

———. "The Unique Tomb of Fathers Zárate and de la Llana in Santa Fe." *New Mexico Historical Review* 40, no. 2 (1965): 101–15.

Cipolla, Carlo M. *Miasmas and Disease: Public Health and the Environment in the Pre-Industrial Age*. Translated by Elizabeth Potter. New Haven: Yale University Press, 1992.

Clement, Jean-Pierre. "El nacimiento de la higiene urbana en la América Española del siglo XVIII." *Revista de Indias* 43, no. 171 (1983): 77–95.

Cogollos Amaya, Silvia, and Martín Eduardo Vargas Poo. "Las discusiones en torno a la construcción y utilidad de los 'dormitorios' para los muertos (Santafé, finales del siglo XVIII)." In *Inquisición, muerte y sexualidad en el Nuevo Reino de Granada*, edited by Jaime Humberto Borja Gómez, 143–67. Bogotá: Editorial Ariel-CEJA, 1996.

———. "Sociedad, muerte y prácticas de enterramiento en el Santa Fe colonial: la concepción de la muerte en el español." *Universitas Humanistica* 22, no. 37 (1993): 35–42.

Coke, Van Deren. *Photography in New Mexico*. Albuquerque: University of New Mexico Press, 1979.

Colegio de San Ildefonso. *Arte y mística del barroco: Colegio de San Ildefonso, Marzo-Junio 1994*. Mexico City: Consejo Nacional para la Cultura y las Artes, 1994.

Coloquio de Metodología Histórica Aplicada. *La documentación notarial y*

la historia. Madrid: Junta de Decanos de los Colegios Notariales de
España, 1984.

Cooper, Donald. *Epidemic Disease in Mexico City, 1761–1813: An
Administrative, Social, and Medical Study.* Austin: University of
Texas Press, 1965.

Corbin, Alain. *The Foul and the Fragrant: Odor and the French Social
Imagination.* 1982. Reprint, Cambridge, MA: Harvard University
Press, 1986.

Córdova, Lorenzo de. *Echoes of the Flute.* Santa Fe: Ancient City
Press, 1972.

Cutter, Charles R. *The Legal Culture of Northern New Spain, 1700–1810.*
Albuquerque: University of New Mexico Press, 1995.

———. *The Protector de Indios in Colonial New Mexico, 1659–1821.*
Albuquerque: University of New Mexico Press, 1986.

Dávalos, Marcela. *Basura e Ilustración: la limpieza de la Ciudad de México
a fines del siglo XVIII.* Mexico City: Instituto Nacional de
Antropología e Historia, 1997.

Deetz, James, and Edwin Dethlefsen. "Some Social Aspects of New
England Colonial Mortuary Art." In *Memoirs of the Society for
American Archeology* 25, edited by James A. Brown, 30–38.
Washington, DC: Society for American Archaeology, 1971.

Del Arco Moya, Juan. "Religiosidad popular en Jaén durante el siglo XVIII:
Actitud ante la muerte." In *La religiosidad popular. Vida y muerte:
La imaginación religiosa,* edited by Carlos Álvarez Santaló, María
Jesús Buxó I Rey, and Salvador Rodríguez Becerra. Barcelona:
Editorial Anthropos, 1989. Vol. II.

Dethlefsen, Edwin, and James Deetz. "Death's Heads, Cherubs and Willow
Trees: Experimental Archaeology in Colonial Cemeteries." In
Passing: The Vision of Death in America, edited by Charles O.
Jackson, 48–59. Westport: Greenwood Press, 1971.

Dickey, Roland. *New Mexico Village Arts.* Albuquerque: University of New
Mexico Press, 1949.

Douglass, Ann. *The Feminization of American Culture.* 1977. Reprint, New
York: The Noonday Press, 1998.

———. "Heaven Our Home: Consolation Literature in the Northern
United States, 1830–1880." *American Quarterly* 26, no. 5 (1974):
496–516.

Dye, Nancy Schrom. "Mother Love and Infant Death, 1750–1920." *The
Journal of American History* 73, no. 2 (Sept. 1986): 329–53.

Ebright, Malcolm, and Rick Hendricks. *The Witches of Abiquiu: The
Governor, the Priest, the Genízaro Indians, and the Devil.*
Albuquerque: University of New Mexico Press, 2006.

Eire, Carlos. *From Madrid to Purgatory: The Art and Craft of Dying in Sixteenth-Century Spain.* Cambridge: Cambridge University Press, 1995.

Eliade, Mircea. "Mythologies of Death: An Introduction." In *Religious Encounters with Death,* edited by Frank E. Reynolds and Earle H. Waugh, 13–23. University Park: Penn State University Press, 1977.

Ellis, Bruce. *Bishop Lamy's Santa Fe Cathedral.* Albuquerque: University of New Mexico Press, 1985.

Espinosa, Aurelio. *The Folklore of Spain in the American Southwest.* Norman: University of Oklahoma Press, 1985.

———. "Romances españoles tradicionales que cantan y recitan los indios de los pueblos de Nuevo Méjico." *Boletin de la Biblioteca de Menéndez y Pelayo* 14 (1932): 98–109.

———. "Spanish Folk-lore in New Mexico." *New Mexico Historical Review* 1, no. 2 (1926): 135–55.

Espinosa, José E. *Saints in the Valleys: Christian Sacred Images in the History, Life and Folk Art of Spanish New Mexico.* Albuquerque: University of New Mexico Press, 1960.

Farrell, James J. *Inventing the American Way of Death, 1830–1920.* Philadelphia: Temple University Press, 1980.

Farriss, Nancy M. *Crown and Clergy in Colonial Mexico: The Crisis of Ecclesiastical Privilege, 1759–1821.* London: Athelone Press, 1968.

Ferguson, Bobbie. "'And They Laid Them to Rest in the Little Plot beside the Pecos': Final Report on the Relocation of Old Seven Rivers Cemetery Eddy County, New Mexico." 2 vols. Denver: Denver Office, Bureau of Reclamation, 1993.

Fernández Ledesma, Gabriel. "El Triunfo de la Muerte." *México en el Arte* 5 (Nov. 1948).

Foucault, Michel. *Discipline and Punish: The Birth of the Prison.* Translated by Alan Sheridan. 1977. Reprint, New York: Vintage Books, 1995.

———. *The History of Sexuality: An Introduction.* Vol. 1. 1978. Reprint, New York: Vintage Books, 1990.

Francaviglia, Richard. "The Cemetery as Evolving Cultural Landscape." *Annals of the Association of American Geographers* 61 (1971): 501–9.

Frank, Larry. *A Land So Remote: Religious Art of New Mexico, 1780–1907.* 3 vols. Santa Fe: Red Crane Books, 2002.

———. *The New Kingdom of the Saints: Religious Art of New Mexico, 1780–1907.* Santa Fe: Red Crane Books, 1992.

Frank, Ross. *From Settler to Citizen: New Mexican Economic Development and the Creation of a Vecino Society, 1750–1820.* Berkeley: University of California Press, 2000.

Frazer, Robert. *New Mexico in 1850: A Military View*. Norman: University of Oklahoma Press, 1968.

French, Stanley. "The Cemetery as Cultural Institution: The Establishment of Mount Auburn and the 'Rural Cemetery' Movement." *American Quarterly* 26 (March 1974): 37–59.

Gallegos, Bernardo P. *Literacy, Education and Society in New Mexico, 1693–1821*. Albuquerque: University of New Mexico Press, 1992.

Gallegos, José Ignacio. *Historia de la iglesia en Durango*. Mexico City: Editorial Jus, 1969.

García Fernández, Máximo. *Los castellanos y la muerte: religiosidad y comportamientos colectivos en el Antiguo Régimen*. Valladolid: Junta de Castilla y León, Consejería de Educación y Cultura, 1996.

———. "Vida y muerte en Valladolid—Un estudio de religiosidad popular y mentalidad colectiva: los testamentos." In *La religiosidad popular. Vida y muerte: La imaginación religiosa*, vol. 2, edited by Carlos Álvarez Santaló, María Jesús Buxó I Rey, and Salvador Rodríguez Becerra. Barcelona: Editorial Anthropos, 1989.

García-Abásolo, Antonio. *La vida y la muerte en Indias*. Córdoba: Publicaciones del Monte de Piedad y Caja de Ahorros, 1992.

García Gascón, María José. "El ritual funerario a fines de la edad moderna: una manifestación de la religiosidad popular." In *La religiosidad popular. Vida y muerte: La imaginación religiosa*, vol. 2, edited by Carlos Álvarez Santaló, María Jesús Buxó I Rey, and Salvador Rodríguez Becerra. Barcelona: Editorial Anthropos, 1989.

Gómez, José Manuel. *Salud pública y medicina en Mérida, 1700–1833*. Merida: Consejo Ciudadano de la Biblioteca Pública Municipal Juan Pablo Forner, 1990.

Góngora, Mario. *Studies in the Colonial History of Spanish America*. Cambridge: Cambridge University Press, 1975.

González Lopo, Domingo. "La actitud ante la muerte en la Galicia occidental de los siglos XVII y XVIII." In *Actas del II coloquio de metodología histórica aplicada: La documentación notarial y la historia*. Santiago de Campostela: Junta de Decanos de los Colegios Notariales de España, Secretariado de Publicaciones de la Universidad de Santiago, 1984.

Grandin, Greg. *The Blood of Guatemala: A History of Race and Nation*. Durham, NC: Duke University Press, 2000.

Greenleaf, Richard E. "The Inquisition in Eighteenth-Century New Mexico." *New Mexico Historical Review* 60, no. 1 (1985): 29–60.

Gutiérrez, Ramón A. *When Jesus Came, the Corn Mothers Went Away: Marriage, Sexuality, and Power in New Mexico, 1500–1846*. Stanford: Stanford University Press, 1991.

Hall, Thomas D. *Social Change in the Southwest, 1350–1880*. Lawrence: University Press of Kansas, 1989.

Halttunen, Karen. *Confidence Men and Painted Women: A Study of Middle-Class Culture in America, 1830–1870*. New Haven: Yale University Press, 1982.

Hendricks, Rick. "The Exile and Return of Fray Isidro Cadelo, 1793–1810." *New Mexico Historical Review* 70, no. 2 (1995): 129–57.

Hernández Sáenz, Luz María. *Learning to Heal: The Medical Profession in Colonial Mexico, 1767–1831*. Series XXI Regional Studies 17. New York: Peter Lang, 1997.

Hoffert, Sylvia D. *Private Matters: American Attitudes Toward Childbearing and Infant Nurturing in the Urban North, 1800–1860*. Urbana: University of Illinois Press, 1999.

Hotz, Gottfried. *The Segesser Hide Paintings: Masterpieces Depicting Spanish Colonial New Mexico*. 1970. Reprint, Santa Fe: Museum of New Mexico Press, 1991.

Hunt, Lynn, ed. *The New Cultural History*. Berkeley: University of California Press, 1989.

Isenberg, Nancy, and Andrew Burstein, eds. *Mortal Remains: Death in Early America*. Philadelphia: University of Pennsylvania Press, 2003.

Jackson, Charles O. *Passing: The Vision of Death in America*. Westport, CT: Greenwood Press, 1977.

Jones Jr., Oakah L. *Los Paisanos: Spanish Settlers on the Northern Frontier of New Spain*. Rev. ed. Reprint, Norman: University of Oklahoma Press, 1996.

Jordan, Terry G. *Texas Graveyards: A Cultural Legacy*. Austin: University of Texas Press, 1982.

Juegos de ingenio y agudeza: La pintura emblemática de la Nueva España. Mexico City: Instituto Nacional de Bellas Artes, 1994.

Kalish, Richard. *Death and Ethnicity*. Los Angeles: University of Southern California, 1976.

Kessell, John L. *The Missions of New Mexico Since 1776*. Albuquerque: University of New Mexico Press, 1980.

Kinnaird, Lawrence and Lucia. "Secularization of Four New Mexican Missions." *New Mexico Historical Review* 54, no. 1 (1979): 35–41.

Knaut, Andrew L. "Yellow Fever and the Late Colonial Public Health Response in the Port of Veracruz." *Hispanic American Historical Review* 77, no. 4 (1997): 619–44.

Koch, Joan K. "Mortuary Behavior Patterning and Physical Anthropology in Colonial St. Augustine." In *Spanish St. Augustine: the Archaeology of a Colonial Creole Community*, edited by Kathleen Deagan, 187–227. New York: Academic Press, 1983.

Korte, Alvin O. "Despedidas As Reflections of Death in Hispanic New Mexico." *Omega* 32, no. 4 (1995–96): 245–67.

Laderman, Gary. *Rest in Peace: A Cultural History of Death and the Funeral Home in Twentieth-Century America.* New York: Oxford University Press, 2003.

———. *The Sacred Remains: American Attitudes Toward Death, 1799–1883.* New Haven: Yale University Press, 1996.

Laqueur, Thomas. "Bodies, Death, and Pauper Funerals." *Representations* I, no. 1 (1983): 109–31.

Larkin, Brian. "The Splendor of Worship: Baroque Catholicism, Religious Reform, and Last Wills and Testaments in Eighteenth-Century Mexico City." *Colonial Latin American Historical Review* 8, no. 4 (1999): 405–42.

Le Goff, Jacques. *The Birth of Purgatory.* Translated by Arthur Goldhammer. Chicago: University of Chicago Press, 1984.

Lecompte, Janet. *Rebellion in the Río Arriba, 1837.* Albuquerque: University of New Mexico Press, 1985.

León León, Marco Antonio. "De la capilla a la fosa común: el cementerio católico parroquial de Santiago, 1878–1932." *Historia* 27 (1993): 331–75.

———. *Sepultura sagrada, tumba profana. Los espacios de la muerte en Santiago de Chile, 1883–1932.* Santiago: LOM Ediciones, 1997.

Ligon de Ita, Nancy. *The Ortiz Family of New Mexico.* San Mateo, CA: Nancy Ligon de Ita, 1998.

López, Roberto J. *Oviedo: Muerte y religiosidad en el siglo XVIII.* Oviedo: Consejería de Educación, Cultura y Deportes del Principato de Asturias, 1985.

López Gómez, José Manuel. *Salud pública y medicina en Mérida, 1700–1833.* Extremadura: Asamblea de Extremadura, 1990.

Lucero-White, A. "Wakes For the Dead and the Saints." *El Palacio* 52, no. 12 (1945): 255–58.

Lynch, John. *Bourbon Spain, 1700–1808.* Southampton: The Camelot Press, Ltd., 1989.

MacFarlane, Alan. "Death and the Demographic Transition: A Note on English Evidence on Death, 1500–1750." In *Mortality and Immortality: The Anthropology and Archaeology of Death*, Proceedings of a meeting of the Research Seminar in Archaeology and Related Subjects held at the Institute of Archaeology, edited by S. C. Humphreys and Helen King, 249–59. London: Academic Press, 1981.

MacLeod, Murdo J. "Death in Western Colonial Mexico: Its Place in Village and Peasant Life." In *The Middle Period in Latin America: Values and Attitudes in the Seventeenth–Nineteenth Centuries*, edited by Mark D. Szuchman, 57–73. Boulder: Lynne Rienner, 1989.

Malvido, Elsa. "Civilizados o salvajes. Los ritos al cuerpo humano en la época colonial mexicana." In *El cuerpo humano y su tratamiento mortuorio*, Serie Antropología Social, coordinated by Elsa Malvado, Gregory Pereira, and Vera Tiesler, 29–49. (Mexico City: Instituto Nacional de Antropología e Historia, 1997).

Martín, Eliseo Serrano, ed. *Muerte, religiosidad y cultura popular, siglos XIII–XVIII*. Zaragoza: Institución Fernando el Católico de la Excma. Disputación de Zaragoza, 1994.

Martínez, Robert D. "Fray Juan José Toledo and the Devil in Spanish New Mexico: A Story of Witchcraft and Cultural Conflict in Eighteenth-Century Abiquiú." Master's thesis, University of New Mexico, 1997.

Martínez Gil, Fernando. *Muerte y sociedad en la España de los Austrias*. Madrid: Siglo Veintiuno, 1993.

Martínez y Alíre, Jerome J. "The Influence of the Roman Catholic Church in New Mexico under Mexican Administration: 1821–1848." In *Four Hundred Years of Faith: Seeds of Struggle, Harvest of Faith: A History of the Catholic Church in New Mexico*, edited by Thomas J. Steele, SJ, Paul Fisher Rhetts, and Barbe Awalt, 329–44. Santa Fe: Archdiocese of Santa Fe, 1998.

Martos, Joseph. *Doors to the Sacred: A Historical Introduction to Sacraments in the Catholic Church*. Garden City, NY: Doubleday & Co., 1981.

Masur, Louis P. *Rites of Execution: Capital Punishment and the Transformation of American Culture, 1776–1865*. New York: Oxford University Press, 1989.

McManners, John. *Death and the Enlightenment: Changing Attitudes to Death Among Christians and Unbelievers in Eighteenth-Century France*. New York: Oxford University Press, 1981.

Merinero Martín, María Jesús. *Percepción social de la enfermedad en tiempos de la ilustración*. Cáceres: Universidad de Extremadura, 1995.

Meschke, Amy. "Women's Lives Through Women's Wills in the Spanish and Mexican Borderlands, 1750–1846." PhD diss., Southern Methodist University, 2004.

Metcalf, Peter, and Richard Huntington. *Celebrations of Death: The Anthropology of Mortuary Ritual*. Cambridge: Cambridge University Press, 1991.

Meyer, Richard E., ed. *Ethnicity and the American Cemetery*. Bowling Green, OH: Bowling Green State University Press, 1993.

Minge, Ward Alan. "The Last Will and Testament of don Severino Martínez." *New Mexico Quarterly* 33 (Spring 1963): 33–56.

Mocho, Jill. *Murder and Justice in Frontier New Mexico, 1821–1846.* Albuquerque: University of New Mexico Press, 1997.

Moll, Aristides A. *Aesculapius in Latin America.* Philadelphia: WB Saunders Co., 1944.

Montgomery, Charles. *The Spanish Redemption: Heritage, Power and Loss on New Mexico's Upper Rio Grande.* Berkeley: University of California Press, 2002.

Montgomery, Russ Gordon, Watson Smith, and John Otis Brew. *Franciscan Awatovi: The Excavation and Conjectural Reconstruction of a Seventeenth-Century Spanish Mission Establishment at a Hopi Indian Town in Northeastern Arizona.* Cambridge, MA: Peabody Museum, Harvard University, 1949.

Morales, María Dolores. "Cambios en las prácticas funerarias. Los lugares de sepultura en la ciudad de México, 1784–1857." *Historias* 27 (Oct. 1991–Mar. 1992): 97–105.

Morin, Edgar. *El hombre y la muerte.* Barcelona: Editorial Kairos, 1974.

Navarro García, Luis. "The North of New Spain as a Political Problem in the Eighteenth Century." In *New Spain's Far Northern Frontier: Essays on Spain in the American West, 1540–1821,* edited by David J. Weber, 201–15. Albuquerque: University of New Mexico Press, 1979.

Norris, Jim. *"After the Year Eighty": The Demise of Franciscan Power in Spanish New Mexico.* Albuquerque: University of New Mexico Press, 2000.

Norton, Mary Beth. *Liberty's Daughters: The Revolutionary Experience of American Women, 1750–1800.* Boston: Little, Brown, 1980.

Obregón, Gonzalo. "La representación de la muerte en el arte colonial." *Artes de México* 145 (1971): 37–57.

Olmsted, Virginia Langham. "The Ortiz Family of New Mexico: The First Six Generations." N.p. 1978.

———. *Spanish and Mexican Colonial Censuses of New Mexico: 1790, 1823, 1845.* Albuquerque: New Mexico Genealogical Society, 1975.

Orts, Paula Mues. "Imágenes corporales: Arte virreinal de los siglos XVII y XVIII en Nueva España." In *El Cuerpo aludido: Anatomías y construcciones México, siglos XVI–XX,* 47–69. Mexico City: Patronato del Museo Nacional de Arte, Conaculta—Instituto Nacional de Bellas Artes, 1998.

Pascua Sánchez, María José de la. "La solidaridad como elemento del 'buen morir.' La preparación de la muerte en el siglo XVIII (El caso de Cádiz)." In *Muerte, religiosidad y cultura popular siglos XIII–XVIII,* edited by Eliseo Serrano Martín, 343–64. Zaragoza: Institución Fernando el Católico, 1994.

Payne, Stanley. *Spanish Catholicism: An Historical Overview.* Madison:

University of Wisconsin Press, 1984.

Pescador, Juan Javier. *De bautizados a fieles difuntos: Familia y mentali-dades en una parroquia urbana: Santa Catarina de México, 1568–1820*. Mexico City: El Colegio de México, 1992.

Petrick, Betsy. "Abiquiu Rebuilds Its Heritage." *Suntrails USA* 1, no. 1 (1978): 18–47.

Rael, Juan. *The New Mexican Alabado*. Stanford: Stanford University Press, 1951.

Reder Gadow, Marion. *Morir en Málaga. Testamentos malagueños del siglo XVIII*. Málaga: Universidad de Málaga, Diputación Provincial de Málaga, 1986.

Reis, João José. *Death is a Festival: Funeral Rites and Rebellion in Nineteenth-Century Brazil*. Translated by H. Sabrina Gledhill. Chapel Hill: University of North Carolina Press, 2003.

———. "'Death to the Cemetery': Funerary Reform and Rebellion in Salvador, Brazil, 1836." In *Riots in the Cities: Popular Politics and the Urban Poor in Latin America, 1765–1910*, edited by Silvia M. Arrom and Servando Ortoll, 93–117. Wilmington, DE: Scholarly Resources Inc., 1996.

Reséndez, Andrés. *Changing National Identities at the Frontier: Texas and New Mexico, 1800–1850*. Cambridge: Cambridge University Press, 2005.

———. "Getting Cured and Getting Drunk: State Versus Market in Texas and New Mexico, 1800–1850." *Journal of the Early Republic* 22, no. 1 (2002), 77–103.

———. "National Identity on a Shifting Border: Texas and New Mexico in the Age of Transition, 1821–1848." *Journal of American History* 86, no. 2 (1999): 668–88.

Reynolds, Frank E., and Earle H. Waugh, eds. *Religious Encounters with Death: Insights From the History and Anthropology of Religions*. University Park: Pennsylvania State University Press, 1977.

Rigau-Pérez, José G. "Surgery at the Service of Theology: Postmortem Cesarean Sections in Puerto Rico and the Royal Cedula of 1804." *Hispanic American Historical Review* 75, no. 3 (1995): 377–404.

Ríos-Bustamante, Antonio José. "New Mexico in the Eighteenth Century: Life, Labor and Trade in la Villa de San Felipe de Albuquerque, 1706–1790." *Aztlán* 7, no. 3 (1976): 357–89.

Risse, Guenter B. "Medicine in the Age of Enlightenment." In *Medicine in Society: Historical Essays*, edited by Andrew Wear, 149–95. New York: Cambridge University Press, 1992.

Rivas Álvarez, José Antonio. *Muerte y piedad: testamentos sevillanos del siglo XVIII*. Seville: Deputación Provincial de Sevilla, 1986.

Rivera, Rowena A., and Thomas J. Steele, SJ. "Territorial Documents and Memories: Singing Church History." *New Mexico Historical Review* 67, no. 4 (1992): 393–413.

Rodríguez Alvarez, María de los Angeles. *Usos y costumbres funerarias en la Nueva España.* Zamora: El Colegio de Michoacán, 2001.

Ruby, Jay. *Secure the Shadow: Death and Photography in America.* Cambridge: MIT Press, 1995.

Sappol, Michael. *A Traffic of Dead Bodies: Anatomy and Embodied Social Identity in Nineteenth-Century America.* Princeton: Princeton University Press, 2002.

Saum, Lewis O. "Death in the Popular Mind of Pre-Civil War America." *American Quarterly* 26 (1974): 477–95.

Scadron, Arlene, ed. *On Their Own: Widows and Widowhood in the American Southwest, 1848–1939.* Urbana: University of Illinois Press, 1988.

Scholes, France V. "Church and State in New Mexico, 1610–1650." *New Mexico Historical Review* 11, no. 1 (1936): 9–76; no. 2 (1936): 145–78; no. 3 (1936): 283–94; no. 4 (1936): 297–349.

———. "Civil Government and Society in New Mexico in the Seventeenth Century." *New Mexico Historical Review* 10, no. 2 (1935): 71–111.

Schroeder, Susan. "Jesuits, Nahuas, and the Good Death Society in Mexico City, 1710–1767." *Hispanic American Historical Review* 80, no. 1 (2000): 43–76.

Seeman, Erik R. *Pious Persuasions: Laity and Clergy in Eighteenth-Century New England.* Baltimore: The Johns Hopkins University Press, 1999.

———. "'She Died Like Good Old Jacob': Deathbed Scenes and Inversions of Power in New England, 1675–1775." *Proceedings of the American Antiquarian Society* 104, no. 2 (1994): 285–314.

Sena, José D. "The Chapel of Don Antonio José Oritz." *New Mexico Historical Review* 13, no. 4 (1938): 347–59.

Serrano Martín, Eliseo, ed. *Muerte, religiosidad y cultura popular, siglos XVII–XVIII.* Zaragoza: Institución Fernando el Católico, 1994.

Shively, Charles. *A History of the Conception of Death in America, 1650–1860.* Harvard Dissertations in American History and Political Science. New York: Garland Publishing, Inc., 1988.

Shorter, Edward. *The Making of the Modern Family.* New York: Basic Books, 1975.

Simmons, Marc. "Hygiene, Sanitation, and Public Health in Hispanic New Mexico." *New Mexico Historical Review* 67, no. 3 (1992): 205–25.

———. "New Mexico's Spanish Exiles." *New Mexico Historical Review* 59, no. 1, (1984): 67–79.

———. "Settlement Patterns and Village Plans in Colonial New Mexico." In

New Spain's Far Northern Frontier, edited by David J. Weber, 97–115. Albuquerque: University of New Mexico Press, 1979.

——. *Spanish Government in New Mexico*. Albuquerque: University of New Mexico Press, 1968. Reprint, Albuquerque: University of New Mexico Press, 1990.

Skansie, Juli Ellen. *Death Is For All: Death and Death-Related Beliefs of Rural Spanish-Americans*. New York: AMS Press, 1985.

Slater, Peter. *Children in the New England Mind: In Death and in Life*. Hamden, CT: Archon, 1977.

Sloane, David Charles. *The Last Great Necessity: Cemeteries in American History*. Baltimore: The Johns Hopkins University Press, 1991.

Stamatov, Suzanne. "Family, Kin, and Community in Colonial New Mexico, 1694–1800." PhD diss., University of New Mexico, 2003.

Stannard, David E. *The Puritan Way of Death: A Study in Religion, Culture, and Social Change*. New York: Oxford University Press, 1977.

Stannard, David E., ed. *Death in America*. Pittsburgh: University of Pennsylvania Press, 1975.

Staples, Anne. "La lucha por los muertos." *Dialogos* 13, no. 5 (1977): 15–20.

——. "Policía y Buen Gobierno: Municipal Efforts to Regulate Public Behavior, 1821–1857." In *Rituals of Rule, Rituals of Resistance: Public Celebrations and Popular Culture in Mexico*, edited by William H. Beezley, Cheryl English Martin, and William E. French, 115–26. Wilmington, DE: Scholarly Resources, Inc., 1994.

Steele, Thomas J., SJ. "The Death Cart: Its Place Among the Santos of New Mexico." *The Colorado Magazine* 55, no. 1 (1978): 1–14.

——. *Santos and Saints: The Religious Folk Art of Hispanic New Mexico*. 1974. Reprint, Santa Fe: Ancient City Press, 1994.

——, ed. *New Mexican Spanish Religious Oratory, 1800–1900*. Albuquerque: University of New Mexico Press, 1997.

Steele, Thomas J., SJ, Paul Fisher Rhetts, and Barbe Awalt. *Seeds of Struggle, Harvest of Faith: The Papers of the Archdiocese of Santa Fe Catholic Cuarto Centennial Conference: The History of the Catholic Church in New Mexico*. Albuquerque: LPD Press, 1998.

Steele, Thomas J., SJ, and Rowena Rivera. *Penitente Self-Government: Brotherhoods and Councils, 1797–1947*. Santa Fe: Ancient City Press, 1985.

Stilgoe, John R. "Folklore and Graveyard Design." *Landscape* 22, no. 3 (1978): 22–28.

Stone, Lawrence. *The Family, Sex and Marriage in England, 1500–1800*. London: Weidenfeld and Nicholson, 1977.

Stubbs, Stanley A., and Bruce T. Ellis. *Archaeological Investigations at the Chapel of San Miguel and the Site of La Castrense Santa Fe, New*

Mexico. Monographs of the School of American Research, Laboratory of Anthropology, Museum of New Mexico, 20. Santa Fe: School of American Research, 1955.

Sudnow, David. *Passing On: The Social Organization of Dying.* Englewood Cliffs, NJ: Prentice-Hall, Inc., 1967.

Sullivan-González, Douglass. *Piety, Power and Politics: Religion and Nation Formation in Guatemala, 1821–1871.* Pittsburgh: University of Pittsburgh Press, 1998.

Tamayo, José Herrera. *La muerte en Lima, 1780–1990.* Lima: Universidad de Lima, Facultad de Ciencias Humanas, 1992.

Taylor, William B. *Magistrates of the Sacred: Priests and Parishioners in Eighteenth-Century Mexico.* Stanford: Stanford University Press, 1996.

Thomas, Alfred Barnaby, ed. and trans. "An Anonymous Description of New Mexico, 1818." *Southwestern Historical Quarterly* 33 (July 1929): 50–74.

Tjarks, Alicia V. "Comparative Demographic Analysis of Texas, 1777–1793." *Southwestern Historical Quarterly* 77 (Jan. 1974): 291–338.

———. "Demographic, Ethnic and Occupational Structure of New Mexico, 1790." *The Americas* 35, no. 1 (1978): 45–88.

———. "Evolución urbana de Texas durante el siglo XVIII." *Revista de Indias* 33–34 (Jan. 1973–Dec. 1974): 605–36.

Toll, H. Wolcott, Nancy J. Akins, Natasha Williamson, Matthew Barbour, and Glenna Dean. "La Garita Camposanto: Work at a Forgotten Cemetery Under Kearny Road, Santa Fe, New Mexico, 2003 and 2005," Archaeology Note 358. Santa Fe, NM: Office of Archaeological Studies, Department of Cultural Affairs, forthcoming.

Torrez, Robert J. "Crime and Punishment in Spanish Colonial New Mexico." Research Paper 34. Albuquerque: Center for Land Grant Studies, 1994.

Valdés, Alma Victoria. *Testamentos, muerte y exequias: Saltillo y San Esteban al despuntar el siglo XIX.* Saltillo, Mexico: Centro de Estudios Sociales y Humanísticos, 2000.

Valle, Rosemary Keupper. "The Cesarean Operation in Alta California During the Franciscan Mission Period (1769–1833)." *Bulletin of the History of Medicine* 48, no. 2 (1974): 265–75.

Vaquero Iglesias, Julio Antonio. *Muerte e ideología en la Asturias del siglo XIX.* Madrid: Siglo Veintiuno, 1991.

Vargas Poo, Martín Eduardo, and Silvia Cogollos Amaya. "La teología de la muerte: Una visión española del fenómeno durante los siglos XVI al XVIII." In *Inquisición, muerte y sexualidad en el Nuevo Reino de Granada,* edited by Jaime Humberto Borja Gómez. Bogota:

Editorial Ariel-CEJA, 1996.

Velázquez B., Carmela. "Morir en el XVII." *Revista de historia* 33 (Jan.–June 1996): 45–66.

Vigil, Cipriano. *Entriegas of Northern New Mexico and Southern Colorado.* Santa Fe: History Library, Museum of New Mexico, 1987.

Viqueira, Juan Pedro. "El sentimiento de la muerte en el México ilustrado del siglo XVIII a través de dos textos de la época." *Relaciones* 2, no. 5 (1981): 27–63.

Viqueira Albán, Juan Pedro. *Propriety and Permissiveness in Bourbon Mexico.* Translated by Sonya Lipsett-Rivera and Sergio Rivera Ayala. Wilmington, DE: Scholarly Resources, 1999.

Voekel, Pamela. *Alone Before God: The Religious Origins of Modernity in Mexico.* Durham, NC: Duke University Press, 2002.

———. "Peeing on the Palace: Bodily Resistance to Bourbon Reforms in Mexico City." *Journal of Historical Sociology* 5, no. 2 (1992): 183–208.

———. "Piety and Public Space: The Cemetery Campaign in Veracruz, 1789–1810." In *Latin American Popular Culture: An Introduction,* edited by William H. Beezley and Linda A. Curcio-Nagy, 1–25. Wilmington, DE: Scholarly Resources, 2000.

———. "Scent and Sensibility: Pungency and Piety in the Making of the *Gente Sensata.* Mexico, 1640–1850." PhD diss., University of Texas at Austin, 1997.

Vovelle, Michel. *Ideologies and Mentalities.* Translated by Eamon O'Flaherty. Chicago: University of Chicago Press, 1990.

Walker, Carolyn Bynum. *Fragmentation and Redemption: Essays on Gender and the Human Body in Medieval Religion.* New York: Zone Books, 1991.

Warner, Louis. "Wills and Hijuelas." *New Mexico Historical Review* 7, no. 1 (1932): 75–89.

Warren, Adam. "Piety and Danger: Popular Ritual, Epidemics, and Medical Reforms in Lima, Peru, 1750–1860." PhD diss., University of California, San Diego, 2004.

Warren, Nancy Hunter. "New Mexico Village Camposantos." *Markers* 4 (1987): 115–29.

———. *Villages of Hispanic New Mexico.* Santa Fe: School of American Research, 1987.

Weber, David J. *Bárbaros: Spaniards and Their Savages in the Age of Enlightenment.* New Haven: Yale University Press, 2005.

———. *The Mexican Frontier, 1821–1846: The American Southwest Under Mexico.* Albuquerque: University of New Mexico Press, 1982.

———. "Mexico's Far Northern Frontier 1821–1854: Historiography Askew." *Western Historical Quarterly* 7 (July 1976): 279–93.

———. *The Spanish Frontier in North America*. New Haven: Yale University Press, 1992.

Weigle, Marta. *Brothers of Light, Brothers of Blood: The Penitentes of the Southwest*. Albuquerque: University of New Mexico Press, 1976. Reprint, Santa Fe: Ancient City Press, 1989.

Weigle, Marta, and Peter White. *The Lore of New Mexico*. Albuquerque: University of New Mexico Press, 1988.

Wilson, Christ. *The Myth of Santa Fe: Creating a Modern Regional Tradition*. Albuquerque: University of New Mexico Press, 1997.

Wright, Robert E., OMI. "How Many Are 'A Few'? Catholic Clergy in Central and Northern New Mexico, 1780–1851." In *Four Hundred Years of Faith: Seeds of Struggle, Harvest of Faith: A History of the Catholic Church in New Mexico*, 219–61. Santa Fe: Archdiocese of Santa Fe, 1998.

Wroth, William. *Christian Images in Hispanic New Mexico*. Colorado Springs: Taylor Museum, 1982.

———. *Images of Penance, Images of Mercy: Southwestern Santos in the Late Nineteenth Century*. Norman: University of Oklahoma Press, 1991.

Zárate Toscano, Verónica. *Los nobles ante la muerte en México: Actitudes, ceremonias y memoria, 1750–1850*. Mexico City: El Colegio de México, Instituto de Investigaciones Dr. José María Luis Mora, 2000.

———. "Los nobles ante la muerte en México: Actitudes, ceremonias y memoria, 1750–1850." PhD diss., El Colegio de México, 1996.

INDEX

The letters *i* or *n* following a page number refer to an illustration or note on that page. The number following the *n* is the note number.

www.ingramcontent.com/pod-product-compliance
Lightning Source LLC
Chambersburg PA
CBHW020658270326
41928CB00005B/174